KOREAN
PHRASEBOOK

J.D. Hilts, Minkyoung Kim

Korean phrasebook
3rd edition – March 2002

Published by
Lonely Planet Publications Pty Ltd ABN 36 005 607 983
90 Maribyrnong St, Footscray, Victoria 3011, Australia

Lonely Planet Offices
Australia Locked Bag 1, Footscray, Victoria 3011
USA 150 Linden St, Oakland CA 94607
UK 72-82 Rosebery Ave, London, EC1R 4RW

Cover illustration
jenny chonsa doing a bit of a dung san by Patrick Marris

ISBN 1 74059 166 6

text © Lonely Planet Publications Pty Ltd 2002
cover illustration © Lonely Planet Publications Pty Ltd 2002

10 9 8   6 5 4 3 2 1

Printed through Colorcraft Ltd, Hong Kong
Printed in Malaysia

About the Authors

Minkyoung Kim is a Seoul native who studies at Korea University, focusing on the field of English education. Jonathan Hilts-Park is a California native who has lived in Seoul since graduating from the University of California at Irvine in the 1990s, and is pursuing graduate studies at Yonsei University focusing on public health issues in Korea. Since working together at Korea's EBS radio and television network, where Minkyoung was a production assistant and Jonathan works as a news commentator and developer of English educational programs, they have collaborated on a number of publishing projects. They welcome comments on their work, which can be forwarded to Lonely Planet Publications.

From the Authors

Minkyoung and Jonathan wish to thank their friend Elizabeth Harriman for sacrificing her time proofreading so much of this book, and hope she'll be satisfied with a free copy and a nice meal at the restaurant of her choosing. They would also like to thank their family and friends who acted as sounding boards for their ideas, as well as Minkyoung's roommate Alexia for not getting angry about the many late night calls when deadlines were approaching. Finally, they would like to thank the Lonely Planet staff for their understanding and patience when Jonathan had an emergency appendectomy right before deadline.

From the Publisher

The *Korean phrasebook* was like wandering up one of Korea's majestic forested mountains. Annelies Mertens worked devotedly from the temple of editing and was attended by Senior Editors Karina Coates and Karin Vidstrup Monk. Adrienne Costanzo ran a careful eye over these pages. Emma Koch and David Burnett stood guard against destroyers of fonts, and Andrew Tudor rendered valuable technical assistance. Designers

Yukiyoshi Kamimura and Belinda Campbell calmly crafted and laid out the manuscript, taking over from Patrick Marris. Patrick's world-renowned illustrations supplemented the text, and he also detailed the colourful view from the summit on the front cover. Senior Designer Fabrice Rocher guided these deft brush strokes and Natasha Velleley brought the map to the working party. Publishing Manager Jim Jenkin oversaw all this and proclaimed it 'the little book of calm'.

Thanks also to Kim Young Ok and Robert Joseph Dowling who wrote the previous edition of the Lonely Planet *Korean phrasebook*, from which this edition developed.

CONTENTS

6   Contents

INTRODUCTION

Korean is the official language of both South and North Korea. Currently around 77 million people speak Korean. The majority of them, nearly 50 million, are in South Korea while approximately 22 million are in North Korea. At least another five million speakers are part of the Korean diaspora, including millions of speakers in northern China. There are many in the former Soviet Union, not only in the Russian Far East, but also in Central Asia. Japan and North America are also home to hundreds of thousands of Korean speakers, as are parts of Europe, South America and Australia.

Korean is part of the Ural-Altaic family of languages (which includes Turkish, Mongolian and Manchu) and was brought to the peninsula by Altaic peoples during Neolithic times. Strong similarities between Korean and Japanese grammar make the two seem so closely related that some linguists feel they should be in a class by themselves. Over time, the Korean vocabulary has also been influenced considerably by Chinese and English.

There are five main dialects of Korean in South Korea, with the dialects' boundaries closely following provincial borders. The dialect of the capital region, Seoul and the surrounding Kyonggi-do (Gyeonggi-do) Province, is considered standard. In North Korea, the dialect in the capital Pyongyang (Pyeongyang) plays the same role. The media in both countries have helped create a uniform language, but regional differences remain strong. Accents can be used as a way to identify a person's province of origin, which sometimes reinforces inter-regional tensions.

Regional dialects differ primarily in terms of intonation and word endings. Generally, the farther away from the capital, the stronger these differences are. Only on the island province of Cheju-do (Jeju-do), in the far south, is the proliferation of non-standard vocabulary so strong that the local speech is difficult for non-locals to understand. Often locals will adopt a more standard form of Korean when speaking with someone from outside the region, especially international visitors.

INTRODUCTION

Linguistic differences between the official varieties in the two Koreas have not been particularly dramatic. Kim Daejung's so-called 'Sunshine Policy' saw a relative flourishing of trade and exchange between the South and the North, and there were very few communication problems. In many ways, the difference between the two standard forms of Korean is probably similar to the degree of difference between North American and British English, with minor vocabulary and spelling differences. Also, Chinese characters are rarely used in North Korea.

HISTORY & LINGUISTIC INFLUENCES

The Korean language itself reflects the history of both North and South Korea.

Long coveted by the neighbouring Chinese, Japanese, Mongolians and Russians, the Korean peninsula has been seen by its neighbours as a channel for cultural exchange, a buffer against invasion, and a staging ground for imperial conquest. Through it all, the resilient and pragmatic Koreans have managed to thrive, but not without their neighbours having a great impact on their history, culture, economy and even language.

But Korea has also experienced a great deal of cultural exchange with these neighbours. Over the centuries, the threat of occupation or absorption by China, Japan and Mongolia has made the Korean people strive to maintain their unique cultural heritage. It has not been easy.

Korean folklore tells us that the Korean language existed from the days when Tan-gun (Dan-gun), the semi-deity whose mother was a bear, founded the country in 2333 BC. Different forms of proto-Korean (or Old Korean) existed in the three major kingdoms of early Korean history, Shilla (Silla), Koguryo (Goguryeo), and Paekche (Baekje), but became uniform when the Shilla Kingdom conquered the other two in the 8th century.

Chinese Influence

Imperial China saw Korea as a loyal 'little brother', its right-hand man, and the two enjoyed a great deal of positive interchange. Korea flourished as a conduit between China and Japan for the flow – especially from China to Korea to Japan – of culture, religion, technology, and social and political institutions.

Chinese cultural and political influence can be seen in the number of Korean words of Chinese origin, approximately 70% of all Korean vocabulary, although the two languages are linguistically distinct. In many ways, the use of Chinese in Korean and Japanese is similar to the use of Latin by Europeans in the post-Roman era. Korea's elite class, called **yangban** (양반), were trained in Chinese classics, and civil service exams were conducted using Chinese characters. Even nowadays, technical words are typically formed by stringing together relevant Chinese characters.

Japanese Influence

The strong similarity between Korean and Japanese grammar appears to many linguists to reflect both voluntary and forced migrations from Korea to Japan over a millennium ago. Japan's nearly half-century occupation of Korea led to a small number of borrowed words, including those from other countries that were filtered through Japan, such as **arŭbait'ŭ** (아르바이트), 'part-time job', from the German word *Arbeit*, 'work'.

In the first half of the 20th century, Japanese military occupiers sought to wipe out any vestiges of a unique Korean culture, including replacing the Korean language with the Japanese language. Korean language instruction was eventually banned, and virtually all Koreans were required to change their Korean names to Japanese ones. Koreans reverted back to using Korean language and Korean names immediately after liberation from Japanese military rule in 1945, but many elderly people today still maintain some Japanese language ability.

American Influence

America's media and economic domination since WWII, not to mention its strong military presence in Korea since the Korean War (1950–53), have led to hundreds of words of purported English origin in everyday use in Korean. Words like **haendŭp'on** (핸드폰), 'mobile phone' (lit: hand phone), **bippi** (삐삐), 'beeper/pager' and **baengmirŏ** (백미러), 'rear-view mirror' (lit: back mirror) have made their way into everyday Korean.

'Pure' Korean

Since liberation from the Japanese at the end of WWII, both North and South Korea have engaged in manipulation of the Korean language for nationalistic purposes. 'Foreign' words in Korean were at one time discouraged by the South Korean regime of Park Chunghee, and the teaching of all but the most basic Chinese characters was once stopped for a period of time. In North Korea, virtually nothing is written in Chinese characters, and the North Korean rulers have succeeded in systematically replacing most 'foreign' words – even Korean words of Chinese origin – with new words composed of 'pure' Korean components.

A good example can be found in the Korean words for 'ice cream'. Koreans originally referred to it as **aisŭk'ŭrim'** (아이스크림), the 'Hangulised' (see below) form of the English word. The North Koreans, on the other hand, coined a new 'pure' Korean term for the dessert, **ŏrŭmposung-i** (얼음보숭이), literally 'ice-fluffy-thing'. However, many North Koreans still use the original term, as do all South Koreans.

WRITTEN KOREAN

Korean was originally written using Chinese characters made up of complex pictographs, meaning that only the educated elite were literate. King Sejong the Great, considered Korea's finest and wisest ruler, headed the creation of a simple script that the masses could easily learn and use. Hangul (lit: Korean letters) was officially adopted in 1446.

The decision to create a simple writing system for the masses was born from incredible foresight and democratic vision. The creation of the alphabet followed scientific principles that closely match linguistic thought today. With the original 28 characters, it was said that any conceivable sound could be written. Hangul is one of the principle reasons the two Koreas are among the most literate countries in the world, both with literacy rates approaching 100%. Both North and South Koreans take enormous pride in their unique alphabet.

Hangul has since been simplified to include ten vowels and 14 consonants. Whereas Chinese characters represent morphemes – elements having a meaning or grammatical function that cannot be subdivided into further elements – and Japanese characters represent independent syllables, each character in Korean represents a sound by itself, making Hangul the only true alphabet native to East Asia.

Korean was traditionally written the same as Chinese: top to bottom in columns running from right to left. It can still be written this way although, due to Western influence, it's now generally written from left to right, in rows going from top to bottom. Most Korean is written in Hangul only, although South Korean newspapers and some textbooks mix in Chinese characters. Many syllables, from everyday words such as **san** (산), 'mountain' or **kang** (강), 'river', as well as most personal and place names, can be represented by Chinese characters called **hantcha** (한자). North Korea's 'Juche' (self-reliance) philosophy has led them to eschew Chinese characters almost completely.

South Koreans are currently taught a minimum of 1000 'everyday' Chinese characters. Even if one is not adept at reading and writing them, knowing their pronunciation as roots is important. Virtually every Chinese character is written only one way in Hangul (unlike Japanese, in which one Chinese character can have multiple spellings). Chinese characters represent only 'Sino-Korean' words – Korean words of Chinese origin – not 'pure' Korean words, which can be written only in Hangul.

KOREAN

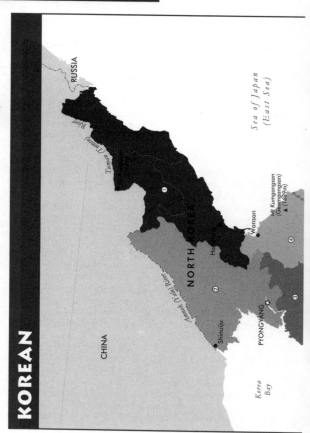

RUSSIA

Tuman (Yuman) River

Amnok (Yalu) River

CHINA

Sinŭiju

NORTH KOREA

Hamhŭng

PYONGYANG

Wŏnsan

Mt Kŭmgangsan
(Geumgangsan)
▲ 1639m

Sea of Japan
(East Sea)

Korea Bay

The decision to create a simple writing system for the masses was born from incredible foresight and democratic vision. The creation of the alphabet followed scientific principles that closely match linguistic thought today. With the original 28 characters, it was said that any conceivable sound could be written. Hangul is one of the principle reasons the two Koreas are among the most literate countries in the world, both with literacy rates approaching 100%. Both North and South Koreans take enormous pride in their unique alphabet.

Hangul has since been simplified to include ten vowels and 14 consonants. Whereas Chinese characters represent morphemes – elements having a meaning or grammatical function that cannot be subdivided into further elements – and Japanese characters represent independent syllables, each character in Korean represents a sound by itself, making Hangul the only true alphabet native to East Asia.

Korean was traditionally written the same as Chinese: top to bottom in columns running from right to left. It can still be written this way although, due to Western influence, it's now generally written from left to right, in rows going from top to bottom. Most Korean is written in Hangul only, although South Korean newspapers and some textbooks mix in Chinese characters. Many syllables, from everyday words such as **san** (산), 'mountain' or **kang** (강), 'river', as well as most personal and place names, can be represented by Chinese characters called **hantcha** (한자). North Korea's 'Juche' (self-reliance) philosophy has led them to eschew Chinese characters almost completely.

South Koreans are currently taught a minimum of 1000 'everyday' Chinese characters. Even if one is not adept at reading and writing them, knowing their pronunciation as roots is important. Virtually every Chinese character is written only one way in Hangul (unlike Japanese, in which one Chinese character can have multiple spellings). Chinese characters represent only 'Sino-Korean' words – Korean words of Chinese origin – not 'pure' Korean words, which can be written only in Hangul.

KOREAN

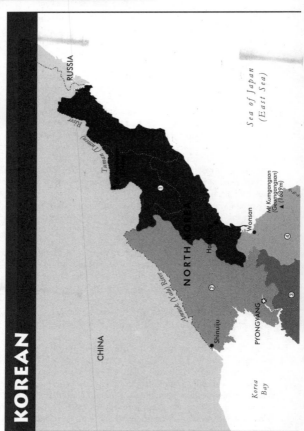

Map 15

INTRODUCTION

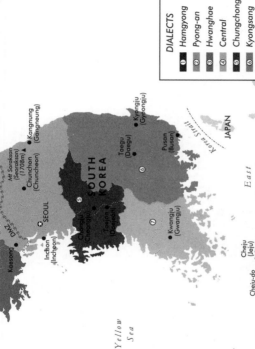

DIALECTS
1 Hamgyong
2 Pyong-an
3 Hwanghae
4 Central
5 Chungchong
6 Kyongsang
7 Cholla
8 Cheju

Kaesong

DMZ

Inchon (Incheon)

SEOUL

Chunchon (Chuncheon)

Mt Soraksan (Seoraksan) (1708m)

Kangnung (Gangneung)

SOUTH KOREA

Chongju (Cheongju)

Taejon (Daejeon)

Taegu (Daegu)

Kyongju (Gyeongju)

Pusan (Busan)

Kwangju (Gwangju)

Korea Strait

JAPAN

East China Sea

Yellow Sea

Cheju (Jeju)

Mt Hallasan (1950m)

Cheju-do Island

0   50   100 km
0   30   60 mi

Both dialectal zones and provincial borders tend to follow traditional regional boundaries

SPOKEN COMMUNICATION

Korean speech ranges from a formal/polite form, used especially with people who are older or of higher rank than oneself, to a casual/polite form used primarily with people of the same age or of similar status, down to a form of speech used only for children. The degree of formal or casual speech is largely indicated by verb endings. For the Korean language beginner, the casual/polite form of speech avoids the awkwardness of being overly formal without showing disrespect and, except where otherwise noted, that's what we have used throughout this book.

Most travellers who visit South Korea, and even those who go to North Korea, would be likely to visit through the few tourist portals opened up by South Korean business ventures, or would travel with mandatory English-speaking tour guides. It's for that reason that we'll use standard South Korean vocabulary when there's a difference between North and South Korean.

South Koreans are now taught English from early elementary school, and the number of people who possess at least basic English communication skills is quite large, so a traveller with no Korean communication skills can generally get by with the use of English, although this may limit his or her opportunities to see parts of the country.

Most Koreans are delighted when overseas visitors try to use their language, and they will happily help even the worst butchers of the language muddle through until they finally make themselves understood. Armed with this book and the right attitude, you are all set to make your cross-cultural journey into the Land of Morning Calm a memorable one.

ABBREVIATIONS USED IN THIS BOOK

adj	adjective	n	noun
f	feminine	neut	neuter
fam	familiar	pl	plural
inf	informal	pol	polite
lit	literal translation	sg	singular
m	masculine	v	verb

PRONUNCIATION

Each of the letters of the Korean alphabet, Hangul, represents a distinct sound. Ten of the letters are vowels and 14 are consonants. There are 11 combination vowels formed from the original ten vowels, and there are five double consonants formed from five of the basic consonants. The result is an alphabet of 40 characters which was designed to be simple to learn. There are a further 11 consonant combinations, but they follow the simple rules of the basic 14 consonants.

If this all sounds confusing, don't worry. Just follow along with the Romanisation we provide, and you'll be able to produce the correct sounds, or at least come very close.

In this chapter, we'll present the various letters of the Hangul alphabet linking them to their corresponding sounds.

So, **shijak halkkayo?** (시작 할까요?), 'Shall we begin?'.

VOWELS

Korean has six basic vowels of essentially the same length, and all are found in English.

Script	Transliteration	Pronunciation
ㅏ	a	as the 'a' in 'father'
ㅓ	ŏ	as the 'o' in 'son'
ㅗ	o	as the 'o' in 'go'
ㅜ	u	as the 'u' in 'nude'
ㅡ	ŭ	as the 'u' in 'put'
ㅣ	i	as the 'ee' in 'keen'

PRONUNCIATION

'Y' Vowels

A 'y' sound like the 'y' in 'yellow' can be added to the first four basic vowels. In the Hangul script, this is represented by a second hash mark:

ㅑ	ya	'y' followed by the 'a' in 'father'
ㅕ	yŏ	'y' followed by the 'o' in 'son'
ㅛ	yo	'y' followed by the 'o' in 'go'
ㅠ	yu	'y' followed by the 'u' in 'nude'

Combination Vowels

Korean has two combination vowels that have a different sound from what might be expected, considering the basic vowels of which they're composed.

ㅐ	ae	as the 'a' in 'bag'
		(ㅏ + ㅣ, but not pronounced as a + i)
ㅔ	e	as the 'e' in 'net'
		(ㅓ + ㅣ, but not pronounced as ŏ + i)

The difference between these two vowels is very subtle, and younger people often don't make the distinction in their speech. They usually pronounce both combination vowels as 'e' (e) in 'net' or something in between the 'e' in 'net' and the 'a' (ae) in bag.

Just as with the basic vowels, a 'y' sound can be added to these by adding a second hash mark to the Hangul. The difference in sound between these two is also very subtle.

ㅒ	yae	'y' followed by the 'a' in 'bag'
		(ㅑ + ㅣ, but not pronounced as ya + i)
ㅖ	ye	'y' followed by the 'e' in 'net'
		(ㅕ + ㅣ, but not pronounced as yŏ + i)

When certain vowels are preceded by **o** (ㅗ) or **u** (ㅜ) this causes them to be pronounced with a 'w' (**w**) sound, like the 'w' in 'water'.

ㅘ	**wa**	'w' followed by the 'a' in 'father' (ㅗ + ㅏ)
ㅙ	**wae**	'w' followed by the 'a' in 'bag' (ㅗ + ㅐ)
ㅝ	**wŏ**	'w' followed by the 'o' in 'son' (ㅜ + ㅓ)
ㅞ	**we**	'w' followed by the 'e' in 'net' (ㅜ + ㅔ)
ㅟ	**wi**	'w' followed by the 'ee' in 'keen' (ㅜ + ㅣ)

Finally, there are two combination vowels that are usually pronounced as two syllables. The first part is briefer than when it's an independent simple vowel, so that it almost sounds like a 'w'.

ㅚ	**oé**	as the 'o' and 'e' in 'no entry',
		but with a shortened 'o' (**o**)
		(ㅗ + ㅣ, but not pronounced as **o** + **i**)
ㅢ	**ŭi**	as the 'ue' in chop suey,
		but with a shortened 'u' (**ŭ**)
		(— + ㅣ, but not pronounced as **ŭ** + **i**)

When **ŭi** is preceded by a consonant, the **ŭ** is dropped, and only **i** is pronounced (as the 'ee' in 'keen'). The word for 'hope/desire', **hŭimang** (희망), is actually pronounced **himang**.

When **ŭi** is used as a possessive however (see Grammar, page 33), it's pronounced -**e**.

MAKING SYLLABLES

A syllable must contain at least one vowel that's always preceded by a consonant (see Consonants from page 20 onwards) and sometimes also followed by a consonant.

All basic vowels are either vertical (ㅏ, ㅑ, ㅓ, ㅕ, or ㅣ) or horizontal (ㅗ, ㅛ, ㅜ, ㅠ, or —). In the case of vowel combinations, it's the leftmost vowel of a combination vowel that dictates whether it's vertical or horizontal.

Vertical Combination Vowels:
ㅐ (**ae**), ㅒ (**yae**), ㅔ (**e**), and ㅖ (**ye**)

Horizontal Combination Vowels:
ㅘ (wa), ㅚ (oé), ㅙ (wae), ㅝ (wǒ), ㅞ (we), ㅟ (wi), and ㅢ (ǔi)

The initial position of a consonant is always to the left of a vertical vowel or above a horizontal vowel. Let's use the consonant ㅁ (m) as an example:

마	ma	모	mo
미	mi	무	mu
매	mae	뭐	mwǒ

Consonants following the vowel always go below the vowel, regardless of whether it is vertical or horizontal. Here are some examples:

| 몸 | mom |
| 맘 | mam |

Consonants preceding or following vertical or horizontal combination vowels follow the same positioning rules.

CONSONANTS
Consonants are usually pronounced as they are in English. However, the pronunciation of most Korean consonants changes depending on their position within a word, or on the letters adjacent to them. Some dialects of English also behave in this way (consider the two different 't' sounds in the American pronunciation of 'total,' or how the 't' changes to 'ch' in 'Don't you?'). In Korean, these sound changes are an integral part of the language.

The following two consonants generally do not change:

| ㄴ | n | as the 'n' in 'nature' |
| ㅁ | m | as the 'm' in 'marry' |

PRONUNCIATION

Aspirated Consonants

Korean has several aspirated consonants (formed by making a puff of air as they're pronounced). Aspirated consonants, when romanised, except for **s** (ㅅ) and **h** (ㅎ), are immediately followed by an apostrophe.

ㅋ	k´	as the 'k' in 'king'
ㅌ	t´	as the 't' in 'talk'
ㅍ	p´	as the 'p' in 'petal'
ㅊ	ch´	as the 'ch' in 'change'
ㅎ	h	as the 'h' in 'happy'
ㅅ	s*	as the 's' in 'sad'

Unaspirated Consonants

There are five more basic consonants. These are unaspirated (pronounced without a puff of air) and they tend to have a different sound depending on their position within a word. As initial sounds (at the beginning of a word or phrase), they appear be pronounced similarly to the aspirated consonants. But it's important that you do not make a puff of air when you pronounce them.

Consonant	Initial sound	Middle sound	Final sound
ㄱ	k-	-g-	-k
ㄷ	t-	-d-	-t
ㅂ	p-	-b-	-p
ㅈ	ch-*	-j-*	-t
ㄹ	r/l-	-r-	-l

The -l at the end of a syllable or word sounds somewhat like a cross between an English 'l' and 'rl' in 'girl' or 'curl'.

Notice the similarity in appearance between the aspirated and unaspirated consonants: ㅋ (k´) and ㄱ (k), ㅌ (t´) and ㄷ (t), ㅍ (p´) and ㅂ (p), and finally, ㅊ (ch´) and ㅈ (ch).

> *Note that s becomes sh when followed by i or ya, yŏ, yo and yu making them shi, sha, shŏ, sho and shu, respectively. Similarly, ch/j followed by ya, yŏ, yo and yu makes them ja, jŏ, jo and ju.

It should also be pointed out that an unaspirated ...
when preceded by **h** (ㅎ) as the final consonant of th...
syllable, becomes aspirated. For example, 안다 is pronounced
anda, 'to hug/embrace', but 않다 is pronounced **ant´a**, 'to not
do something'. (See below for the vowel consonant (ㅇ) at the
beginning of these words.)

Final Sound Changes

A total of five consonants are pronounced like a 't' sound when
they're the final sound of a word: ㅅ (**s**), ㅌ (**t´**), ㅊ (**ch´**), ㄷ (**t/d**),
and ㅈ (**ch/j**). In such cases, they'll all be transliterated as **t**.

The 'Vowel' Consonant

Korean has an unusual consonant (ㅇ), which is either silent
or pronounced, depending on its position within a syllable. At
the beginning of a syllable it's silent, serving as a place holder –
occupying the place where a consonant would be – for syllables
that begin with a vowel sound. However, at the end of a syllable, it's pronounced **ng**. Thus the two ㅇ's found in the syllable
앙 (**ang**), as in chung-ang (중앙), 'central', are completely
different: the first is silent, but the second is pronounced **ng**.

If the 'vowel' consonant is immediately preceded by a
consonant, the pronunciation of that consonant sound is 'moved'
to the position of the 'vowel' consonant. For example, 작아요 ,
'It is small', may appear to be pronounced as **chag-a-yo**, but it
would actually be pronounced as **cha-ga-yo**. Other examples:

	Apparent pronunciation	Actual pronunciation
물어요 (It bites.)	mur-ŏ-yo	mu-rŏ-yo
녹아요 (It melts.)	nog-a-yo	no-ga-yo

Double Consonants

Four unaspirated consonant characters (ㄱ, ㄷ, ㅂ, ㅈ) can be
used to make double consonant characters that, in terms of initial
and middle sounds, may seem almost the reverse of their singular
counterparts (see page 21). As initial sounds, they're pronounced
somewhat more quickly and forcefully than their corresponding
letters in English. The consonant ㅅ can also be used to form a
double consonant.

Character	Initial sound	Middle sound	Final sound
ㄲ	g-	-kk-	-k
ㄸ	d-	-tt-	-
ㅃ	b-	-pp-	-
ㅆ	ss-	-ss-	-t
ㅉ	j-	-tch-	-

Similarly, two ㄹ as the final consonant of one syllable and the first consonant of the following syllable end up pronounced as l.

모래 (one ㄹ)   **morae** ('sand')
몰래 (two ㄹ)   **mollae** ('secretly, without letting anybody know')

Complex Consonants

In addition, there are 11 complex consonants composed of two regular consonants. These are always in the final consonant position within a syllable. How they're pronounced depends on whether the following syllable starts with a vowel or not, but even then there are some inconsistencies. Most of these complex consonants are not common.

	Next syllable starts with a vowel	Next syllable starts with a consonant	Not followed by another syllable
ㅄ	-ps	-p	-p
ㄵ	-nj	-n	-n
ㄺ	-lg	-l	-k
ㄶ	-n	-n	-n
ㄳ	-gs	-k	-k
ㄻ	-rm	-m	-m
ㄼ	-rb	-p	-p
ㄽ	-rs	-l	-l
ㄾ	-rt'	-l	-l
ㄿ	-rp'	-p	-p
ㅀ	-r	-l	-l

For example, the complex consonant ㄺ would be pronounced as:

-lg in 밝아요 (**palgayo**), 'It's bright.', because the next syllable starts with a vowel

-l 밝다 in (**palta**), 'to be bright', because the next syllable starts with a consonant

-k in 닭 (**tak**), 'chicken', because the complex consonant is not followed by another syllable

Other Consonant Changes

There's one feature that complicates Korean pronunciation. Although the pronunciation of a consonant changes according to its position within a word, it can also change depending on the consonant that immediately precedes or follows it. These sound changes occur especially when k/g (ㄱ) and p/b (ㅂ) are followed by r/l (ㄹ), n (ㄴ), or m (ㅁ). These sound changes are mostly the result of positions of the tongue in the mouth. For example, if it's hard to pronounce the sound 'k' (k) when followed by the sound 'm' (m), the sound of the k will change to a sound that's closer to the m and easier to pronounce in conjunction with the m. An example is the word for 'Chinese language' (lit: China + talk):

중국말   chung**guk** + mal

The k/g (ㄱ) followed by m (ㅁ) changes into ng + m, with the result being **chungungmal**.

Other examples:

	Apparent pronunciation	Actual pronunciation
입니다 ('am/is/are', pol)	ibnida	imnida
독립문 ('Independence Gate')	togribmun	tongnimmun
있는 ('being/having/ existing')	itnŭn	innŭn

We'll always provide actual pronunciation throughout the book when we romanise these kinds of words.

STRESS

Unlike some other East Asian languages, stress in Korean is the same for all syllables. The meaning of words does not change depending on stress or pitch.

INTONATION

Rising intonation at the end of a sentence can indicate a question, as is the case in English.

THE HANGUL ALPHABET

consonants:

ㄱ ㄲ ㄴ ㄷ ㄸ ㄹ ㅁ ㅂ ㅃ ㅅ ㅆ ㅇ ㅈ ㅉ ㅊ ㅋ ㅌ ㅍ ㅎ

vowels:

ㅏ ㅑ ㅐ ㅒ ㅓ ㅕ ㅔ ㅖ ㅗ ㅘ ㅙ ㅚ ㅛ ㅜ ㅝ ㅞ ㅟ ㅠ ㅡ ㅢ ㅣ

Refer to pages 17-19 for details on vowels and pages 20-24 for consonants.

TRANSLITERATION SYSTEM

There are a number of transliteration systems to represent Korean by means of the Roman alphabet, but the most widely used was developed in the 1930s by two important academics in Korea, George McCune and Edwin Reischauer – the McCune-Reischauer system (M-R).

In late 2000, however, a South Korean Government agency unilaterally decreed that the Government would henceforth scrap M-R in favour of a 'new' system – the Korean Government system – that was actually based on an older system.

Today various competing Romanisation systems are in use and opinions differ greatly on which system is best suited to transliterate Hangul into Roman characters.

The South Korean Government has been going through the process of changing road signs to reflect the 'new' Romanisation system, as well as to include more Chinese character place names. The process is long, though, and even by the Government's own estimates, will still be underway in 2007. In the meantime, you can expect to encounter signs, maps and tourist literature

PRONUNCIATION

with at least two different Romanisation systems. North Korea however, officially tends to use a form of M-R.

In this book we have used a Romanisation system closely modelled on the Government's pre-2000 version of M-R. It has been our experience that this system is easy to use by Korean language newbies to pronounce Korean words. We'll provide place names in both the McCune-Reischauer and Government systems (also see the list of place names in Getting Around, page 81).

In this book, hyphens are used in the transliterations:

- to avoid confusion between two sounds that might be represented by the same letters:

ng	chung-ang taehakkyo	중앙 대학교	Chungan University
n-g	han-gang	한강	Han River
oé	hoé	회	raw fish
o-e	hakkyo-e	학교에/ 학교의	to school; of a school
ae	shinae	시내	downtown
a-e	k'aenada-e	캐나다에/ 캐나다의	to Canada; Canadian
eu	euljiro	을지로	Euljiro district
e-u	se-uda	세우다	to stop
ae-u	sae-u	새우	shrimp

- before certain components of words – such as -do (一도), -dong (一동), -ku (一구) (all referring to place names), -sa (一사) for temples, -kung (一궁) for palaces, -kang (강) for rivers and before titles, eg -shi (一씨) – to separate them from the first part of the word, because this is what you'll see on signs in Korea.

Despite a strong Chinese influence on Korean vocabulary, Korean grammar is completely different from that of Chinese. There are, however, very strong similarities between Korean grammar and Japanese grammar, which makes learning one much easier if you've already been exposed to the other. Korean grammar ranges from respectful forms of speech, **chondaemal** (존대말), to 'low' forms of speech, **panmal** (반말).

This book presents a practical middle ground – the familiar-high form – between the high form, characterised by the verb endings **-mnida** and **-mnikka**, and lower forms of speech characterised by reduced verb endings or no verb endings at all. The high form is appropriate when first meeting, but would sound awkward if over-used in everyday situations; conversely, using the low form to people with whom you're not familiar will definitely offend the listener.

WORD ORDER

To a large extent, Korean word order (typically subject-object-verb) differs from that of English (typically subject-verb-object). The subject is not always necessary, but when used, it usually comes first, as in English, but direct objects usually precede verbs, eg:

I came from Australia.   (**chŏnŭn**) **hojuesŏ wassŏyo**
                         (lit: [I-nŭn] Australia-from came)

I like spicy food.   (**chŏnŭn**) **maeunŭmshigŭl choahaeyo**
                     (lit: [I-nŭn] spicy food-ŭl like)

(See page 32 for the particles -ŭn/-nŭn and -ŭl/-rŭl.)

When the subject is clear – and sometimes even when it's not – it may be dropped altogether. Rather than saying 'I came from Australia', it's perfectly acceptable to omit the subject if it's clear that you're speaking about yourself and say 'came from Australia'. In fact, it may even sound awkward if you repeatedly say 'I' at the beginning of each sentence. Still, what's clear to the speaker might not be so clear to the listener, so don't be afraid to interject **nugayo?**, the subject form of 'who'.

ARTICLES

Articles are completely absent in Korean. Whether or not the speaker is referring to 'a car', 'the car' or 'cars' is determined by context. A specific thing (indicated by 'the' in English) can be designated by the use of the demonstratives 'this' and 'that' (see page 37) as in 'this car', or by possessive adjectives as in 'our school'.

this car (near the speaker)	i ch'a
that car (near the listener, or one that has previously been mentioned)	kŭ ch'a
that car (visible, but away from both listener and speaker)	chŏ ch'a
our school	uri hakkyo (lit: we school)

NOUNS

Korean is devoid of the feminine, masculine and neuter noun forms that torture many learners of European languages. Even the words for 'he' or 'she' are rarely used.

Plurals

Korean does have a simple way of turning singular nouns into a plural form – by adding -**dŭl** to the noun – but this is usually omitted.

person/people	saram
people	saramdŭl

GRAMMATICAL TERMS

A number of basic grammatical terms are used in this chapter:

adjective	adds information about a noun *big* backpack
adverb	adds information about a verb or adjective He runs *quickly*. The backpack is *very* big.
conjunction	joins together sentences or parts of a sentence Walk to the station *and* deposit the luggage.
noun	a person (John), object (book), place (beach) or concept (happiness)
object	refers to the noun or pronoun that is affected by the verb
direct indirect	The guide showed *a map*. The guide showed *us* a map.
particle	displays the function of the preceding noun or pronoun in a sentence; sometimes acts as a preposition
prefix/suffix	an element added to a word to create a different form; a prefix precedes and a suffix follows the word eg, *un-* (prefix) and *-able* (suffix) in *un*believ*able*
preposition	often introduces information about location, time or direction *at* the market *towards* the train
pronoun	usually takes the place of a noun *she* travels instead of Paula travels
subject	refers to the noun or pronoun that is performing an action *The backpacker* washes his clothes.
verb	an action or doing word He *ran* for the ferry.

PRONOUNS

Pronouns are generally not used in Korean, especially in the third person ('he/him', 'she/her' and 'they/them'). Instead, the person about whom you're speaking is referred to by their name, their title, or especially their relationship to the speaker or listener, expressed in the form of speech (see page 27).

One thing that makes Korean very different from English is that even the pronoun 'you' is often replaced by a third-person reference, especially when speaking to someone in a higher position (see Forms of Address in Meeting People, page 59). As for the third person, there are no real pronouns in Korean. Instead they're usually expressed by combining the words for 'this' and 'that' (see page 37) with the noun.

There are some pronouns that are commonly used. These pronouns can be used interchangeably for males or females.

SINGULAR		PLURAL	
I (pol)	che		
I (inf)	nae		
me (pol)	chŏ	we/us	uri
me (inf)	na		
you (pol)	tangshin		
you (inf)	nŏ	you (inf)	nŏhidŭl
she/her/he/him (pol)	kŭbun		
she/her (inf)	kŭnyŏ	they/them (inf)	kŭdŭl
he/him (inf)	kŭ		

PARTICLES

Korean nouns and pronouns are usually followed by a particle whose role it is to show the function of the preceding noun in the sentence (eg, the subject of the sentence, the direct object etc), as in Korean this is not always clear from the word order. Other particles act as prepositions designating where someone is going to, to whom someone is giving something, where something is coming from, etc.

GRAMMAR

Note that in conversational speech, subject and direct object particles are frequently omitted, especially when the subject or object is clear (for the omission of the subject and object also see page 28).

Because particles are attached to the noun, they essentially become part of the pronunciation of the noun itself. Which form of the particle to use often depends on whether the noun ends in a vowel or a consonant. In the following, for particles which have different forms, we show the form to be used if the noun ends in a consonant first, then the form to be used if the noun ends in a vowel.

Also keep in mind that the particles may alter the pronunciation of the consonant that precedes it (which changes from being a final consonant to a middle consonant. See Pronunciation, page 21).

Subject Particle

The subject particle -i/-ga (after consonant/vowel respectively) is attached to the noun that functions as the subject of the sentence.

mountain(s)	**san**
The mountains are beautiful.	**sani arŭmdawŏyo**
	(lit: mountain-**i** be-beautiful)
I (as a subject)	**che**
I will do it.	**chega hagessŏyo**
	(lit: I-**ga** do-will)

GRAMMAR

THOSE TINY THINGS

Korean grammar is very different from English grammar, especially when it comes to word order and particles. Many people starting out with the Korean language get confused about which particle is appropriate, especially when it comes to choosing between the subject particle and the topic particle. The fact is that even if you make a mistake with these, you're still likely to be understood, so don't get bogged down with the details.

Topic Particle

The topic particle -ŭn/-nŭn (after consonant/vowel respectively) is used to show the subject of the sentence when you want to emphasise another part of the sentence besides the subject. A topic particle can also be used to mention what the sentence is about. Topic particles tend to replace subject particles, and although there's a subtle difference between the two, there may seem to be no difference to an English speaker.

Pusan	pusan
Pusan isn't cold.	pusanŭn ch'upji anayo
('not being cold' is the emphasis)	(lit: Pusan-ŭn cold-not)
I	chŏ
I'm a student.	chŏnŭn haksaeng-ieyo
('being a student' is the emphasis)	(lit: I-nŭn student-am)

ㄱㄲㄴㄷㄸㄹㅁㅂㅃㅅㅆㅇㅈㅉㅊㅋㅌㅍㅎ
ㅏㅐㅑㅒㅓㅔㅕㅖㅗㅘㅙㅚㅛㅜㅝㅞㅟㅠㅡㅢㅣ

GRAMMAR

Direct Object Particle

The direct object particle -ŭl/-rŭl (after consonant/vowel respectively) is used to indicate the noun or pronoun that's affected by the verb.

book	ch'aek
My friend wants to buy a book.	che ch'in-guga ch'aegŭl sago ship'ŏhaeyo
	(lit: my friend-ga book-ŭl buy want)
bus	bŏsŭ
I'm riding the bus.	bŏsŭrŭl t'ayo
	(lit: bus-rŭl ride)

Indirect Object Particle

The indirect object particles -**hante** and -**ege** are used to show to whom something is given. In English, this would be translated simply as 'to'. There's no real difference between these two particles, so choice is one of personal preference.

that woman	kŭyŏjabun
I gave that woman my ticket.	kŭyŏjabunhante p'yorŭl juŏssŏyo (lit: that-woman-hante ticket-rŭl gave)

child	ŏrini
I gave the child a cookie.	ŏriniege kwajarŭl juŏssŏyo (lit: child-ege cookie-rŭl gave)

Possessive Particle

The possessive particle in Korean is -**ŭi**, but it's almost always pronounced -**e**. It's used to indicate that a word belongs to the previous word.

Mr Kim	misŭtŏ kim
Mr Kim's car	misŭtŏ kime ch'a (lit: Mister Kim-e car)

Japan	ilbon
the Japanese economy	ilbone kyŏngje (lit: Japan-e economy)

When the possession is clear, however, the possessive particle is frequently dropped in Korean. In a series of nouns, the subsequent noun (or nouns) are assumed to belong to the preceding noun.

our school's carpark	uri hakkyo chuch'ajang (lit: we school carpark)

GRAMMAR

Special possessive pronouns for 'my' or 'your' have developed based on the possessive particle -e.

I (pol)	chŏ	my (pol)	che (from chŏ + e)
I (inf)	na	my (inf)	nae (from na + e)
you (inf)	nŏ	your (inf)	ne (from nŏ + e)

In the case of 'your', nŏe (from nŏ + e) can still be used, especially since the pronunciation of nae, 'my' (inf), and ne, 'your' (inf), are so similar. Also see Pronouns, page 30.

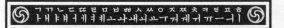

Location Particle

The location particle -e is used to indicate time, location or destination. Because of the context there's rarely any confusion with the possessive particle -e.

• Time	Wednesday	on Wednesday
	suyoil	**suyoire** (suyoil + e)
	four o'clock	at four o'clock
	neshi	**neshie**
	2002 (as in the year)	in 2002
	ichŏninyŏn	**ichŏninyŏne**
• Location	home	at home
	chip	**chibe** (chip + e)
	Korea	in Korea
	han-guk	**han-guge** (han-guk + e)
• Destination	Seoul	to Seoul
	sŏul	**sŏure** (sŏul + e)

(See Pronunciation page 20 for the changes in pronunciation of the consonants.)

Direction Particle

The particle -ŭro/-ro (after consonant/vowel respectively) is used to indicate direction and is very similar in function to the preceding location particle.

market	shijang
towards the market	shijangŭro
	(lit: market-**ŭro**)

school	hakkyo
in the direction of school	hakkyoro
	(lit: school-**ro**)

This particle is also used to indicate that something is done through or by something else.

telephone	chŏnhwa
by telephone	chŏnhwaro
	(lit: telephone-**ro**)

bus	bŏsŭ
I came by bus.	bŏsŭro wassŏyo
	(lit: bus-**ro** came)

Action Location Particle

The action location particle -esŏ is used to indicate the location of an action. When describing where someone started from, it functions as the word 'from'. The same particle is used regardless of whether the preceding noun starts with a consonant or a vowel, although it may alter the pronunciation of a preceding consonant.

Let's call from the hotel.	hoteresŏ chŏnhwa hapshida
	(lit: hotel-**esŏ** phone do-let's)

I'm sleeping at my friend's house.	ch'in-gu chibesŏ chayo
	(lit: friend house-**esŏ** sleep)

I came from New York yesterday.	ŏje nyuyogesŏ wassŏyo
	(lit: yesterday New York-**esŏ** came)

Together Particles

Both **-gwa/-wa** (after consonant/vowel respectively) and **-hago** are used to string nouns together, functioning as 'and' or 'with'. Whether to use **-hago** or **-gwa/-wa** is a matter of preference.

my cousin and my friend	**uri sachonhago che ch'in-gu** (lit: we cousin-**hago** my friend) **uri sachongwa che ch'in-gu** (lit: we cousin-**gwa** my friend)
my friend and my cousin	**che ch'in-guwa uri sachon** (lit: my friend-**wa** we cousin)

GRAMMAR

Certain nouns and particles that commonly follow them can be contracted, as 'I am' or 'there is' are shortened to 'I'm' and 'there's' in English.

	full form	contracted
I (pol) + topic particle	chŏnŭn	chŏn
I (inf) + topic particle	nanŭn	nan
you (inf) + topic particle	nŏnŭn	nŏn
here + action location particle	yŏgiesŏ	yŏgisŏ
there + action location particle	kŏgiesŏ	kŏgisŏ
over there + action location particle	chŏgiesŏ	chŏgisŏ
where + action location particle	ŏdiesŏ	ŏdisŏ
object + subject particle	kŏshi	ke
object + topic particle	kŏsŭn	kŏn
object + direct object particle	kŏsŭl	kŏl

DEMONSTRATIVES

Korean demonstratives have three ways of indicating distance:
i-, **kŭ-** and **chŏ-**.

- The prefix **i-** ('this') is used to indicate something or someone close to the speaker.
- The prefix **kŭ-** ('that') is used to indicate something or someone close to the listener, or something that was previously mentioned.
- The prefix **chŏ-** ('that over there') is used to indicate someone or something away from both the speaker and the listener, but that is still visible.

this	**i-**
this photo	**i sajin**
that	**kŭ-**
that cell phone	**kŭ haendŭp′on**
that over there	**chŏ-**
that restaurant over there	**chŏshiktang**

Keep in mind that the pronunciation of the subsequent noun's first consonant may be altered, as it's now in a 'middle' position.

street	**kil**
that street (over there)	**chŏgil**

The same prefixes are used to form the words 'here' and 'there'.

here	**yŏgi**
(lit: the place where the speaker is)	
there	**kŏgi**
(lit: that place where the listener is, or a place that has been mentioned)	
there	**chŏgi**
(lit: that place over there)	

VERBS

In Korean, verbs go at the end of the sentence and don't change according to the subject. The word **kayo** can mean 'I go' or 'she goes'. There are three basic tenses: past, present and future, all of which are easily conjugated.

Verb endings are not used only to refer to past, present or future, but also express the relationship between the speaker and the listener, or the speaker and the subject (see forms of speech page 27). This can get very complex, however, so we will stick to the multi-purpose 'familiar polite' form, which is useful in almost all situations.

In a Korean dictionary, verbs are always listed in their basic form, which is made up of the verb stem plus the ending -**da**. In order to use a verb in its past, present or future tense, you need to know the verb stem.

Finally, you also need to keep in mind that the pronunciation of consonants may change when endings are added (see Pronunciation page 20).

In the following, the asterisk (*) indicates that the personal pronoun 'I' can be replaced by 'you', 'she', 'he', 'it', 'we' or 'they'.

Present

The present tense is usually formed by adding **a** or **o** to the verb stem. To make the sentence polite -**yo** is added as a final ending.

• Verb stems ending in a consonant

To form the present tense, you need to look at the last vowel of the verb stem, even if the final letter of the verb stem is a consonant. If the last vowel is **a** or **o**, and the verb stem ends in a consonant, the verb ending for the present tense is -**ayo**.

look for, search	**ch´aj-**	I* look for	**ch´ajayo**
	(last vowel **a**)		(**ch´aj** + **ayo**)
melt	**nok-**	It melts.	**nogayo**
	(last vowel **o**)		(**nok** + **ayo**)

• Verb stems ending in **a** (with no consonant following)
If a verb stem ends with **a** but without a consonant following it
(as in **ka-da**, 'to go', or **cha-da**, 'to sleep'), -**yo** is added instead
of -**ayo**, to avoid an awkward-sounding double **a**.

| go | **ka-** | I* go | **kayo** (not **kaayo**) |
| sleep | **cha-** | I* sleep | **chayo** (not **chaayo**) |

• Verb stems ending in **o** (with no consonant following)
If a verb stem ends with **o** but without a consonant following it
(as in **po-da**, 'to see/watch'), -**oayo** at the end (the verb stem's **o**
+ -**ayo**) can be changed to -**wayo**. In the case of **o-da**, 'to come',
it must change to **wayo**.

| see/watch | **po-** | I* see/watch | **pwayo** (or **poayo**) |
| come | **o-** | I* come | **wayo** (can't be **oayo**) |

• Verb stems ending with **ŭ**
If the last vowel of the verb stem is **ŭ**, then the present tense verb
is conjugated by replacing the **ŭ** with -**ŏyo**.

| use | **ssŭ-** | → I* use | **ssŏyo** (ssŭ - ŭ + ŏyo) |

• Verb stems ending with other vowels
If the last vowel of the verb stem is other than **a**, **o** or **ŭ** (ie ŏ, **u**, **i**,
or one of the combination vowels), then the present tense verb
is conjugated by adding -**ŏyo**. Keep in mind consonant sound
changes when suffixes are added.

| eat (inf) | **mŏk-** | I* eat | **mŏgŏyo** (mŏk + ŏyo) |
| laugh | **us-** | I* laugh | **usŏyo** (us + ŏyo) |

• Irregular Verbs

Fortunately, Korean has very few irregular verbs, but they're also among the most common.

ha-da, 'to do'

This verb is one of the most commonly used in Korea, as it's often used to turn nouns into verbs (eg, 'make a reservation' is literally 'reservation do'). Although it ends in **a**, it's not conjugated by adding **-ayo** or **-yo**. Instead the vowel **a** changes into **ae**.

do	**ha-**
I* do	**haeyo**

toé-da, 'to become'

This verb can be conjugated like any other verb, **toéŏyo** (**toé** + **ŏyo**), but it's usually conjugated as **twaeyo**.

-rŭ verbs

The last major set of irregular verbs are the ones whose verb stem ends with **-rŭ**. There aren't many of these verbs, but there are a few that are commonly used.

How to conjugate **-rŭ** verbs depends on the vowel in the syllable preceding **-rŭ**: if the preceding syllable contains an **a** or **o**, you replace **-rŭ** with **-llayo**; if the preceding syllable contains any other vowel, you replace **-rŭ** with **-llŏyo**.

not know	**morŭ-**
I* do not know	**mollayo**
	(**morŭ - rŭ + llayo**)
cut	**charŭ-**
I* cut	**challayo**
	(**charŭ - rŭ + llayo**)
call (someone)	**purŭ-**
I* call (someone)	**pullŏyo**
	(**purŭ - rŭ + llŏyo**)

Past

Once you know how to conjugate verbs in the present tense, the past tense is easy. The same rules apply, depending on the last vowel of the stem.

- Verb stems whose final vowel is **a** or **o**

If the last vowel is **a** or **o**, add -**assŏyo** or -**ssŏyo**.

I* looked for	**ch′ajassŏyo** (ch′aj + assŏyo)
It melted.	**nogassŏyo** (nok + assŏyo)
I* went	**kassŏyo** (ka + ssŏyo)
I* slept	**chassŏyo** (cha + ssŏyo)
I* came	**wassŏyo** (o + assŏyo)
I* saw/watched	**pwassŏyo** (po + assŏyo)

The asterisk (*) indicates that the personal pronoun 'I' can be replaced by 'you', 'she', 'he', 'it', 'we' or 'they'.

- Verb stems ending with **ŭ**

If the last vowel of the verb stem is **ŭ**, drop **ŭ** and add -**ŏssŏyo** to make the past tense.

I* used	**ssŏssŏyo** (ssŭ - ŭ + ŏssŏyo)

- Verb stems ending with other vowels

If the last vowel is other than **a**, **o** or **ŭ** (eg, **ŏ**, **u**, **i** or one of the combination vowels), then the verb ending for the past tense will be -**ŏssŏyo**.

I* ate	**mŏgŏssŏyo** (mŏk + ŏssŏyo)
I* laughed	**usŏssŏyo** (us + ŏssŏyo)

- Irregular verbs

In similar fashion, the irregular verbs **ha-da**, 'to do', and **toé-da**, 'to become', as well as the -**rŭ** verbs, like eg **morŭ**, 'not know', are conjugated in the past tense by adding -**ssŏyo**

I* did	**haessŏyo**
I* became	**twaessŏyo**
I* did not know	**mollassŏyo**

See the previous page for the present tense of these irregular verbs.

Future

The future tense isn't complicated. If the verb stem ends with a consonant, you simply add **-ŭl kŏeyo**. If the verb stem ends with a vowel, you add **-l kŏeyo**. These can also appear as **-ŭl kkeyo** and **-l kkeyo**, respectively. An alternative form of the future tense is to add **-gessŏyo** to the verb stem, but it's less common.

look for, search	ch'aj-
I* will look for	ch'ajŭl kŏeyo
	(ch'aj + ŭl kŏeyo)
eat	mŏk-
I* will eat	mŏgŭl kŏeyo
	(mŏk + ŭl kŏeyo)
go	ka-
I* will go	kal kŏeyo
	(ka + l kŏeyo)

Even the irregular verbs **ha-da**, 'to do' and **toé-da**, 'to become' follow this pattern:

do	ha-
I* will do	hal kŏeyo
	(ha + l kŏeyo)
become	toé-
I* will become	toél kŏeyo
	(toé + l kŏeyo)

BETTER SAFE THAN SORRY

In Korean you must always include linguistic elements to keep your speech polite, except when talking with close friends, younger family members, or people who are much younger. If you omit these, it can easily be taken as an insult. Non-Koreans can avoid such offense by adding **-yo** to their sentences, even if only replying with a one-word answer.

GRAMMAR

There Is/Are

There are two words used for saying whether something exists:
issŏyo for positive situations (ie, 'there is/are') and **ŏpsŏyo** for
negative situations (ie, 'there isn't/aren't'). They're frequently
used with the location particle **-e** (see page 34).

Taegyong is at the university.	**t´aegyŏng-shiga taehakkyo-e issŏyo** (lit: Taegyong-Miss-**ga** university-**e** exist)
Hyonu is not at his company.	**hyŏnu-shiga hoésa-e ŏpsŏyo** (lit: Hyonu-Mister-**ga** company-**e** not-exist)
There's a book.	**ch´aegi issŏyo** (lit: book-**i** exist)
There's no book.	**ch´aegi ŏpsŏyo** (lit: book-**i** not exist)

The same words are used to express possession. In this case, the
object that's possessed is the subject of the sentence, and the
possessor is the topic of the sentence (see Subject Particle and
Topic Particle, page 31-32).

I have a car.	**chŏnŭn ch´aga issŏyo** (lit: I-**nŭn** car-**ga** exist)
I have no house.	**chŏnŭn chibi ŏpsŏyo** (lit: I-**nŭn** house-**i** not-exist)

In such cases, the subject particle is sometimes dropped for
convenience.

To Be

In Korean, the verb 'to be' is rendered not by one single verb as in English, but by various verbs. Something or someone can 'be' ('exist') somewhere, in which case **issŏyo/ŏpsŏyo** is used (see page 43). When using most adjectives (eg, 'She's smart') the various forms of 'to be' are built into the adjective itself (see Adjectives, page 50). But when talking about who you are or what you do (eg, 'I'm a tourist') or what something is (eg, 'It's a dictionary'), the verb to use is **i-da**. Its conjugation for the polite familiar form is **-ieyo** if the preceding word ends with a consonant, and **-eyo** if the preceding word ends with a vowel.

I'm a student.	**(chŏnŭn) haksaeng-ieyo** (lit: (I-**nŭn**) student be)
This is a school.	**hakkyo-eyo** (lit: school be)
We're Australians.	**urinŭn hojusaram-ieyo** (lit: we-**nŭn** Australia-people-be)

The negative for 'to be' is **anieyo**, regardless of whether the previous word ends with a vowel or consonant.

This isn't our hotel.	**uri hoteri anieyo** (lit: we hotel-**i** be-not)

The past tense of **-ieyo/-eyo** is **-iŏssŏyo**, and the past tense of anieyo is **aniŏssŏyo**

I was a student.	**chŏn haksaeng iso** (lit: I student be-not)
I was not a student.	**chŏn haksaeng-i aniso** (lit: I student-**i** was-not)

Who/That Does

To express 'a person who does something' or 'a thing that does something', simply take the verb stem and add the suffix **-nŭn**. To express the same clause in the past tense, you'll need to use the suffixes **-ŭn** (if the verb stem ends with a consonant) and **-n** (if the verb stem ends with a vowel). Similarly, the suffixes **-ŭl** (if the verb stems ends in a consonant) and **-l** (if the verb stem ends in a vowel) are used to express this clause in the future tense.

Verb stem	Suffix	'Person'	Example
mŏk- (eat)	**-nŭn**	saram	**mŏngnŭn saram** the person who eats (lit: eat-**nŭn** person)
kongbuha- (study)	**-nŭn**	saram	**kongbuhanŭn saram** the person who studies (lit: study-do-**nŭn** person)
mŏk- (eat)	**-ŭn**	saram	**mŏgŭn saram** the person who ate
ka- (go)	**-n**	saram	**kan saram** the person who went
mŏk- (eat)	**-ŭl**	saram	**mŏgŭl saram** the person who will eat
kyŏlhonha- (get married)	**-l**	saram	**kyŏlhonhal saram** the person who will get married

Note that the suffixes **-nŭn**, **-ŭn** and **-ŭl** may change the pronunciation of the preceding consonant (as the verb stem **mŏk-** shows).

Commands & Requests

Commands can be made politely by adding **-ŭseyo** to verb stems ending with a consonant, and **-seyo** to verb stems ending with a vowel. As this verb ending is polite in itself, the word 'please' is implied.

sit	**anj-** (ends with a consonant)
Please sit down.	**anjŭseyo (anj + ŭseyo)**
eat	**chapsu-** (ends with a vowel)
Please eat. (pol)	**chapsuseyo**

An alternative ending with the same meaning is **-ŭshipshio/ -shipshio**, but it's less common.

Sometimes **-ŭseyo/-seyo** is used in place of **-ŏyo/-ayo** to form polite questions.

Where are you going? (pol)	**ŏdi kaseyo?**
	(lit: where go-**seyo**)
What are you doing? (pol)	**mwŏ haseyo?**
	(lit: what do-**seyo**)

A more polite, less direct way to ask someone to do something for you is to turn the verb stem into what we could call the compound form of the verb, and then add **-juseyo** (or **-jushipshio**), the command form of 'give'. Making a verb stem into its compound form is easy: it's simply the present tense without the verb ending **-yo**.

Please buy it for me.	**sajuseyo (sa + juseyo)**
	(lit: buy-**juseyo**-command)
Please take me there.	**kajuseyo (ka + juseyo)**
	(lit: go-**juseyo**-command)
Please do it for me.	**haejuseyo (hae + juseyo)**
	(lit: do-**juseyo**-command)

MODALS

Modals are verbs that modify the meaning of another verb. They express an ability, necessity, desire or need, as in 'can read', 'need to go' and 'want to drink'. The English verbs 'can', 'may', 'must', 'should', 'to want' and 'to need' are often called modals.

Must; Have To; Need To

To say someone 'must' or 'has to' do something, you take the compound form of a verb – the present tense without the verb ending -yo – and add the suffix -ya, followed by the conjugated form of the verb **ha-da**, 'to do', or **toé-da**, 'to become; to be okay; to be acceptable'. There's no difference between the two choices, but **toé-da** is more common.

| He must go. | **kunŭn kaya twaeyo**
(lit: he-**nŭn** go-ya okay) |
| I have to buy (it). | **chŏnŭn (kŭgŏl) saya haeyo**
(lit: I-**nŭn** that thing-I buy-ya do) |

Instead of saying 'you don't have to (do something)', Koreans would say 'it's okay if you do not (do something)'. Simply add -**ji anado twaeyo** to the verb stem of the action that doesn't need to be done.

| You don't have to pay. | **tangshinŭn naeji anado twaeyo**
(lit: you-**ŭn** pay-**ji** not-**do** okay) |

The negative of must – as in 'you must not' – is expressed by adding the conjunction -**myŏn**, 'if', to the verb stem of the action that you must not do, followed by the phrase **an-dwaeyo**, 'no good'.

| go in | **tŭrŏga-** |
| You must not go in there. | **tŭrŏgamyŏn andwaeyo**
(lit: go-in-**myŏn** not-okay) |

Can; To Be Able

To express the ability to do something, add -ŭl to a verb stem that ends with a consonant, or simply -l to a verb stem that ends with a vowel. You then add **su issŏyo**, which literally means 'ability exists'.

eat	**mŏk-** (ends with a consonant)
can eat	**mŏgŭlsu issŏyo**
	(**mŏk + ŭl + su issŏyo**)
I can eat spicy food.	(**chŏnŭn**) **maeun ŭmshigŭl mŏgŭlsu issŏyo**
	(lit: (I-**nŭn**) spicy food-**ŭl** eat-**ŭl su issŏyo**)
go	**ka-** (ends with a vowel)
can go	**kalsu issŏyo** (**ka + l + su issŏyo**)
I can go tomorrow.	(**chŏnŭn**) **naeil kalsu issŏyo**
	(lit: (I-**nŭn**) tomorrow go-**l su issŏyo**)

Can't

There are two ways to express 'can't'. A negative can be made simply by replacing **issŏyo** with its negative, **ŏpsŏyo**. Literally this means 'ability does not exist'.

She can't speak Japanese.	**kŭnyŏnŭn ilbonmarŭl halsu ŏpsŏyo**
	(lit: she-**nŭn** Japan-talk do-**l su ŏpsŏyo**)

Alternatively, the prefix **mot** can be put in front of any verb to express 'can't'. This suffix may alter the pronunciation of the following verb.

I can't sleep.	(**chŏnŭn**) **mot chayo**
	(lit: (I-**nŭn**) can't-sleep)

May

Expressing the verb 'may' (as in 'having permission') is done by taking the compound form of a verb (see page 46) and adding **-do dwaeyo**.

You may take a photo.

(tangshinŭn) sajin tchigŏdo dwaeyo
(lit: (you-ŭn) photo take-**do** okay)

To Want

If you want to say that you would like 'an item', simply use that item as a direct object (followed by **-ŭl/rŭl**, see page 32) and the verb **wonha-**, 'to want'.

I want ice cream.

chŏnŭn aisŭ-k'ŭrimŭl wonhaeyo
(lit: I-**nŭn** ice cream-**ŭl** want)

To express that you want to 'do something' in the first person, simply follow that action's verb stem with **-go/-ko ship'ŏyo**. If you want to talk about someone wanting to do something in the third person, follow that action's verb stem with **-go/-ko ship'ŏhaeyo**. The pronunciation of **-go/-ko** will depend on the final consonant of the verb stem that precedes it.

I/We want to visit the hot springs.

onch'ŏne kago ship'ŏyo
(lit: hot-springs-**e** go-**go** want)

My husband wants to do some sightseeing.

uri namp'yŏnŭn kugyŏng hago ship'ŏhaeyo
(lit: we husband-**ŭn** do-sightseeing-**go** want)

ADJECTIVES

Basic adjectives in Korean are very similar in structure and function to verbs: they're conjugated in the same way as verbs – following the same rules of conjugation that depend on the final vowel of the stem (see pages 38–42) – and they come at the end of a sentence. If you were to translate them into English, they would include the word 'be'.

> (be) high
> The mountain is high.
> **nop′-** (last vowel is **o**)
> **sani nop′ayo (nop′ + ayo)**
> (lit: mountain-**i** be-high)

> (be) big
> The park is big.
> **k′ŭ-** (last vowel is **ŭ**)
> **kong-wŏni k′ŏyo (k′ŭ - ŭ + ŏyo)**
> (lit: park-**i** be-big)

An adjective can precede the noun it modifies by adding **-ŭn** or **-n** to it (similar to the way in which a verb phrase can modify a noun, see page 45). If the adjective ends with a consonant, **-ŭn** is added to that syllable. If the adjective ends with a vowel, then **-n** is added.

> (be) high
> This is a high mountain.
> **nop′-** (ends with a consonant)
> **nop′ŭn sanieyo**
> (lit: high mountain-be)

> (be) big
> It's a big park.
> **k′ŭ-** (ends with a vowel)
> **k′ŭn kong-wonieyo**
> (lit: big park-be)

(See page 44 for the verb To Be.)

Adjectives involving people or places are also made using the possessive particle **-e**, although it's often dropped. In that case, the first noun modifies the second one.

> Canadian mountain(s)
> **k′aenada-e san**
> (lit: Canada-**e** mountain)

> educational policy
> **kyoyuk chedo**
> (lit: education policy)

Irregular Adjectives

There's only one main type of irregular adjective: that ending with **p**. When conjugating this adjective, you simply replace **p** with **u**. It can then be conjugated like any other adjective or verb ending in **u** (by adding **-ŏyo** which, together with **u**, becomes **-wŏyo**).

be hot (as in spicy)	**maep-**
'useable' form	**maeu (maep - p + u)**
hot/spicy	**maeun (maeu + n)**
It's spicy.	**maewŏyo (maeu + ŏyo)**

be cold (as in weather)	**ch'up-**
'useable' form	**ch'u-u (ch'up - p + u)**
cold	**ch'u-un (ch'u - u + n)**
It's cold.	**ch'uwŏyo (ch'u - u + ŏyo)**

Comparatives

Comparatives are made by adding the prefix **tŏ-**, 'more', at the beginning of an adjective:

hot (spicy)	**maeun**
hotter (spicier)	**tŏ maeun**

The particle **-boda/-poda** functions as the word 'than' in English. However, it follows the word being compared against, rather than preceding it, and its pronunciation – **b** or **p** – depends on the preceding letter.

Kimchi is spicier than wasabi.	**kimch'inŭn**
	wasabiboda maewŏyo
	(lit: kimchi-**nŭn**
	wasabi-than be-spicy)

Superlatives

Superlatives are easily created by putting the words **cheil** (lit: 'number one') or **kajang** ,'most', before the adjective or adverb to be modified. The difference between the two is a matter of choice.

pretty	yeppŭn
prettiest	cheil yeppŭn; kajang yeppŭn
the prettiest girl	cheil/kajang yeppŭn yŏja (lit: most pretty girl)

ADVERBS

Adverbs are usually made by taking the adjective stem and adding -**ge/-ke**. Keep in mind that this may change the pronunciation of the preceding consonant. Adverbs come before the verb they modify.

be safe	anjŏnha-
safely	anjŏnhage
drive safely	anjŏnhage unjŏn haeyo (lit: safely drive)

There are a few special adverbs that sound completely unlike their adjectival counterparts. For example, there are two words for 'slowly': **nŭrige**, from the adjective **nŭri-**, and the unrelated **ch'ŏnch'ŏnhi**. The more common of these will be in the dictionary (see page 239 onwards).

QUESTIONS

In the polite familiar form, there's no difference in the word order or verb ending of statements and questions. As often in English, a rising tone at the end indicates a question.

QUESTION WORDS

Where?	ŏdi
Where is it?	ŏdi issŏyo?
When?	ŏnje
When's …?	…-ŭn/nŭn ŏnje-eyo?
Who? (as subject)	nuga
Who? (as direct object)	nugu
Who is it? (pol)	nugurŭl ch'ajayo?
Why?	wae
Why can't I go there?	wae mot kayo?
How?	ŏttŏk´e
How do you do it?	ŏttŏk´e haeyo?
What? (as subject, pol)	mwŏga (pronounced similarly to **moga**)
What? (as subject, inf)	mwŏ (pronounced similarly to **mo**)
What is it?	mwŏeyo? (often pronounced similarly to **moeyo**)
What? (as direct object, pol)	muŏsŭl
What? (as direct object, inf)	mwŏl
What are you eating?	mwŏl dŭsŏyŏ
Which?	ŏnŭ
Which one?	ŏnŭ gŏeyo?

Note that these question words usually come towards the end of a sentence, just before the verb.

Where's the train station?	kich´ayŏgŭn ŏdieyo? (lit: train station-ŭn where is)
When does the bank open?	ŭnhaeng munŭn ŏnje yŏrŏyo? (lit: bank door-ŭn when open)

GRAMMAR

YES & NO

Answering questions in Korean and in English can be somewhat different. A Korean may answer 'yes' or 'no' depending on agreement or disagreement with the question. This can be confusing when the question itself is negative. An English speaker might answer the question, 'You're not a student?' with 'no' (meaning 'No, I'm not') but a Korean might answer 'yes' (meaning 'Yes, that's right').

yes	**ne**
Yes, that's right.	**ne, majayo** (lit: yes, be-right)
Yes, it is.	**ne, kŭraeyo** (lit: yes, be-like-that)
no	**anio**
No, it's not.	**anio, an-gŭraeyo** (lit: no be-like-that)

NEGATIVES

There are two simple ways to make a negative sentence in Korean. The difference between them is primarily a matter of preference. The first is to precede the verb or adjective with **an-**, which functions as 'not'.

It's not spicy.	**anmaewŏyo** (lit: not-spicy)
I'm not going.	**an-gayo** (lit: not-go)
He/She didn't come.	**anwassŏyo** (lit: not-came)

Note that the negative prefix **an-** may cause a sound change if the verb or adjective begins with certain consonants that are pronounced differently depending on their position (see Pronunciation, page 20).

I'm sleeping.	**chayo**
I'm not sleeping.	**anjayo**

The second way of making a negative is by adding -**ji anayo** to the verb stem.

go	**ka-**
I'm not going.	**kaji anayo** (ka + ji anayo)

The negative verb ending -**ji anayo** can be conjugated in the past tense as -**ji anassŏyo**.

I didn't sleep.	**chaji anassŏyo**

CONJUNCTIONS

Korean conjuctions, as a rule, come between the two clauses they connect. They usually alter the conjugation of the verb in the first part of the sentence, but the way they alter the verb differs according to each conjunction, as well as whether or not the verb stem ends with a consonant or a vowel.

- **and**

Two actions performed by the same person(s) can be connected with the conjunction **-go/-ko**. The pronunciation depends on the verb stem that precedes it.

They're eating lunch   **kŭdŭrŭn chŏmshim**
and talking.   **mŏkko yaegihaeyo**
         (lit: they-**ŭn** lunch eat-**ko** story-do)

- **but**

Two contrasting clauses can be connected by ending the first one with **-jiman**, which functions as 'but'. This conjunction follows the verb stem ending.

I want to go, but   **kago ship'jiman, shigani ŏpsŏyo**
I have no time.   (lit: go-**go** want-**jiman** time not-exist)

- **if**

This is made by adding **-ŭmyŏn** to the verb stem if it ends in a consonant, and **-myŏn** if it ends in a vowel. Unlike in English, the word 'if' goes at the end of the clause it refers to.

be small   **chak-** (ends in a consonant)
If it's small, ...   **chagŭmyŏn, ...** (**chak** + **ŭmyŏn**)
         (lit: small-**ŭmyŏn**)

- **while**

There are two ways to express 'while' in Korean. The first one is to attach **-ŭmyŏnsŏ** to the verb stem if it ends with a consonant, or **-myŏnsŏ** if it ends with a vowel. This way of expressing 'while' is used when the subject of the first part of the sentence and the subject of the second part of the sentence are the same.

While I sleep, I dream.   **chamyŏnsŏ, gumŭl kkwŏyo**
         (lit: sleep-**myŏnsŏ** dream-**ŭl** dream)

GRAMMAR

The second way of expressing 'while' or 'during' is by using the suffix **dong-an**. The preceding word can be a noun or a verb (in the form of the verb stem + **-ŭn/-nŭn**). The pronunciation depends on the preceding letter.

study	**kongbuha-**
while studying	**kongbuhanŭn dong-an**
	(lit: study do-**nŭn** during)

• **because**

There are two ways to form the conjunction 'because'. The first is expressed by taking the compound form of a verb (see page 46) and adding the suffix **-sŏ** to it.

ticket(s)	**p'yo**
Because there were no tickets, we went home.	**p'yoga ŏpsosŏ chibe kassŏyo**
	(lit: ticket-**ga** not-exist-**sŏ** home-**e** went)

The second way is to put a noun or an adjective/verb stem + **gi** in front of **-ttaemune**.

be expensive	**pissa-**
because it is expensive	**pissagittaemune**
	(lit: be-expensive-**gi** because)

사람들 만나기

Koreans will go out of their way to accommodate visitors or help solve any problem that may come up. You might find, if you ask for directions, a local will escort you to your destination even if it's many blocks away.

Foreign visitors, **oégugin** (외국인) or more formally **oégukpun** (외국분), are not expected to be adept at all Korean social customs, including intricate forms of speech such as formal, casual, same-level, low-form and high-form speech.

Koreans in general are an outgoing and friendly bunch around people they know, but are often reserved around strangers. Young Koreans are now required to learn English from elementary school, but many are self-conscious about their perceived linguistic shortcomings. Consequently, some people will be a little embarrassed at first when approached by someone speaking English, but they'll still try to help.

And while your attempts to speak Korean might elicit giggles initially, your efforts to communicate are sure to be highly appreciated.

YOU SHOULD KNOW

알아두세요

Hello.	**annyŏng haseyo**	안녕하세요.
Goodbye. (pol, when leaving)	**annyŏnghi kyeseyo**	안녕히계세요.
Goodbye. (pol, when staying)	**annyŏnghi kaseyo**	안녕히가세요.
Bye. (inf)	**annyŏng**	안녕.
Yes./No.	**ne/anio**	네./아니오.
Excuse me. (pol, for attention)	**shille hamnida**	실례합니다.
Excuse me. (pol, apologising)	**choésong hamnida**	죄송합니다.

In Korean, there are two common ways to say 'thank you'. The two words are different only in their origin, the first being 'pure' Korean, the second 'Sino-Korean'.

Thank you. (pol)	**komapsŭmnida**	고맙습니다.
Thank you. (pol)	**kamsa hamnida**	감사합니다.
Many thanks.	**chŏngmal**	정말
	komapsŭmnida	고맙습니다.

There's no 'please' in the sense of 'Please do this ...'. Instead, in Korean you would combine the verb **ha-** (compound form **hae-**), 'do', with the verb **juseyo** (주세요), 'give'. Otherwise, any command spoken in high form already has 'please' built into it.

When asking someone to 'please take this' (as in the case of food, drinks or a gift), you simply use the high form of 'receive', **padŭseyo** (받으세요) or, when talking about food or drinks, **tŭseyo** (드세요), literally 'eat (this)', or **mani dŭseyo** (많이 드세요), literally 'eat a lot'.

The word **chebal** (제발), 'please', by itself, to reinforce a request, is rarely used in Korean.

Please ... (when asking someone to do something for you)
Please do this.	**haejuseyo**	해 주세요.
Please do ... for me.	**... haejuseyo**	... 해 주세요.
Please buy this for me.	**sajuseyo**	사 주세요.
Please go to ...	**...e kajuseyo**	...에 가 주세요.
(to a taxi driver)		

Please. (to reinforce a request; used only in extreme situations)
| | **chebalyo** | 제발요. |

PARDON THE EXPRESSION

English speakers may feel inclined to use the expression **choésong hamnida** (죄송합니다) whenever they're bumped into on the street. Koreans generally reserve **choésong hamnida** (죄송합니다) for something more serious.

GREETINGS & GOODBYES   인사와 작별

Korean doesn't have a separate greeting for morning, noon, afternoon and evening. At all times of the day **annyŏng haseyo** (안녕하세요), 'hello', is appropriate.

Hello; Hi; Good morning/day/afternoon/evening.
| (pol) | **annyŏng haseyo** | 안녕하세요. |
| (inf) | **annyŏng** | 안녕. |

However, it's not uncommon for Koreans to greet someone they know by asking **shiksa hashŏssŏyo?** (식사하셨어요?), 'Did you eat?'. A simple **ne** (네), 'yes', is all that's expected, for if you go into detail about what you ate, you may be met with bewildered looks.

CIVILITIES   공손한 말

Korean society is based on a rigid social hierarchy in which a person who's older or has seniority is accorded more respect – and this is reflected in the language and word choice. Even when speaking to someone younger or with less seniority than yourself, it's considered good manners to use the following expressions in the polite form. With the less formal younger generation, though, informal expressions are perfectly acceptable.

Thank you (very much).	**kamsa hamnida**	감사합니다.
You're welcome. (pol)	**ch'ŏnmaneyo**	천만에요.
You're welcome. (inf)	**anieyo/mwŏryo**	아니에요/뭘요.

FORMS OF ADDRESS   호칭

Although there are traditional forms of address, many Koreans tend to favor the Western forms of Mister or Miss. These have been 'hangulised' into **misŭtŏ** (미스터) and **misŭ** (미스). The term **misŭ** (미스) is used even for married women, although **misesŭ** (미세스) for 'Mrs' is also becoming common. These forms precede the surname of the person to whom you are referring. When addressing Westerners, though, many Koreans will use **misŭtŏ** or **misŭ** before the addressee's given name, such as 'Mister David' or 'Miss Eleanor'. Korean women do not take the surname of their husband.

Traditional Titles   평범한 호칭

Koreans still use more traditional forms of address. These generally follow the addressee's given name. The higher the level of the person (relative to the speaker), or the less familiar you are to the speaker, the more likely you'll address that person by his or her surname. You would never refer to a much older person by his or her given name.

Mr/Ms/Mrs ...	...-shi/-ssi	...씨
Taejin (given name)	t'aejin-shi	태진 씨
Taegyong (given name)	t'aegyŏng-shi	태경 씨
Mr Park Taejin	pak t'aejin-shi	박태진 씨
Ms Kim Taegyong	kim t'aegyŏng-shi	김태경 씨

In contrast, when calling a child or a close friend the same age or younger than you, you can use their first name only, followed by -a (-아) if the name ends in a consonant or -ya (-야) if the name ends in a vowel:

Yumi!	yumiya!	유미야!
Sujin!	sujina!	수진아!

There are also special forms of address for:

Dr (Cho)	(cho)-paksanim	(조)박사님
teacher (Paul)	(p'ol)-sŏnsaengnim	(폴)선생님
person in your group		
(older than you or	sŏnbaenim	선배님
at a higher level)		
(younger than you	hubae	후배
or at a lower level)		
President (of a company)	sajangnim	사장님
President/Chairman	(kang)-sajangnim	강 사장님
(Kang)		
Professor (Lee)	(i)-kyosunim	(이)교수님

The titles **sŏnsaengnim** (선생님) and **sŏnbaenim** (선배님) both mean something like 'higher person', and are very useful if you're not sure what form to use. Not knowing the relative position of an overseas 'guest', many Koreans will refer to him or her simply as **sŏnsaengnim** (선생님). If a traveller looks sufficiently young or not business-like, he or she may be referred to simply as **haksaeng** (학생), which literally means 'student'.

It's also important to note that Koreans frequently refer to each other directly in the third person, rather than using the informal and polite forms of 'you', **nŏ** (너) and **tangshin** (당신).

'Relative' Titles   친척과 관계된 호칭

Koreans consider themselves one big family, and there are several titles to refer to a person that reflect this. An older man or woman might be called 'uncle' or 'aunt' and an elderly man or woman would be called 'grandfather' or 'grandmother'.

older woman (pol)	**ajumŏni** (lit: aunt)	아주머니
older woman (less pol)	**ajumma** (lit: auntie)	아줌마
older man	**ajŏshi** (lit: uncle)	아저씨
elderly woman (pol)	**halmŏni** (lit: grandmother)	할머니
elderly man (less pol)	**harabŏji** (lit: grandpa)	할아버지

In modern Korean culture, there's some uncertainty as to how to refer to a young man or woman who's unknown to the speaker. Calling a young man **ajŏshi** (아저씨), 'uncle' seems odd, but there's no other appropriate 'relative' expression. On the other hand, the word **agashi** (아가씨), literally 'husband's younger sister' for a young woman is now out of favour. In restaurants young people are tending to call someone over by simply saying **yŏgiyo!** (여기요!). This is 'over here' with a polite ending and although it may sound rude to English speakers, it's considered acceptable in Korean.

A LEE BY ANOTHER NAME

If you meet the parents of your Korean friends, chances are you'll never learn their names. To show respect, you'd refer to them in the third person, using your friend's name followed by **ŏmŏni** (어머니), 'mother', and **abŏji** (아버지), 'father', as the case may be.

Older 'Siblings'   손위 형제 자매

You can refer to classmates, colleagues, and other 'close' people of similar ages as 'older sister', 'older brother' or 'younger sibling'. Which word to use, however, depends on the gender of the speaker. The following forms of address are sometimes attached to the person's name:

older sister (if speaker is female)	**ŏnni**	언니
older brother (if speaker is female)	**oppa**	오빠
older sister (if speaker is male)	**nuna**	누나
older brother (if speaker is male)	**hyŏng**	형
younger sibling	**tongsaeng**	동생
(regardless of speaker's gender)		

FIRST ENCOUNTERS   첫 만남

When first meeting someone, Koreans will often be shy, but may then open up with a barrage of questions about your background. Be prepared for some topics that could often be considered personal in English-speaking countries such as age, marital status and why you came to Korea. These questions arise from curiosity and a desire to figure out where you fit in the relative social hierarchy.

How are you?
   annyŏng haseyo?   안녕하세요?
Fine. And you?
   ne. annyŏng haseyo?   네. 안녕하세요?
What's your name?
   irŭmŭl yŏtchŏbwado   이름을 여쭤봐도
   doélkkayo?   될까요?
My name is ...
   che irŭmŭn ...(i)eyo   제 이름은 ...(이)에요.
   (if the name ends in a consonant:
   ieyo follows; if a vowel: **eyo**)
I'd like to introduce you to ...
   (ibunŭn) ...imnida   (이분은) ...입니다.

Note that **ibunŭn** (이분은) may be omitted, but the expression should then be accompanied with an open palm gesturing towards the person being introduced.

This is my ...	(ibunŭn) ...	(이분은) ...
business partner	che hoésa-tongnyo-eyo	제 회사동료에요
boyfriend	che namja ch'in-gueyo	제 남자 친구에요
girlfriend	che yŏja ch'in-gueyo	제 여자 친구에요
husband	uri namp'yŏnieyo	우리 남편이에요
wife	uri annae-eyo	우리 아내에요

Although there's a direct word for someone you're romantically involved with, **ae-in** (애인), literally meaning 'love person', Koreans prefer the more euphemistic **yŏja ch'in-gu** (여자 친구), 'female friend' or **namja ch'in-gu** (남자 친구), 'male friend', respectively.

I'm pleased to meet you. (pol)
mannasŏ pan-gapsŭmnida　　　만나서 반갑습니다.

MAKING CONVERSATION　　대화하기

Many Koreans, especially young people, love to practise English, so if you're looking for conversationalists, you'll have no problem finding them. Some people, though, keenly aware of their shortcomings in speaking English, will simply giggle if you talk to them. Still, the same phrases you would use back home are generally good icebreakers in Korea as well. This is especially true when talking about the weather, as Korea's extremes in weather patterns – icy Manchurian winters and humid subtropical summers – are generally on people's minds. The expressions **nŏmu ch'uwŏyo!** (너무 추워요!), 'It's so cold!' or **nŏmu tŏwŏyo!** (너무 더워요!), 'It's so hot!', are great conversation starters.

Do you live here?	yŏgisŏ saseyo?	여기서 사세요?
Where are you going?	ŏdi kaseyo?	어디 가세요?
What are you doing?	mwŏ haseyo?	뭐 하세요?

Can I take a photo (of you)?
  **tangshine sajin chom
  tchigŏdo doélkkayo?**

당신의 사진 좀
찍어도 될까요?

What's this called?
  igŏl mwŏrago pullŏyo?

이걸 뭐라고 불러요?

Beautiful, isn't it?
  arŭmdamneyo

아름답네요.

It's great here.
  igosŭn nŏmuna chonneyo

이곳은 너무나 좋네요.

Are you waiting too?
  **tangshindo kidarigo
  kyeseyo?**

당신도 기다리고
계세요?

Are you here on holiday?
  yŏhaeng harŏ oshŏssŏyo?

여행하러 오셨어요?

BODY LANGUAGE

Koreans will greet each other with a bow, or a bow and a simultaneous handshake. The same is used when saying goodbye. They rarely hug in public, except for emotional goodbyes. In general, touching wouldn't be considered rude though. It's not as common as in Western countries, however, and you definitely should avoid touching people on the head, except for small children.

When offering anything with your hands, it's best if done with two hands or the following way – the left hand should be open, with the palm facing up, supporting the right forearm, just next to the wrist. This is also true when pouring alcohol.

Also, it's considered rude to pour one's own alcoholic beverage. When drinking in a group, someone is sure to fill your glass when it starts to look empty. It's considered very polite for you to do the same.

I'm here ...	... wassŏyo	... 왔어요.
for a holiday	yŏhaeng harŏ	여행하러
on business	saŏp daemune	사업 때문에
to study	kongbuharŏ	고부하러

How long are you here for?
yŏgie ŏlmadong-an   여기에 얼마동안
kyeshil kŏeyo?   계실 거에요?
I'm/We're here for ... weeks/days.
...dal/il-dong-an   ...달/일 동안
issŭl kŏeyo   있을거에요.
Do you like it here?
igoshi maŭme tŭrŏyo?   이곳이 마음에 들어요?
I/We like it here very much.
nŏmuna maŭme tŭrŏyo   너무나 마음에 들어요.

Sure.	mullonijo	물론이죠.
Just a minute.	chamkkanmanyo	잠깐만요.
It's OK.	kwaenchanayo	괜찮아요.
It's important.	chung-yo haeyo	중요해요.
It's not important.	chung-yo haji anayo	중요하지 않아요.
It's (not) possible.	(pul)kanŭng haeyo	(불)가능해요.
Look at that!	chŏgŏt poseyo!	저것 보세요!
Look at this!	igŏt poseyo!	이것 보세요!
Listen (to this).	igŏl tŭrŏboseyo	이걸 들어보세요.
I'm ready.	chunbi dwaessŏyo	준비 됐어요.
Are you ready?	chunbi dwaessŏyo?	준비 됐어요?
Good luck!	haeng-unŭl pirŏyo;	행운을 빌어요;
	hwait'ing!	화이팅!

MEETING PEOPLE

Note that **hwait'ing!** is the 'hangulised' form of 'fighting!', originally thought by Koreans to be an English cheer.

NATIONALITIES   국적

Koreans have two different ways of naming countries: a 'hangulised' form of the original name, as in k'aenada (캐나다) for 'Canada', or the Korean pronunciation of the Chinese characters for that name, as in miguk (미국) or 'beautiful country' for 'America' and ilbon (일본) or 'sun's origin' for 'Japan'.

If your country isn't listed here, try pointing on a map.

Where are you from? (pol)
ŏdisŏ oshŏssŏyo?   어디서 오셨어요?

I'm/We're from ...	...-esŏ wassŏyo	…에서 왔어요.
Australia	hoju	호주
Canada	k'aenada	캐나다
England	yŏngguk	영국
Europe	yurŏp	유럽
Germany	togil	독일
India	indo	인도
Ireland	aillaendŭ	아일랜드
Japan	ilbon	일본
New Zealand	nyujillaendŭ	뉴질랜드
the Philippines	p'illip'in	필리핀
Russia	rŏshia	러시아
Scotland	sŭkot'ŭllaendŭ	스코틀랜드
the USA	miguk	미국
Wales	weilsŭ	웨일스

YO! ... BE POLITE!

Politeness is an important part of speaking Korean. Speaking in an overly casual way, especially to someone older, can be extremely offensive. A simple way to ensure a minimal level of politeness is to add yo (요) – for example, when asked where you're from, answer hojuyo (호주요) for Australia, rather than hoju (호주).

MEETING PEOPLE

I live in/at the/a ...	...-esŏ sarayo	...에서 살아요.
city	toshi	도시
countryside	shigol	시골
mountains	san	산
seaside	haebyŏn	해변
suburbs of ...	...-e kyo-oé	...의 교외
local	chibang-e	지방의
national	kukka-e	국가의

CULTURAL DIFFERENCES

문화의 차이

How do you do this
in your country?
    **han-gugesŏnŭn igŏl
ŏttok′e haeyo?**

한국에서는 이걸
어떻게 해요?

Is this a local or national
custom?
    **han-guge kwansŭbin-gayo,
ijibang-mane
kwansŭbin-gayo?**

한국의 관습인가요,
이 지방만의
관습인가요?

I don't want to offend you.
    ohae hajinŭn maseyo

오해하지는 마세요.

I'm sorry, it's not the custom
in my country.
    **choésong hamnida
urinara-esŏnŭn kŭrŏk′e
haji ank′ŏdŭnyo**

죄송합니다.
우리나라에서는 그렇게
하지 않거든요.

MEETING PEOPLE

I'm not accustomed to this.		
igŏse iksukaji anayo		이것에 익숙하지 않아요.
I don't mind watching, but		
I'd prefer not to participate.		
hajinŭn ank'o,		하지는 않고
pogiman halkkeyo		보기만 할게요.

I'm sorry,	**choésong hajiman,**	죄송하지만,
it's against my ...	**kŭgŏsŭn chŏ-e**	그것은저의
	...-e wibae dwaeyo	...에 위배돼요.
culture	**munhwa**	문화
religion	**chonggyo**	종교

(But) I'll give it a go.		
(hajiman) hanbŏn		(하지만) 한번
haebolkkeyo		해 볼게요.

AGE 나이

How old are you?		
(to a child)		
myŏssarini?		몇 살이니?
(to an adult who is younger		
or about the same age as the		
speaker)		
naiga ŏttŏk'e twaeyo?		나이가 어떻게 돼요?
(to someone older)		
yŏnse-ga ŏttŏk'e toéseyo?		연세가 어떻게 되세요?

How old is your daughter/son?		
dare/adŭre naiga		딸의/아들의 나이가
ŏttŏk'e dwaeyo?		어떻게 돼요?
I'm ... years old.		
chŏnŭn ... sarieyo		저는 … 살 이에요.

(See Numbers & Amounts, page 209, for your age.)

OCCUPATIONS

직업

What (work) do you do?

musŭn irŭl haseyo? 무슨 일을 하세요?

I'm a/an ...	**chŏnŭn ...(i)eyo**	저는 ...(이)에요.
businessperson	**saŏpka**	사업가
chef	**yorisa**	요리사
doctor	**ŭisa**	의사
engineer	**enjiniŏ**	엔지니어
farmer	**nongbu**	농부
homemaker	**kajŏngjubu**	가정주부
journalist	**kija**	기자
labourer	**nodongja**	노동자
lawyer	**pyŏnhosa**	변호사
mechanic	**kigyegong**	기계공
nurse	**kanhosa**	간호사
office worker	**hoésa jigwŏn**	회사 직원
professor	**kyosu**	교수
scientist	**kwahakcha**	과학자
soldier	**kunin**	군인
student	**haksaeng**	학생
teacher	**sŏnsaengnim**	선생님
waiter	**weitŏ**	웨이터
writer	**chakka**	작가

ㄱㄲㄴㄷㄸㄹㅁㅂㅃㅅㅆㅇㅈㅉㅊㅋㅌㅍㅎ
ㅏㅐㅑㅒㅓㅔㅕㅖㅗㅘㅙㅚㅛㅜㅝㅞㅟㅠㅡㅢㅣ

I'm retired.

chŏnŭn t'oéjik haessŏyo 저는 퇴직했어요.

I'm unemployed.

chŏnŭn hyŏnjae 저는 현재
chigŏbi ŏpsŏyo 직업이 없어요.

What are you studying?

musŭn kongburŭl haseyo? 무슨 공부를 하세요?

I'm studying ...	chŏnŭn ...rŭl/ŭl kongbu haeyo	저는 ...를/을 공부해요.
art	misul	미술
arts/humanities	inmunhak	인문학
business	kyŏng-yŏnghak	경영학
engineering	konghak	공학
English	yŏng-ŏ	영어
Korean	han-gugŏ	한국어
languages	ŏnŏ	언어
law	pŏphak	법학
medicine	ŭihak	의학
science	kwahak	과학
teaching	kyoyuk	교육

FEELINGS   감정

When describing yourself or another person, the subject, eg, **chŏnŭn** (저는), 'I', is omitted if it's understood between the speaker and the listener.

Are you ...?	tangshinŭn ...?	당신은 ...?
I'm ...	chŏnŭn ...	저는 ...
afraid	musŏwŏyo	무서워요
angry	hwanassŏyo	화났어요
cold	ch'uwŏyo	추워요
happy	haengbok haeyo	행복해요
hot	tŏwŏyo	더워요.
hungry	paegop'ayo	배고파요
in a hurry	kŭp'aeyo	급해요
sad	sŭlp'ŏyo	슬퍼요
sleepy	chollyŏyo	졸려요
sorry (regret)	huhoé haeyo	후회해요
thirsty	mongmallayo	목말라요
tired	p'igon haeyo	피곤해요
well	kŏn-gang haeyo	건강해요
worried	kŏkchŏng dwaeyo	걱정돼요

BREAKING THE LANGUAGE BARRIER

언어 장벽 허물기

Do you speak English? (pol)
yŏng-ŏ haseyo?

영어 하세요?

Yes. (I do.)
ne

네.

No. (I don't.)
anio

아니오.

Does anyone speak English? (pol)
**yŏng-ŏ hashinŭnbun
kyeseyo?**

영어 하시는 분
계세요?

I speak a little. (pol)
chega chogŭm haeyo

제가 조금해요.

Do you understand? (pol)
ara dŭrŭshŏssŏyo?

알아 들으셨어요?

Yes. (I understand.)
ne

네.

I don't understand.
anio/modaradŭrŏssŏyo

아니오/못 알아들었어요.

Please speak more slowly. (pol)
**chom ch'ŏnch'ŏnhi
malhaejuseyo**

좀 천천히
말해 주세요.

Please repeat that. (pol)
tashi hanbŏn malhaejuseyo

다시 한번 말해 주세요.

Could you please write it down?
chŏgŏ jushillaeyo?

적어 주실래요?

How do you say ...?
...rŭl/ŭl mwŏrago haeyo?

...를/을 뭐라고 해요?

What does ... mean?
...ga/i musŭn dŭshieyo?

...가/이 무슨 뜻이에요?

You speak Korean/English
very well.

    han-gungmal/yŏng-ŏ   한국말/영어
    chŏngmal chal hashineyo   정말 잘 하시네요.

I don't do it well.

    chŏn chal moťaeyo   전 잘 못 해요.

You're very good at it.

    chŏngmal chal hashineyo   정말 잘 하시네요.

KONGLISH

The English language is put to great use in Korea. It's often possible – with the help of gestures – to make simple thoughts or requests understood through common English words.

Koreans also borrow words from English. Many of these Korean-style English terms (called Konglish) are created by truncating English words. An 'apartment' is called **apatŭ** (아파트), for example. Some Konglish phrases are coined by combining English words in a way that makes sense to Korean ears: a 'mobile phone' is a **haendŭ-p'on** (핸드폰), 'hand-phone'.

Beware though! The meaning of the original English words and that of the Konglish terms don't always add up. A **hattogŭ** (핫도그) from 'hot dog', for example, is actually a 'corn dog' and a **k'ondo** (콘도), 'condo', refers to a time-share.

MEETING PEOPLE

돌아다니기 GETTING AROUND

South Korea has an extensive public transport network that is clean, safe, comfortable (except during rush hour), efficient, and affordable. Most bus and subway passengers use a pre-paid electronic transit pass, **kyot'ong k'adŭ** (교통카드).

FINDING YOUR WAY   길 찾기

Where's the ...?	...i/ga ŏdi issŏyo?	...이/가 어디있어요?
bus to ...	...e kanŭn bŏsŭ	...에 가는 버스
road to ...	...e kanŭn gil	...에 가는 길
train to ...	...e kanŭn kich'a	...에 가는 기차
bus station	bŏsu t'ŏminŏl	버스 터미널
bus stop	bŏsu chŏngnyujang	버스 정류장

What time does the ... leave/arrive?	...i/ga ŏnje dŏnayo/tochak-haeyo?	...이/가 언제 떠나요/도착해요?
aeroplane	pihaenggi	비행기
boat	pae	배
ferry	hanggu	항구
bus	bŏsŭ	버스
train	kich'a	기차

What ... is this?	yŏgiga musŭn ...(i)eyo?	여기가 무슨 ...(이)에요?
street	kil	길
city	toshi	도시
village; small town	maŭl	마을

What number bus goes to ...?
myŏppŏn bŏsŭga ...e kayo? 몇 번 버스가 ...에 가요?

How do we get to ...?
...e ŏttok'e kayo? ...에 어떻게 가요?

Is it close by?
kakkawŏyo? 가까워요?

Where is it on this map?
ijidosang-esŏ ŏdieyo? 이 지도상에서 어디에요?

GETTING AROUND

Directions
방향 찾기

Turn at the ...	...esŏ toseyo	...에서 도세요.
next corner	taŭm mot'ung-i	다음 모퉁이
traffic light	shinhodŭng	신호등
pedestrian crossing	kŏnnŏlmok	건널목
pedestrian underpass	chihado	지하도
pedestrian overpass	yukkyo	육교

> **DID YOU KNOW ...**
>
> In Korea, many businesses will print a useful **yakto** (약도), or 'local neighbourhood map', on the back of their business card so that patrons can find them easily.

Straight ahead.
dokparo kaseyo 똑바로 가세요.

To the left/right.
wentchogŭro/orŭntchogŭro 왼쪽으로/오른쪽으로
kaseyo 가세요.

Thank you (for showing me/us the way).
komapsŭmnida 고맙습니다.

behind ...	... dwi-e	... 뒤에
far	mŏlli	멀리
here	yŏgie	여기에
in front of ...	... ape	... 앞에
near	kakkai	가까이
opposite	pandaep'yŏne	반대편에
over there	chŏgie	저기에

north	puktchok	북쪽
south	namtchok	남쪽
east	tongtchok	동쪽
west	sŏtchok	서쪽

ADDRESSES   주소

Postal addresses, or **chuso** (주소), are written in reverse order from those in the West: they go from the largest administrative unit to the smallest administrative unit, with the house or apartment number last. Neighbourhoods are divided into block numbers and house numbers which are not always in sequential order. There are no street names in the address.

You might encounter following administrative units:

metropolitan prefecture (the latter only for Seoul)	**kwang-yŏkshi/ t´ŭkpyŏlshi**	광역시/ 특별시
province	**-do**	-도
city in province	**-shi**	-시
urban area (subdivision of city)	**-ku/gu**	-구
neighbourhood (subdivision of urban area)	**-dong**	-동
county	**-kun**	-군
district	**-ŭp**	-읍
township	**-myŏn**	-면
village	**-ri**	-리

FEAR OF FOUR

Step into the lift of many modern Korean buildings, and you'll see still see 1, 2, 3, F, 5, 6 ... In Korean, the pronunciation of the number four sounds similar to a word for 'death' and many architects who were aware of superstitions surrounding that pronunciation avoided using the number four when referring to the fourth floor of buildings. The solution they came up with was designating the fourth floor in elevators, office listings etc, with the letter 'F'.

GETTING AROUND

A sample address might go this way:

대한민국   **taehan min-guk**
서울특별시   **sŏul-t'ŭkpyŏlshi**
용산구 남영동   **yongsan-ku, namyŏng-dong**
삼우 APT 106동 501호 **samu apt. 106-dong 501-ho**
김태경귀하   **kim t'aegyŏng-kwiha**
우편번호 140-151   **upyŏnbŏnho 140-151**

In English, we would read this in the following order:

To: Kim Taegyong
Samu Apartments
Apt #501 Bldg #106
Namyong-dong, Yongsan-ku
Postal Code 140-151
Seoul, Republic of Korea

When writing an address in English, it's acceptable to write it in the order addresses are written in the West, from local to national.

BUYING TICKETS   표 사 기

Where can I buy a ticket?
    p'yo ŏdisŏ salsu issŏyo?   표 어디서 살 수 있어요?
We want to go to ...
    ...e karyŏgo hanŭndeyo   ...에 가려고 하는데요.
Do I need to book?
    yeyak haeyadwaeyo?   예약해야돼요?
I'd like to book a seat to ...
    ... kanŭn p'yo hanjang   ... 가는 표 한 장
    yeyak haejuseyo   예약 해 주세요.
It's full.
    mansŏk imnida;   만석입니다;
    chariga ŏpsŭmnida   자리가 없습니다.
Can I get a stand-by ticket?
    taegi p'yorŭl salsu issŏyo?   대기 표를 살 수 있어요?

I'd like (a) ...	... chuseyo	... 주세요.
one-way ticket	p'yŏndo p'yo (hanjang)	편도 표 (한 장)
return ticket	wangbok p'yo (hanjang)	왕복 표 (한 장)
two tickets	tujang	두 장
student's fare	haksaengp'yo (hanjang)	학생 표 (한 장)
child's fare	ŏrinip'yo (hanjang)	어린이 표 (한 장)
senior citizen's fare	noin/kyŏngno p'yo (hanjang)	노인/경로 표 (한 장)

dining car	shiktangch'a	식당차
first-class seat	ildŭngsŏk	일등석
seat	chwasŏk	좌석
second-class seat	idŭngsŏk	이등석
sleeper car	ch'imdaech'a	침대차
standing-room ticket	ipsŏk	입석

AIR   공항에서

Air travel to and from Korea is safe and convenient. Korea has many domestic airports, and most domestic flights take less than an hour.

airline terminal 1	cheil ch'ŏngsa	제1청사
airline terminal 2	che-i ch'ŏngsa	제2청사
domestic terminal	kungnae ch'ŏngsa	국내 청사

When's the next flight to ...?
   ...e kanŭn daŭm   …에 가는 다음
   pihaenggiga ŏnje issŏyo?   비행기가 언제 있어요?
How long does the flight take?
   pihaeng shigani ŏlmana dwaeyo? 비행시간이 얼마나 돼요?
What time do I have to
check in at the airport?
   myŏshie ch'ek'ŭinŭl   몇 시에 체크인을
   haeya dwaeyo?   해야돼요?
Where's the baggage claim?
   chim buchinŭn goshi ŏdieyo? 짐 부치는 곳이 어디에요?
My luggage hasn't arrived.
   che jimi ajik anwassŏyo   제 짐이 아직 안 왔어요.

At Customs   세관에서

I have nothing to declare.
shin-go hal gŏshi ŏpsŭmnida   신고할 것이 없습니다.
I have something to declare.
shin-go hal gŏshi issŭmnida   신고할 것이 있습니다.
Do I have to declare this?
igŏtto shin-go haeya hanayo?   이것도 신고해야 하나요?
This is all my luggage.
ige che chim chŏnbu imnida   이게 제 짐 전부입니다.
That's not mine.
kŭgŏn che gŏshi anindeyo   그건 제 것이 아닌데요.
I didn't know I had to declare it.
shingo haeya hanŭnjul   신고해야 하는 줄
morŭgo issŏssŭmnida   모르고 있었습니다.

BUS   버스

Korea has five major types of buses:

shinae bŏsŭ   시내버스
regular metropolitan buses that go from one district of the city to another; some go to nearby cities

chwasŏk bŏsŭ   좌석버스
first-class metropolitan buses usually servicing the same routes as **shinae bŏsu** (시내버스), as well as long-distance routes to the suburbs or to destinations like the airport; twice as expensive

maŭl bŏsŭ   마을버스
cheaper buses that snake through the local neighbourhood

kosok bŏsŭ   고속버스
long-distance inter-city buses that crisscross the country

chik'aeng bŏsŭ   직행버스
rural inter-town buses running between major towns and stopping at local bus stops in between

With the exception of deluxe buses servicing destinations that overseas visitors are likely to visit, most of the buses have maps and destinations printed in Korean only.

Where's the bus stop?
bŏsŭ chŏng-yujang-i ŏdieyo? 버스 정류장이 어디에요?
Which bus goes to ...?
myŏppŏn bŏsŭga ...e kayo? 몇 번 버스가 ...에 가요?
Does this bus go to ...?
ibŏsŭ ...e kayo? 이 버스 ...에 가요?
How often do buses come?
bŏsŭga myŏppunmada 버스가 몇 분마다
wayo? 와요?
Please let me off here!
naeryŏjuseyo! 내려 주세요!

What time's	**...e kanŭn bŏsŭ**	...에 가는 버스
the ... bus?	**myŏshi-e issŏyo?**	몇 시에 있어요?
next	**taŭm**	다음
first	**ch'ŏt**	첫
last	**majimak**	마지막

Could you let me know
when we get to ...?
...e tochak halttae chege ...에 도착할 때 제게
chom allyŏjushillaeyo? 좀 알려 주실래요?
Where do I get the bus for ...?
...e kanŭn bŏsŭ ŏdisŏ t'ayo? ...에 가는 버스 어디서 타요?

TRAIN 기차

Korea has an extensive network of affordable and comfortable
trains. They're fast and extremely punctual. There are various
types of trains:

saemaŭl-ho 새마을호
the more expensive, but comfortable, express trains that hit
only a few cities on their cross-country journey

mugunghwa-ho 무궁화호
cheaper but not quite as fast; stop at more stations

t'ong-il-ho 통일호
cheaper still, but stop at most stations, so they take longer to
make their journey

GETTING AROUND

What station is this?
yŏgiga musŭn yŏgieyo?
여기가 무슨 역이에요?

What's the next station?
taŭm yŏgi ŏdieyo?
다음 역이 어디에요?

How many stops until ...?
...kkaji myŏt chŏnggŏjang namassŏyo?
...까지 몇 정거장 남았어요?

Does this train stop at ...?
igicha ...esŏ sŏyo?
이 기차 ...에서 서요?

The train is delayed.
kich'aga yŏnch'ak toélgŏshimnida
기차가 연착 될 것입니다.

The train is cancelled.
kich'aga ch'wiso doé-ŏssŭmnida
기차가 취소 되었습니다.

How long will it be delayed?
ŏlmana yŏnch'ak dwaeyo?
얼마나 연착돼요?

How long does the trip take?
ŏlmana orae kanayo?
얼마나 오래 가나요?

Is it a direct route?
ige chikhaeng nosŏnieyo?
이게 직행 노선이에요?

Is that seat taken?
ijari imja issŏyo?
이 자리 임자 있어요?

I want to get off at ...
...esŏ naeriryŏgo hanŭndeyo
...에서 내리려고 하는데요.

I'd like to store my luggage.
chim pogwanhami issŏssŭmyon hanŭndeyo
짐 보관함이 있었으면 하는데요.

TO KYŎNGJU OR GYEONGJU?

South Korea is blessed with an excellent public transport system and an extensive road and highway network, all well-marked in Korean, English and even Chinese characters. But one thing that any English-speaking traveller will quickly notice is that the English isn't always consistent. The official Romanisation system has changed many times, so you might see variations in the spelling of place names. Here are some of the more popular destinations:

1984 system	2000 system	Variations	Hangul
Ch'ungch'ŏng-namdo	Chungcheong-namdo	Choongcheong-namdo	충청남도
Cheju-do	Jeju-do	Chejoo-do, Jejoo-do	제주도
Chinju	Jinju	Chinjoo, Jinjoo	진주
Chŏlla	Jeolla	Junra, Jeonra	전라
Inch'ŏn	Incheon	Inchon	인천
Kangnam	Gangnam	Gahngnahm	강남
Kangnŭng	Gangneung	Gangreung	강릉
Kangwon-do	Gangwon-do	Gangweon-do	강원도
Kimp'o	Gimpo	Kimpo, Geempo	김포
Kwangju	Gwangju	Kwangjoo, Gwangjoo	광주
Kyŏngbokkung	Gyeongbok-gung	Gyeongbok-goong	경복궁
Kyŏnggi-do	Gyeonggi-do	Kyungki-do	경기도
Kyŏngju	Gyeongju	Kyongjoo, Gyeongjoo	경주
Kyŏngsang-bukdo	Gyeongsang-bukto	Gyeongsang-bookdo	경상북도
P'yŏngyang	Pyeongyang	Pyongyang	평양
Pusan	Busan	Boosan	부산
Puyŏ	Buyeo	Booyeo	부여
Seoul	Seoul	Sŏul	서울
Shinch'on	Sinchon	Shinchon	신촌
Sŏraksan	Seoragsan	Seolagsan	설악산

TO KYŎNGJU OR GYEONGJU?

1984 system	2000 system	Variations	Hangul
Taegu	Daegu	Taegoo, Daegoo, Daigoo	대구
Taejŏn	Daejeon	Taejun, Daejun, Daijun	대전
Tŏksugung	Deoksugung	Deogsoogoong	덕수궁
Tongdaemun	Dongdaemun	Dongdaemoon	동대문
Tongnimmun	Dongnimmun	Dogribmoon, Doglipmoon	독립문
Ulsan	Ulsan	Woolsan	울산

SUBWAY   지하철

Korea's major metropolitan areas all have clean and modern subway systems. Seoul's network is one of the longest in the world. All of the subway systems are bilingual (Korean and English) or even trilingual (with Chinese characters) and are colour coordinated, so that they're extremely convenient and easy for getting around.

entrance number 1	ilbŏn ch'ulgu	일번출구/1번출구
subway	chihachŏl	지하철
subway entrance	chihachŏripku	지하철입구
subway line	chihachŏl nosŏn	지하철노선
subway station	chihachŏlyŏk	지하철역
ticket counter	p'yo p'anŭn-got	표 파는 곳
ticket vending machine	p'yo chapan-gi	표 자판기
transfer point	karatanŭn-got	갈아타는 곳

SEOUL'S SUBWAY

line 1 (dark blue line)	ilhosŏn	일호선/1호선
line 2 (green line)	ihosŏn	이호선/2호선
line 3 (orange line)	samhosŏn	삼호선/3호선
line 4 (blue line)	sahosŏn	사호선/4호선
line 5 (purple line)	ohosŏn	오호선/5호선
line 6	yuk'osŏn	육호선/6호선
line 7	ch'ilhosŏn	칠호선/7호선
line 8	p'alhosŏn	팔호선/8호선
National Rail line	kukch'ŏl	국철

BOAT
배

Boats are no longer a common form of transport in Korea, although you'll need to take one if you travel to some of the beautiful islands along the west and south coasts. International ferries between Korea, Japan and China are economical – but much slower – ways to travel.

Where does the boat leave from?
paega ŏdisŏ ch'ulbal haeyo?   배가 어디서 출발해요?

Is this a sightseeing boat?
ige yuramsŏnieyo?   이게 유람선이에요?

How many islands does
this boat go to?
ibaega sŏmŭl   이 배가 섬을
myŏkkaena kŏch'ŏgayo?   몇 개나 거쳐가요?

Can I take my car on the boat?
ch'arŭl pae-e shilkko   차를 배에 싣고
kalsu issŏyo?   갈 수 있어요?

TAXI
택시

There are two kinds of taxis: regular **t'aekshi** (택시) and more expensive deluxe taxis, **mobŏm t'aekshi** (모범택시).

As regular taxis legally can take only four passengers (not including the driver), a third type of taxi has popped up, the so-called **chŏmbo t'aekshi** (점보택시), 'jumbo taxi', a kind of minivan.

Taxi drivers who don't speak English have a number to call to hook you up with someone who will translate.

Is this taxi free?
it'aekshi muryo-eyo?   이 택시 무료에요?

Please take me to ...
...e kajuseyo   ...에 가 주세요.

How long will it take to get there?
ŏlmana kŏllyŏyo?   얼마나 걸려요?

How much is it to go to ...?
...kkaji kanŭnde ŏlma-eyo?   ...까지 가는데 얼마에요?

How much do I owe you?
ŏlma-eyo?   얼마에요?

GETTING AROUND

Please don't pick up another passenger.	
hapsŭng haji maseyo	합승하지 마세요.
It's OK to pick up another passenger.	
hapsŭng hashŏdo dwaeyo	합승하셔도 돼요.

Instructions 방향 지시

Please continue.	
kyesok kajuseyo	계속 가 주세요.
The next street to the left/right.	
ibŏne chwahoéjŏn/uhoéjŏn haejuseyo	이번에 좌회전/우회전 해 주세요.
Please slow down.	
ch'ŏnch'ŏnhi kajuseyo	천천히 가 주세요.
Please wait here.	
yŏgisŏ kidaryŏ jushillaeyo?	여기서 기다려 주실래요?
Stop here.	
yŏgisŏ sewŏjuseyo	여기서 세워 주세요.
Stop at the corner.	
mot'ung-iesŏ sewŏjuseyo	모퉁이에서 세워 주세요.

TAXI TACTICS

As Korean taxis are very cheap, taxi drivers try to find ways to boost their earnings. Driving as fast as possible seems to be the preferred method, but picking up multiple fares is another. Even with passengers already in the car, taxi drivers might slow down for would-be passengers on the side of the road, who shout their destination to the driver. The taxi driver will pick up that fare if he or she is going in the same direction as the person(s) already in the car.

This practice is called **hapsŭng** (합승), and although technically illegal, it's quite common. It offers no savings benefit for the passengers, but can dramatically increase the likelihood of getting a taxi at busy times. Be prepared to shout out your destination or you may be standing around for a long time.

CAR   자동차

Driving in Korea is not for the fainthearted, especially in big cities
where beginner drivers abound and buses and taxis often ignore
traffic laws. Driving in the countryside is relatively more pleasant.

Where can I rent a car?
ŏdisŏ ch´a rentŭ   어디서 차 렌트
halsu issŏyo?   할 수 있어요?

How much is it daily/weekly?
harue/iljuire   하루에/일주일에
ŏlmaeyo?   얼마에요?

Does that include
insurance/mileage?
pohŏm/mailliji   보험/마일리지
p´oham haesŏyo?   포함해서요?

Where's the next
petrol station?
taŭm juyusoga   다음 주유소가
ŏdi issŏyo?   어디 있어요?

What kind of fuel does this take?
musŭn yŏllyorŭl ssŏyo?   무슨 연료를 써요?

Please fill the tank.
kadŭk ch´aewŏjuseyo   가득 채워 주세요.

I'd like ... litres.
... ritŏ nŏ-ŏjuseyo   ... 리터 넣어 주세요.

diesel	**dijel**	디젤
LPG	**elp´iji**	엘피지
(unleaded) petrol	**(muyŏn) hwibalyu**	(무연)휘발유

GETTING AROUND

Please check the ...	... chom ch'ek'ŭ haejuseyo	... 좀 체크 해 주세요.
oil	o-il	오일
tyre pressure	t'aiŏ amnyŏk	타이어 압력
water	naenggaksu	냉각수

Can I park here?
yŏgi chuch'a haedo dwaeyo?
여기 주차해도 돼요?

How long can we park here?
yŏgi ŏlma-dong-an chuch'a halsu issŏyo?
여기 얼마동안 주차 할 수 있어요?

How much does it cost to park here?
chuch'a hanŭnde ŏlmaeyo?
주차하는데 얼마에요?

Does this road lead to ...?
igil daragamyŏn ...e kal-su issŏyo?
이 길따 라가면 ...에 갈 수 있어요?

Where's the express way?
kosoktoroga ŏdieyo?
고속도로가 어디에요?

What major street is it near?
chuwie k'ŭn-giri issŏyo?
주위에 큰 길이 있어요?

PARKING PROBLEMS

Because of the astronomical price of real estate, large buildings are designed with massive above-ground parking structures, or with giant parking lifts that cover only 20 or so square meters of land, but rise up 10 floors or more.

air	e-ŏ	에어
battery	baet'ŏri	배터리
brakes	bŭreik'ŭ	브레이크
clutch	k'ŭllŏch'i	클러치
drivers licence	unjŏnmyŏnhŏjŭng	운전면허증
engine	enjin	엔진
fuel (all types)	kirŭm	기름
garage	ch'ago	차고
headlight	hedŭrait'ŭ	헤드라이트
indicator	panghyang jishigi;	방향 지시기;
	gambagi	깜박이
international	kukche myŏnhŏjŭng	국제면허증
drivers licence		
lights (interior)	pul/shillaedŭng	불/실내등
main road	chuyodoro	주요 도로
oil	o-il	오일
puncture	p'ŏngk'ŭ	펑크
radiator	rajiet'a/	라지에타/
	radieit'ŏ	라디에이터
roadmap	torojido	도로지도
seatbelt	anjŏnbelt'ŭ	안전벨트
self-service	selp'ŭ sŏbisŭ	셀프 서비스
speed limit	chehan-sokto	제한 속도
tollbooth	yogŭm naenŭn-got	요금 내는 곳
tyres	t'ai-ŏ	타이어
unleaded petrol	muyŏn hwibalyu	무연 휘발유
windscreen	amnyuri	앞유리

Car Problems   자동차 수리하기

We need a mechanic.
    chŏngbi-gong-i p'ilyo haeyo   정비공이 필요해요.
What make is it?
    ŏnŭ hoésa ch'a-eyo?   어느 회사 차에요?
What model is it?
    musŭn model ch'a-eyo?   무슨 모델 차에요?
What year is this car?
    myŏnnyŏnhyŏng ch'a-eyo?   몇 년 형 차에요?

GETTING AROUND

The car broke down at ...
    ...esŏ ch'aga kojang nassŏyo ...에서 차가 고장났어요.
The battery's flat.
    baet'ŏriga nagassŏyo 배터리가 나갔어요.
The radiator's leaking.
    rajiet'aga saeyo 라지에타가 새요.
I have a flat tyre.
    t'aiŏ-e p'ŏngk'u nassŏyo 타이어에 펑크 났어요.
It's overheating.
    kwayŏl/obŏhit'ŭ dwaessŏyo 과열/오버히트 됐어요.
It's not working.
    chaktong-i andwaeyo 작동이 안 돼요.
I've lost my car keys.
    ch'a yŏlsoérŭl
    irŏbŏryŏssŏyo 차 열쇠를
     잃어버렸어요.
I've run out of fuel.
    kirŭmi dŏrŏjŏssŏyo 기름이 떨어졌어요.

ROAD SIGNS

어린이 보호구역	BEWARE OF CHILDREN
버스전용 차선	BUS-ONLY LANE
위험	DANGER
낙석주의	FALLING ROCKS
안개지역	FOG ZONE
무료주차	FREE PARKING
주차금지	NO PARKING
일방통행	ONE-WAY
좌신호시	ON LEFT TURN ARROW ONLY
적신호시	ON RED LIGHT ONLY
유료주차	PAID PARKING
보행금지	PEDESTRIANS PROHIBITED
천천히	SLOW
정지	STOP
견인지역	TOW-AWAY ZONE
비보호	TURN WHEN SAFE

BICYCLE   자전거

Between crowded pavements and busy streets, there isn't much room for bicycles in the city, and in many neighbourhoods it's dangerous to ride. However, Korean parks have lately been designed with cycling in mind. It's also not a bad way to move around in rural areas. Bike rentals can be hard to find, but good multi-speed bikes can easily be purchased.

Is it within cycling distance?
**chajŏn-gŏro kalsu
innŭn kŏrieyo?**
자전거로 갈 수
있는 거리에요?

Is there a bike path?
chajŏn-gŏ doroga issŏyo?
자전거 도로가 있어요?

Where can I hire a bicycle?
**chajŏn-gŏ ŏdisŏ rent'ŭ
halsu issŏyo?**
자전거 어디서 렌트
할 수 있어요?

Where can I find second-hand bikes for sale?
**chunggo chajŏn-gŏ ŏdisŏ
kuhalsu issŏyo?**
중고 자전거 어디서
구할 수 있어요?

I have a flat tyre.
t'aiŏ-e p'ŏngkŭ nassŏyo
타이어에 펑크 났어요.

How much is it for ...?	...e ŏlma-eyo?	...에 얼마에요?
the afternoon	**ohudong-an**	오후 동안
the day	**haru**	하루
an hour	**han shigan**	한 시간
the morning	**ojŏndong-an**	오전 동안

bike	chajŏn-gŏ	자전거
bicycle path	chajŏn-gŏ doro	자전거 도로
brakes	bŭreik'ŭ	브레이크
gear stick	kiŏ sŭt'ik	기어 스틱
go cycling	chajŏn-gŏ t'ayo	자전거 타요
handlebars	haendŭl	핸들
helmet	helmet	헬멧
inner tube	t'yubŭ	튜브
lights	rait'ŭ	라이트
mountain bike	sanak chajŏn-gŏ	산악 자전거
padlock	chamulsoé	자물쇠
pump	p'ŏmp'ŭ	펌프
puncture	p'ŏngk'ŭ	펑크
racing bike	kyŏngjuyong chajŏn-gŏ	경주용 자전거
saddle	anjang	안장
tandem	i-inyong chajŏn-gŏ	2인용 자전거
wheel	pak'wi	바퀴

숙박　ACCOMMODATION

'Western-style' hotels can be found just about anywhere in Korea. They range from cheap (but clean) small rooms that are also used for late-night rendezvous or by businessmen too drunk to go home on their own, to expensive deluxe hotels where you can expect every employee to speak English.

Camping has only recently started to gain popularity, and most people travelling to national parks or beaches still tend to stay in motels or **minbak** (민박), small family-run facilities that cater for people on holiday.

FINDING ACCOMMODATION　　숙소 찾기

I'm looking for a ...	...rŭl/ŭl ch'akko issŏyo	...를/을 찾고 있어요.
camping ground	k'aemp'ŭjang	캠프장
guesthouse	minbakchip	민박집
hotel	hotel	호텔
motel	motel/yŏgwan/ yŏinsuk	모텔/여관/ 여인숙
youth hostel	yusŭ hosŭt'el	유스 호스텔

See In the Country, page 179, for specific words and phrases on Camping.

Where can I find a ... hotel?	... hoteri ŏdi issŏyo?	... 호텔이 어디 있어요?
good	choŭn	좋은
nearby	kakkaun	가까운
clean	gaekkŭt'an	깨끗한

Where's the cheapest hotel?
**kajang ssan hoteri
ŏdi issŏyo?**　가장 싼 호텔이
어디 있어요?

ACCOMMODATION

What's the address?
    chusoga ŏttŏk'e dwaeyo?   주소가 어떻게 돼요?
Please write down
the location.
    wich'i chom chŏgŏjuseyo   위치 좀 적어 주세요.

> **DID YOU KNOW ...**
>
> When giving an address or telephone number to someone, Koreans will write in any colour but red. Red ink conveys a message of unfriendliness.

BOOKING AHEAD   예약하기

I'd like to book a room, please.
    pang yeyak haryŏgo   방 예약하려고
    hanŭndeyo   하는데요.
Do you have any rooms/beds
available?
    pang issŏyo?   방 있어요?

| double | **dŏbŭl** | 더블 |
| single | **shinggŭl** | 싱글 |

How much for ...?   **...e ŏlma-eyo?**   ...에 얼마에요?
  one night   **haruppam**   하룻 밤
  (three) nights   **(sam)bak**   (삼)박
  a week   **ilchuil**   일주일
  two people   **tu saram**   두 사람

I'll/We'll be arriving at ...
    ...e tochak hal   ...에 도착 할
    yejŏng-ieyo   예정이에요.
My name's ...
    che irŭmŭn ...(i)eyo   제 이름은 ...(이)에요.

Can I pay by credit card?
k'ŭredit'ŭ k'adŭro
kyesan dwaeyo?

크레디트 카드로
계산돼요?

Do you accept travellers
cheques?
yŏhaengja sup'yo padayo?

여행자 수표 받아요?

YES OR NO OR YES OR NO?

Keep in mind that answering questions in Korean
and in English can be somewhat different. A Korean
may answer 'yes' or 'no' depending on agreement or
disagreement with the question. This can be confusing
when the question itself is negative. An English speaker
might answer the question, 'You're not a student?'
with 'no' (meaning 'No, I'm not.'), but a Korean might
answer 'yes' (meaning 'Yes, that's right.').

CHECKING IN   체크 인

Larger motels and hotels will provide beds in every room
(Western-style rooms), but smaller places may have rooms with
no bed (Korean-style rooms), instead offering **yo** (요), 'sleeping
mats' to sleep on. In winter, when the **ondol** (온돌), 'heated
floors' are turned on, the floor is extremely comfortable.

Do you have a room
with two beds?
ch'imdae dugae innŭn
bang issŏyo?

침대 두개있는
방 있어요?

Do you have a room with
a double bed?
dŏbŭl ch'imdae innŭn
bang issŏyo?

더블 침대있는
방 있어요?

ACCOMMODATION

Do you have a
Western-style room?
  yangshik bang issŏyo?   양식 방 있어요?
Do you have a room with
sleeping mats?
  yo kkalgo chanŭn   요 깔고 자는
  bang issŏyo?   방 있어요?
Sorry, we're full.
  choésong hajiman namnŭn 죄송하지만 남는
  bang-i ŏpsŏyo   방이 없어요.

I'd like ...	...ro/ŭro halkkeyo	...로/으로 할게요.
to share a room	kachi ssŭnŭn bang	같이 쓰는 방
a single room	shinggŭl rum	싱글 룸

I/We want a room with a ...	... bang-ŭro halkkeyo	... 방으로 할게요.
bathroom	yokshiri innŭn	욕실이 있는
shower	shawŏshiri innŭn	샤워실이 있는
TV	t'ellebijŏn innŭn	텔레비전 있는
view	chŏnmang-i choŭn	전망이 좋은
cable TV	k'eibŭl t'ibiga naonŭn	케이블 티비가 나오는

Can I see it?
  pang chom polsu issŏyo? 방 좀 볼 수 있어요?
Are there any others?
  tarŭn bang-ŭn ŏpsŏyo? 다른 방은 없어요?
Where's the bathroom?
  yokshiri ŏdie issŏyo?   욕실이 어디에 있어요?
Is there hot water all day?
  onsu harujong-il nawayo? 온수 하루 종일 나와요?
When is the hot water on?
  onsuga ŏnje nawayo?   온수가 언제 나와요?

Is there a discount for
(children; students; senior citizens)?
    (ŏrini/haksaeng/kyŏngno)   (어린이/학생/경로)
    harin issŏyo?   할인있어요?
It's fine. I'll take it.
    chonneyo. ibang-ŭro   좋네요. 이 방으로
    halkkeyo   할께요.

REQUESTS & QUERIES   요구 사항과 질문

Where's the bathroom?
    yokshiri ŏdi issŏyo?   욕실이 어디있어요?
Is breakfast served?
    ach'im shiksaga nawoyo?   아침 식사가 나와요?
Does it come with a
Western breakfast?
    sŏyangshik ach'im shiksaga   서양식 아침 식사가
    nawoyo?   나와요?
Is there somewhere to
wash clothes?
    set'ak'-hal goshi issŏyo?   세탁할 곳이 있어요?
Can we use the telephone?
    chŏnhwa ssŏdo dwaeyo?   전화 써도 돼요?
Do you have a safe where
I can leave my valuables?
    kwijungpumdŭrŭl nŏŭl   귀중품들을 넣을
    pogwanham issŏyo?   보관함 있어요?
Do you change money here?
    yŏgisŏ hwanjŏn halsu   여기서 환전할수
    issŏyo?   있어요?
Is there a message for me?
    chege on meshiji ŏpsŏyo?   제게 온 메시지 없어요?
Can you call a taxi for me?
    t'aekshi chom   택시 좀
    pullŏjushillaeyo?   불러 주실래요?
Please wake us at (seven).
    (ilgopshie) gaewŏjuseyo   (일곱시에) 깨워 주세요.

ACCOMMODATION

ACCOMMODATION

Could we have ...?	... jushilsu issŏyo?	... 주실 수 있어요?
an extra blanket	tamnyo	담요
	hanjang tŏ	한장 더
a mosquito net	mogijang	모기장
our key	pang yŏlsoé	방 열쇠

I've locked myself out
of my room.

yŏlsoé ŏpshi pangmunŭl   열쇠없이 방문을
chamgŭgo nawabŏryŏssŏyo   잠그고 나와 버렸어요.

COMPLAINTS   불평하기

I can't open/
close the window.

ch'angmuni an   창문이 안
yŏllyŏyo/dach'ŏyo   열려요/닫혀요.

I don't like this room.

pang-i mame andŭrŏyo   방이 맘에 안 들어요.

The toilet won't flush.

hwajangshil muri   화장실 물이
annaeryŏgayo   안 내려가요.

Can I change to another?

tarŭn bang-ŭro   다른 방으로
omgilsu issŏyo?   옮길 수 있어요?

It's too ...	nŏmu ...	너무 ...
cold	ch'uwŏyo	추워요
dark	ŏduwŏyo	어두워요
expensive	pissayo	비싸요
light/bright	palgayo	밝아요
noisy	shikkŭrŏwŏyo	시끄러워요
small	chagayo	작아요

This ... is not clean.	i ...nŭn/ŭn gaekkŭt′ajiga anneyo	이 ...는/은 깨끗하지가 않네요.
blanket	tamnyo	담요
pillowcase	pegaennitt	베갯잇
pillow	pegae	베개
sheet	shit′ŭ	시트

CHECKING OUT

체크 아웃

What time do we have to check out?
  ŏnje pang-ŭl piwŏyadwaeyo?
언제 방을 비워야 돼요?

I'm/We're leaving now.
  chigŭm dŏnayo
지금 떠나요.

We had a great stay, thank you.
  yŏrŏgajiro komapsŭmnida
여러가지로 고맙습니다.

I'd like to pay the bill.
  kyesan halkkeyo
계산할게요.

Can I pay with a
travellers cheque?
  yŏhaengja sup′yo padŭseyo?
여행자 수표 받으세요?

There's a mistake in the bill.
  **kyesansŏ-e chalmot
  toén gŏshi innŭn-gŏt kat′ayo**
계산서에 잘못
된 것이 있는 것 같아요.

Can I leave my backpack/
bag/suitcase here until tonight?
  **onŭl bamkkaji paenang-ŭl/
  kabang-ŭl/chim-ŭl yŏgi
  nwadwŏdo doélkkayo?**
오늘 밤까지 배낭을/
가방을/짐을 여기
놔둬도 될까요?

We'll be back in (three) days.
  (sam)irane tora-olkkeyo
(삼)일 안에 돌아올 게요.

ACCOMMODATION

RENTING 방 빌리기

In Korea, renting apartments or homes for short-term stays is virtually unheard of. Renting individual rooms in boarding houses, however, is quite common, and can be arranged through **pudongsan** (부동산), 'real estate offices', for a small fee. Boarding houses, or **hasukchip** (하숙집), are easy to find, especially around universities, and they are a great place to meet local Koreans. Some motels will also rent out rooms for extended periods of time, at a discount.

Do you have any rooms to rent?
pang pillilsu issŏyo?   방 빌릴 수 있어요?
Could I see it?
chom polsu issŭlkkayo?   좀 볼 수 있을까요?

How much is it per ...?   **...e ŏlma-eyo?**   ...에 얼마에요?
   week   **ilchuil**   일주일
   month   **handal**   한 달

I'd like to rent it for (one) month.
(han)daldong-an pillilkkeyo   (한)달 동안 빌릴게요.

A SMILE WILL DO

Cultural differences will pop up right and left when you come to Korea, and one that is particularly bewildering to Westerners is the tendency for Koreans (especially middle-aged or older) to smile when they've made a mistake. Many Westerners misinterpret the smile to mean the person is not taking the mistake or its consequences seriously. But smiling is actually a show of embarrassment, and is generally meant to defuse anger in a difficult situation.

apartment	**apat'ŭ**	아파트
boarding house	**hasukchip**	하숙집
condo	**pilla**	빌라
dormitory	**kisuksa**	기숙사
furnished	**kagu wanbidoén**	가구 완비된
house	**chip**	집
partly furnished	**kaguga**	가구가
	pubunchŏgŭro	부분적으로
	put'ŭn	붙은
real estate office	**pudongsan**	부동산
room	**pang**	방
studio apartment	**wonrŭm**	원룸
	(lit: one-room)	
time-share	**k'ondo**	콘도
unfurnished	**kaguga ŏmnŭn**	가구가 없는

ACCOMMODATION

PAPERWORK
서류 작성

As a foreign visitor, virtually any document you'll have to fill out will be in English or bilingual. There may be some odd occasions, though, where you'll have to provide personal information on a form that's in Korean only.

name	**irŭm/sŏngmyŏng**	이름/성명
address	**chuso**	주소
date of birth	**saengnyŏnwŏril/**	생년월일/
	saeng-il	생일
place of birth	**ch'ulsaengji**	출생지
age	**nai/yŏllyŏng**	나이/연령
sex	**sŏngbyŏl**	성별
nationality	**kukchŏk**	국적
religion	**chonggyo**	종교
profession/work	**chigŏp**	직업
marital status	**kyŏlhon yumu**	결혼유무
single	**mihon**	미혼
married	**kihon**	기혼
divorced	**ihon**	이혼

ACCOMMODATION

identification card	shinbunjŭng	신분증
passport number	yŏkwŏnbŏnho	여권번호
visa	bija	비자
drivers licence	unjŏnmyŏnhŏjŭng	운전면허증
customs	segwan	세관
immigration	ipkuk kwalli;	입국 관리;
	ipkuk shimsa	입국 심사
purpose of visit	pangmun mokchŏk	방문 목적
reason for travel	yŏhaeng mokchŏk	여행 목적
visiting relatives	ch'inch'ŏk pangmun;	친척 방문;
	ch'inji pangmun	친지 방문
visiting the homeland	kohyang pangmun	고향 방문
holiday	yŏhaeng	여행
business	saŏp	사업

DID YOU KNOW ...   UNESCO (United Nations Educational, Scientific and Cultural Organisation) gives out a prize every year to a person who contributed a great deal to the promotion of literacy. The prize is called the King Sejong Prize, in honour of King Sejong, for his development of Hangul which promoted literacy in Korea.

AROUND TOWN

Korea boasts 5000 years of history, as its many palaces, temples, gates and other cultural sites attest. It seems there's an historical marker on every street corner. At the same time, Korea is a technological leader with excellent public transport and highly efficient banking and postal systems.

LOOKING FOR ...   ... 찾기

Where's a/an/the ...?	...i/ga ŏdi issŏyo?	...이/가 어디 있어요?
art gallery	misulgwan	미술관
bank	ŭnhaeng	은행
cinema	yŏnghwagwan	영화관
city centre (downtown)	shinae jungshimga	시내 중심가
consulate	yŏngsagwan	영사관
embassy	taesagwan	대사관
hotel	hotel	호텔
market	shijang	시장
museum	pangmulgwan	박물관
police station	kyŏngchalsŏ	경찰서
post office	uch'eguk	우체국
public telephone	kongjung jŏnhwa	공중전화
public toilet	hwajangshil	화장실
telephone centre	chŏnhwaguk	전화국
tourist information office	kwan-gwang annaeso	관광 안내소

SIGNS

관계자외 출입금지	AUTHORISED PERSONNEL ONLY
영업 안 합니다; 휴무; 휴업	CLOSED
입구	ENTRANCE
출구 나가는 곳	EXIT
들어가지 마시오; 출입 금지	NO ENTRY
사진 촬영 금지	NO PHOTOGRAPHY
금연	NO SMOKING
영업중; 영업합니다	OPEN
… 금지	… PROHIBITED
흡연 구역	SMOKING AREA
화장실	TOILET
신사용	MEN
숙녀용	WOMEN
머리조심	WATCH YOUR HEAD

AT THE BANK   은행에서

Banking in Korea tends to be done electronically, with the help of automatic teller machines that are found almost everywhere. Most banks will have at least someone who can help you in English.

The local currency is called **won** (원). You'll have to get used to carrying around lots of bills as even the largest denominations still represent modest amounts of money. Koreans bypass the need to carry lots of bills by using **sup'yo** (수표), a kind of 'cheque' that can come in fixed denominations (especially 100,000 won) or can be created in specific amounts.

I want to change (a) ...	...rŭl/ŭl pakkuryŏgo hanŭndeyo	...를/을 바꾸려고 하는데요.
cash/money	hyŏn-gŭm/ton	현금/돈
cheque; money order	sup'yo	수표
travellers cheque	yŏhaengja sup'yo	여행자 수표

Can I use my credit card
to withdraw money?
**k'ŭredit'ŭ k'adŭro hyŏn-gŭm
inch'ul halsu issŏyo?**
크레디트 카드로 현금
인출 할 수 있어요?

Can I exchange money here?
hwanjŏn halsu issŏyo?
환전 할 수 있어요?

What's the exchange rate?
hwanyuri ŏttŏk'e dwaeyo?
환율이 어떻게 돼요?

What's your commission?
k'ŏmishŏnŭn ŏlmana haeyo?
커미션은 얼마나 해요?

How many won per dollar?
**dallŏdang wŏnhwaga
ŏlmana haeyo?**
달러당 원화가
얼마나 해요?

What time does the bank open?
**ŭnhaeng munŭl
ŏnje yŏrŏyo?**
은행 문을
언제 열어요?

Where can I cash a
travellers cheque?
**yŏhaengja sup'yorŭl
ŏdisŏ hyŏn-gŭmŭro
pakkulsu issŏyo?**
여행자 수표를
어디서 현금으로
바꿀 수 있어요?

Can I transfer money here
from my bank?
**che ŭnhaeng-esŏ
i ŭnhaeng-ŭro
song-gŭmi dwaeyo?**
제 은행에서
이 은행으로
송금이 돼요?

Has my money arrived yet?
che toni tochak haessŏyo?
제 돈이 도착했어요?

Can I transfer money overseas?
oégugŭro songgŭm
halsu issŏyo?

외국으로 송금
할 수 있어요?

The automatic teller machine
(ATM) swallowed my card.
hyŏn-gŭmjigŭpkiga che
tonŭl mŏgŏbŏryŏssŏyo

현금지급기가 제
돈을 먹어 버렸어요.

ㄱㄲㄴㄷㄸㄹㅁㅂㅃㅅㅆㅇㅈㅉㅊㅋㅌㅍㅎ
ㅏㅐㅑㅒㅓㅔㅕㅖㅗㅘㅙㅚㅛㅜㅝㅞㅟㅠㅡㅢㅣ

AT THE POST OFFICE   우체국에서

Postal services in Korea are cheap and efficient. Large post offices
also offer some banking services. Most forms are available in
English as well as Korean. Sending and receiving faxes is usually
done at hotels or **munbanggu** (문방구), 'stationery stores'.

I want to buy ...	**...rŭl/ŭl saryŏ-go**	...를/을 사려고
	hanŭndeyo	하는데요.
postcards	**yŏpsŏ**	엽서
stamps	**up'yo**	우표

I want to send a ...	**...rŭl/ŭl puchiryŏ-go**	...를/을 부치려고
	hanŭndeyo	하는데요.
letter	**p'yŏnji**	편지
parcel	**sop'o**	소포
postcard	**yŏpsŏ**	엽서

I'd like to send a fax.
p'aeksŭrŭl ponaeryŏgo
hanŭndeyo

팩스를 보내려고
하는데요.

Please send it by air mail.
hanggong p'yŏnŭro
ponaejuseyo

항공편으로
보내 주세요.

Please send it by surface mail.
sŏnbak p'yŏnŭro
ponaejuseyo

선박편으로
보내 주세요.

How much does it cost
to send this to ...?
  igŏl ...e ponaenŭnde toni   이걸 ...에 보내는 데 돈이
  ŏlmana tŭrŏyo?   얼마나 들어요?
Where's the poste-restante
section?
  yuchi up'yŏnŭn   유치 우편은
  ŏdisŏ padayo?   어디서 받아요?
Is there any mail for me?
  chege on up'yŏnmul ŏpsŏyo?   제게 온 우편물 없어요?

air mail	**hanggong up'yŏn**	항공우편
envelope	**pongt'u**	봉투
express mail	**barŭn up'yŏn**	빠른 우편
mailbox	**uch'et'ong**	우체통
parcel	**sop'o**	소포
pen	**bolp'en**	볼펜
postcode	**up'yŏnbŏnho**	우편번호
registered mail	**tŭnggiup'yŏn**	등기우편
surface mail	**sŏnbakp'yŏn**	선박편

AROUND TOWN

TELECOMMUNICATIONS   통신

From landlines to mobile phones, the telephone service in
Korea is extremely cheap and very reliable. Mobile phone users
now outnumber landline customers.

Prior to the mobile phone craze, South Korea had the fourth-
highest number of payphones in the world. Payphones are still
plentiful in public areas.

Where's the nearest
public phone?
  kakkaun kongjungjŏnhwaga   가까운 공중전화가
  ŏdi issŏyo?   어디있어요?
Could I please use the telephone?
  chŏnhwa chom ssŏdo dwaeyo?   전화 좀 써도 돼요?

I want to call ...
   ...hante chŏnhwahago
    ship'ŏyo

...한테 전화하고
싶어요.

I want to make a long-distance
call to (Australia).
   (hoju)e changgŏri
   chŏnhwarŭl haryŏgo
   hanŭndeyo

(호주)에 장거리
전화를 하려고
하는데요.

I want to make a collect call.
   sushinjabudam chŏnhwarŭl
   haryŏgo hanŭndeyo

수신자부담 전화를
하려고 하는데요.

It's engaged.
   t'onghwajung-ieyo

통화중이에요.

I've been cut off.
   t'onghwaga
   gŭnk'yŏbŏryŏssŏyo

통화가
끊겨 버렸어요.

mobile/	hyudaep'on/	휴대폰/
cell phone	haendŭp'on	핸드폰
operator	kyohwanwŏn	교환원
phone book	chŏnhwabŏnhobu	전화번호부
phone box	chŏnhwa baksŭ	전화박스
phonecard	chŏnhwa k'adŭ	전화카드
telephone	kunae yŏn-gyŏl	구내 연결
extension	bŏnho	번호

Making a Call 전화걸기

Hello, is ... there?
   yŏboseyo, ... issŏyo?

여보세요, ... 있어요?

Hello, is ... there?
(when an older person answers)
   yŏboseyo, ... chom
   pakkwŏ jushigessŏyo?

여보세요, ... 좀
바꿔 주시겠어요?

Hello. (answering a call)
   yŏboseyo

여보세요.

Who's calling?	죄송하지만
choésong hajiman, nugushindeyo?	누구신데요?
It's ... (referring to the caller)	
...indeyo	...인데요.
Yes, he's/she's here.	
ne, issŏyo	네, 있어요.
One moment, (please).	
chamkkanmanyo	잠깐만요.
I'm sorry, he's/she's not here.	
chigŭm ŏmnŭndeyo	지금 없는데요.
What time will he/she be back?	
ŏnje toraonŭndeyo?	언제 돌아오는데요?
Can I leave a message?	
meshiji namgilsu issŏyo?	메시지 남길 수 있어요?
Please tell ... I called.	
...hante chega chŏnhwa haettago chŏnhaejuseyo	...한테 제가 전화했다고 전해 주세요.
I'll call back later.	
chega tashi chŏnhwa halkkeyo	제가 다시 전화할게요.

AROUND TOWN

HELLO-YO? IT'S ME-YO!

Remember that in Korean you must always include linguistic elements to keep your speech polite, except when talking with close friends, younger family members, or people who are much younger. If you omit these, it can easily be taken as an insult. You can avoid such offense by adding **-yo** (–요) at the end of your sentences, even if only replying with a one-word answer.

The Internet   인터넷

You can take advantage of cheap, high-speed connections at the ubiquitous 24-hour **p'ishibang** (PC 방), literally 'PC room', a kind of simple 'Internet cafe'.

Is there a local Internet cafe?
**chubyŏne int'ŏnet
k'ap'ega issŏyo?**   주변에 인터넷
                                            카페가 있어요?
I'd like to get Internet access.
**int'ŏnesŭl haryŏgo
hanŭndeyo**   인터넷을 하려고
                                            하는데요.
I'd like to check my email.
**imeil hwagin haryŏgo
hanŭndeyo**   이 메일 확인하려고
                                            하는데요.
I'd like to send an email.
**imeirŭl ponaeryŏgo
hanŭndeyo**   이 메일을 보내려고
                                            하는데요.

computer	**k'ŏmp'yut'ŏ**	컴퓨터
fax	**p'aeksŭ**	팩스
Internet cafe	**p'ishibang;**	PC 방;
	intŏnet k'ap'e	인터넷 카페
modem	**modem**	모뎀

SIGHTSEEING   구경하기

Although its cities are modern and high-tech, Korea is a wondrous place of mountain peaks and isolated islands, with historic temples and palaces thrown in for good measure. Kyongju (Gyeongju) is called 'a museum without walls'.

History has not always been kind to Korea: many historical sites were burned down during invasions of centuries past, only to be rebuilt again. Unfortunately, though, many were lost during the Korean War.

Where's the tourist office?	
kwan-gwang annaesoga ŏdi issŏyo?	관광안내소가 어디 있어요?
Do you have a local map?	
shinae jido issŏyo?	시내 지도 있어요?
I'd like to see ...	
...rŭl/ŭl pogo ship'ŏyo	...를/을 보고 싶어요.
Can we take photographs?	
sajin tchigŏdo dwaeyo?	사진 찍어도 돼요?
I'll send you the photograph.	
chega sajin ponaedŭrilkkeyo	제가 사진 보내 드릴게요.
Could you take a photograph of me?	
che sajin chom tchigŏjushillaeyo?	제 사진 좀 찍어 주실래요?

Getting In   입장하기

What time does it open/close?	
mun ŏnje tadayo/yŏrŏyo?	문 언제 닫아요/열어요?
Is there an admission charge?	
ipjangnyo issŏyo?	입장료 있어요?

Is there a discount for ...?	**... harin issŏyo?**	... 할인 있어요?
children	**ŏrini**	어린이
students	**haksaeng**	학생
Korean War veterans	**han-gukchŏn ch'amjŏn yongsa**	한국전 참전용사
senior citizens	**kyŏngno**	경로

The Sights   경치

What's that building?	
chŏ kŏnmuri mŏeyo?	저 건물이 뭐에요?
What's this monument?	
i kinyŏmbiga mŏeyo?	이 기념비가 뭐에요?
It's crowded.	
pumbyŏyo	붐벼요.

amusement park	yuwonji	유원지
castle	sŏng	성
church/cathedral	kyohoé/sŏngdang	교회/성당
hot springs	onch'ŏn	온천
Independence Memorial Hall	tongnip kinyŏmgwan	독립기념관
Itaewon	it'aewon	이태원
Kyongbok-kung Palace	kyŏngbok-kung	경복궁
Namsan Tower	namsan t'awŏ	남산 타워
national park	kungnip kong-won	국립공원
Panmunjom/DMZ	p'anmunjŏm; pimujang jidae	판문점; 비무장 지대
palace	kung	궁
park	kong-won	공원
Pulguk-sa Temple	pulguk-sa	불국사
Secret Garden	piwŏn	비원
Seoul Arts Center	yesure chŏndang	예술의 전당
statue	tongsang	동상
temple	chŏl	절
Toksu-gung Palace	tŏksu-gung	덕수궁
Tongdaemun (East Gate)	tongdaemun	동대문

AROUND TOWN

Tours

여행/투어

Are there regular tours we can join?
uriga ch'amyŏ halmanhan chŏnggijŏgŭro chegongdoénŭn yŏhaeng sangpum ŏmnayo?

우리가 참여 할만한 정기적으로 제공되는 여행 상품 없나요?

Can we hire a guide?
gaidŭ kuhalsu issŏyo?

가이드 구할 수 있어요?

How much is the tour?
yŏhaenghanŭnde ŏlma-eyo?

여행하는데 얼마에요?

How much is a guide?
gaidŭ kuhanŭnde ŏlma-eyo?

가이드 구하는데 얼마에요?

How long is the tour?
**yŏhaeng hanŭnde
ŏlmana kŏllyŏyo?**

여행하는데
얼마나 걸려요?

Is there a tour in English?
**yŏng-ŏro sŏlmyŏng haejunŭn
yŏhaeng issŏyo?**

영어로 설명해 주는
여행 있어요?

Have you seen a group
of (Australians)?
**(hoju) yŏhaenggaek kŭrup
poshinjŏk issŏyo?**

(호주) 여행객 그룹
보신 적 있어요?

나가서 즐기기   GOING OUT

For better or worse, drinking is a national pastime in Korea. Until recently, a man or woman who didn't go drinking with his or her buddies after work or school was seen as antisocial and could even be ostracised.

If getting drunk isn't your idea of fun, another of Korea's favourite pastimes may be right up your alley: singing. The **noraebang** (노래방), literally 'song rooms', are businesses divided into small rooms with karaoke machines, perfect for up to a dozen people to get together and wail out the latest single by Cho Sungmo or an oldie from the Beatles.

WHERE TO GO   어디에 갈까?

Besides drinking, Koreans like to socialise over coffee at one of the millions of cafes found in every nook and cranny of the country. Film is also popular, as is the theatre, where even Shakespeare is performed in Korean.

Some of Korea's traditional markets have become all-night centres of activity with a party-like atmosphere, as locals and foreigners alike throng to get their hands on the latest shipments from elsewhere in Korea and beyond.

What's there to do in the evenings?
  chŏnyŏge halsu innŭn   저녁에 할 수 있는
  chaeminnŭnil issŏyo?   재미있는 일 있어요?
What's on tonight?
  onŭl bame mwŏ chaemi   오늘 밤에 뭐
  innŭnil issŏyo?   재밌는 일있어요?
Where can I find out what's on?
  musŭn halkŏridŭri innŭnji 무슨 할 거리들이 있는지
  ŏdisŏ arabolsu issŏyo? 어디서 알아볼 수 있어요?

I feel like ...	... ship'ŏyo	... 싶어요.
a stroll	sanch´aek hago	산책하고
dancing	ch'um-ch'ugo	춤추고
going for a	kŏp´i/sul	커피/술
coffee/drink	mashirŏ kago	마시러 가고

I feel like going to a/the …	… kago ship'ŏyo	… 가고 싶어요.
bar/pub	sul mashirŏ	술 마시러
cafe	k'ŏp'i-shobe	커피숍에
cinema	yŏnghwagwane	영화관에
concert	kong-yŏnjang-e	공연장에
karaoke bar	karaok'e ba	가라오케 바
nightclub	nait'ŭ-e	나이트에
opera	opera-e	오페라에
restaurant	shiktang-e	식당에
theatre	kŭkjang-e	극장에
traditional teahouse	chŏnt'ong ch'atchibe	전통 찻집에
traditional music performance	kugak kong-yŏne	국악 공연에

INVITATIONS

초대

What are you doing
this evening?
   onŭlbame mwŏ haseyo?   오늘 밤에 뭐 하세요?

What are you doing
this weekend?
   ibŏnjumare mwŏ haseyo?   이번 주말에 뭐 하세요?

Do you know a good
restaurant (that's cheap)?
   ŏdi (ssago) choŭn   어디 (싸고) 좋은
   ŭmshikchŏm ŏpsŏyo?   음식점 없어요?

Would you like to go for a drink?
   sul mashirŏ kalkkayo?   술 마시러 갈까요?

Would you like to go for a meal?
   papmŏgŭrŏ kalkkayo?   밥 먹으러 갈까요?

My shout. (I'll buy.)
   chega salkkeyo   제가 살게요.

Do you want to come to the
{music style; name of artist}
concert with me?
   {...} kong-yŏne kach'i   {...} 공연에 같이
   kashillaeyo?   가실래요?

We're having a party.
   uri p'at'i-rŭl halkkŏeyo   우리 파티를 할 거에요.

Come along.
   kachi kayo   같이 가요.

ANNYŎNG ANY OL' TIME

Korean doesn't have a separate greeting for morning,
noon, afternoon and evening. At all times of the day
annyŏng haseyo (안녕하세요), 'hello', is appropriate.

Responding to Invitations   초대에 응하기

Sure!
   mullonijo!   물론이죠!
Yes, I'd love to.
   ne, tang-yŏnhi kayajo   네, 당연히 가야죠.
Yes. Where shall we go?
   ne. ŏdi kalkkayo?   네. 어디 갈까요?
No, I'm afraid I can't.
   choésong hande   죄송한데
   mot kalgŏt kat'ayo   못 갈 것 같아요.
What about tomorrow?
   naeirŭn ŏttaeyo?   내일은 어때요?

NIGHTCLUBS & BARS   나이트와 술집

Districts of big cities that cater to foreign residents usually have some Western-style dance clubs. Lately, Latin dancing has gained quite a few followers. Drinks are generally expensive, and if you decide to sit down at a table, be prepared to order some fruit or French fries (called **anju** (안주), or 'side dishes') at astronomical prices.

Are there any good nightclubs?
   choŭn nait'ŭ issŏyo?   좋은 나이트 있어요?
How do you get to this club?
   i nait'ŭ-e ŏttŏk'e   이 나이트에 어떻게
   kayo?   가요?
Do you want to dance?
   ch'um ch'ushillaeyo?   춤 추실래요?

I'm sorry, I'm a terrible dancer.
 **choésong hande, chŏ ch'um
 jal mot ch'wŏyo**

죄송한데, 저 춤
잘 못 춰요.

Come on!
 ŏsŏyo!

어서요!

What type of music do
you prefer?
 **ŏttŏn ŭmagŭl
 choa haseyo?**

어떤 음악을
좋아하세요?

I really like (reggae).
 **chŏn (rege) ŭmagŭl
 choahaeyo**

전 (레게) 음악을
좋아해요.

Where can we dance
some (salsa)?
 **(salsa) ch'um ch'ulsu
 innŭn-got issŏyo?**

(살사) 춤 출 수
있는 곳 있어요?

Do you want to go to a
norae-bang? (see page 113)
 noraebang kashillaeyo?

노래방 가실래요?

Do you have to pay to enter?
 ipchangnyo issŏyo?

입장료 있어요?

No, it's free.
 anio, muryo-eyo

아니오, 무료에요.

Yes, it's ...
 ne, ...wonieyo

네, ...원이에요.

This place is great.
 yŏgi nŏmu choŭndeyo

여기 너무 좋은데요.

I'm having a great time.
 nŏmu chaemi issŏyo

너무 재미있어요.

I don't like the music here.
 **yŏgi ŭmagi maŭme
 andŭneyo**

여기 음악이 마음에
안 드네요.

Shall we go somewhere else?
 tarŭn gosŭro kalkkayo?

다른 곳으로 갈까요?

ARRANGING TO MEET   약속잡기

In Korea, it's rare to pick someone up at their home. Instead, the two parties will arrange to meet at a well-known location near the place they plan to visit. Because of long subway or bus commutes to get back home, it's customary not to stay out too late (eg, past 10 pm).

What time shall we meet?
myŏshie mannalkkayo?   몇 시에 만날까요?
Where will we meet?
ŏdisŏ mannalkkayo?   어디서 만날까요?
Let's meet at (eight o'clock)
at {name of place}.
(yŏdŏlshi)e {...}esŏ   (여덟시)에 {...}에서
mannayo   만나요.
Agreed/OK.
kŭrŏk′e haeyo   그렇게 해요.
I'll pick you up at (nine).
(ahopshi)e terirŏ   (아홉시)에 데리러
olkkeyo   올게요.
See you later/tomorrow.
ittaga/naeil poéyo   이따가/내일 봬요.
Sorry I'm late.
nŭjŏsŏ choésong haeyo   늦어서 죄송해요.

DATING & ROMANCE   데이트와 로맨스

Korea is a conservative country where different standards for the men's and women's behaviour still apply. A woman's reputation is often closely guarded whereas men have considerably more freedom.

Casual sex is not common in Korea, and excessive talk about sex is considered offensive by many people.

GOING OUT

The Date

데이트

Would you like
to go see a movie
or something …?

... mannasŏ
yŏnghwarado
kach'i polkkayo?

... 만나서
영화라도
같이 볼까요?

tomorrow

naeil

내일

tonight

onŭlbam

오늘 밤

at the weekend

chumare

주말에

Yes. (I'd love to.)
ne

네.

I'm afraid I'm busy.
choésong hande,
nŏmu pappasŏyo

죄송한데,
너무 바빠서요.

Where would you like to go?
ŏdi kago ship'ŭseyo?

어디 가고 싶으세요?

Can I see you again?
ŏnje do polsu issŭlkkayo?

언제 또 볼 수 있을까요?

Can I call you?
chŏnhwahaedo dwaeyo?

전화해도 돼요?

I'll call you tomorrow.
naeil chŏnhwa halkkeyo

내일 전화 할게요.

Classic Pick-Up Lines

전형적인 말걸기

Would you like a drink?
mwŏ kach'i mashilkkayo?

뭐 같이 마실까요?

Do you have a light?
rait'ŏ issŭseyo?

라이터 있으세요?

Do you mind if I sit here?
yŏgi anjado dwaeyo?

여기 앉아도 돼요?

Shall we get some fresh air?
sanch'aek halkkayo?

산책 할까요?

Do you have a boyfriend/girlfriend?
namjach'in-gu/yŏjach'in-gu
issŭseyo?

남자친구/여자친구
있으세요?

He's/She's just a friend.
kŭnyang chin-gueyo

그냥 친구에요.

Classic Rejections

전형적인 거절

I'm sorry but I'd rather not.
  choésong-hande,
  an-doél-gŏt kanneyo

죄송한데
안 될 것 같네요.

I'm here with my
boyfriend/girlfriend.
  namjachin-gurang/
  yŏjachin-gurang
  kach'i wassŏyo

남자친구랑/
여자친구랑
같이 왔어요.

Stop hassling me.
  kŭmanhaseyo

그만하세요.

Excuse me, I have to go now.
  choésong hande, chigŭm
  ŏdi kabwaya dwaeyo

죄송한데 지금
어디 가봐야 돼요.

I'm not interested.
  kwanshim ŏpsŏyo

관심없어요.

가족

FAMILY

Family cohesion is important in Korea, with most young people living at home long after they would have moved out in Western countries. Living with one's parents until marriage is the norm. Although many senior citizens now prefer to remain living independently, three-generation families are very common, as the oldest son – and especially his wife – end up caring for the elderly parents.

QUESTIONS & ANSWERS   질문, 대답

Are you married?
kyŏlhon hashŏssŏyo?   결혼하셨어요?

I'm ...	**chŏnŭn ...**	저는 ...
divorced	**ihon haessŏyo**	이혼했어요
married	**kyŏlhon haessŏyo**	결혼했어요
separated	**pyŏlgŏjungieyo**	별거중이에요
single	**mihonieyo**	미혼이에요

How many children do you have?
chanyŏga myŏnmyŏng-iseyo?   자녀가 몇 명이세요?

I don't have any children.
chanyŏga ŏpsŏyo   자녀가 없어요.

I have a daughter/son.
dal/adŭl hanmyŏng issŏyo   딸/아들 한명이 있어요.

FAMILY TIES

Marriage prospects among Koreans are limited by the fact that, in traditional Confucian culture, it's considered incestuous to marry someone with the same surname. Given that there are only a few hundred surnames in Korea and over 20% of the population uses the surname Kim, and 15% Lee, this certainly limits marriage prospects.

FAMILY

FAMILY MEMBERS 가족 구성원

Reflecting the importance of family relations, Koreans have very specific words for various relatives. Here are the more common kinship terms:

baby	agi	아기
boy	namja-ai	남자아이
brother	hyŏngje	형제
children	chanyŏ	자녀
dad (inf)	appa	아빠
daughter	dal	딸
family	kajok	가족
father (pol)	abŏji	아버지
father-in-law		
(speaker is f)	shi-abŏji	시아버지
(speaker is m)	chang-inŏrŭn	장인어른
girl	yŏja-ai	여자아이
grandfather	harabŏji	할아버지
grandmother	halmŏni	할머니
husband	nampyŏn	남편
mother (pol)	ŏmŏni	어머니
mother-in-law		
(speaker is f)	shi-ŏmŏni	시어머니
(speaker is m)	changmonim	장모님
mum/mom (inf)	ŏmma	엄마
sister	chamae	자매
son	adŭl	아들
wife	anae	아내

TALKING WITH PARENTS 부모와 대화하기

Korean parents love to dote on their children – compliments will be most welcome.

When is the baby due?
  **ch'ulsan yejŏng-iri   출산 예정일이
  ŏnje-eyo?   언제에요?**
Is this your first child?
  chŏt agieyo?   첫 아기에요?

How old are your children?
 **chanyŏdŭre naiga
 ŏttŏk'e dwaeyo?**

자녀들의 나이가
어떻게 돼요?

Does he/she attend school?
 hakkyo tanyŏyo?

학교 다녀요?

Do you have grandchildren?
 sonju issŭseyo?

손주 있으세요?

What's the baby's name?
 agi irŭmi mwŏ-eyo?

아기 이름이 뭐에요?

Is it a girl or a boy?
 darieyo, adŭrieyo?

딸이에요, 아들이에요?

He's/She's very big for
his/her age.
 naie pihae k'ŭneyo

나이에 비해 크네요.

What a cute child.
 nŏmu kwiyŏundeyo

너무 귀여운데요.

He/She looks like you.
 talmannŭndeyo

닮았는데요.

IF IT LOOKS LIKE A DUCK

Although many Koreans will give themselves an English
moniker when learning the language, their use doesn't
usually extend to formal settings. Nevertheless many
Koreans try to make Korean names easier for foreigners
to read or pronounce, sometimes by manipulating the
spelling. When a syllable in someone's name sounds like
a word in English, he or she may be tempted to use that
word's spelling in his or her name. So a person named
sŏngdŏk (성덕) might be tempted to spell his name
Sung-Duck, and **yŏngju** (영주) might be tempted to write
her name as Young-Jew. It's possible to see members of
the **won** (원), **yu** (유) and **pak** or **park** (both are 박) clans
writing their surname as One, You and Bach.

FAMILY

FAMILY

TALKING WITH CHILDREN　아이들과 대화하기

Small children who are just beginning to learn English are often delighted to show off their command of 'Hello!' and 'How are you?'. You should expect that some children will be very shy about talking with a non-Korean.

Note that the form of speech used in the phrases below is specifically for talking to children; using these verb endings when talking to an adult may cause offence.

What's your name?
irŭmi mwŏya?　　　　　　　이름이 뭐야?

How old are you?
myŏssarini?　　　　　　　　몇 살이니?

How many siblings do you have?
hyŏngjega myŏnmyŏng-iya?　형제가 몇 명이야?

How old are they?
myŏssarinde?　　　　　　　　몇 살인데?

Do you go to school or kindergarten?
hakkyo tanyŏ,　　　　　　　학교 다녀,
yuch'iwon tanyŏ?　　　　　유치원 다녀?

Is your teacher nice?
sŏnsaengnim choa?　　　　　선생님 좋아?

Do you like school?
hakkyo taninŭn-gŏt chonni?　학교 다니는 것 좋니?

Do you learn English?
yŏng-ŏ paeuni?　　　　　　　영어 배우니?

We speak a different language
in my country so I don't
understand you very well.
urinara-esŏnŭn yŏng-ŏ　　　우리 나라에서는 영어
ssŭgittaemune, nan　　　　　쓰기때문에 난
hangungmal chal mot'ae　　　한국말 잘 못 해.

Plymouth District Library
Thank you for using self-checkout!

Checked Out Items 7/11/2018 15:35
XXXXXXXXXX7592

Item Title	Due Date
33387005782554	8/1/2018 23:59
SAT prep plus 2018	
33387005434891	8/1/2018 23:59
Cracking the SAT	
33387003073444	8/1/2018 23:59
Korean phrasebook	
33387003072727	8/1/2018 23:59
Korean dictionary _phrasebook	
33387003075233	8/1/2018 23:59
Mastering Korean, Level 1 [cdbook]	

Renew online at plymouthlibrary.org
or by phone 734-453-0750, option 3

관심사, 여러가지 활동

INTERESTS & ACTIVITIES

One of the questions you'll almost certainly be asked by Koreans you first meet is 'What are your hobbies?'. Koreans are keen on joining hobby-oriented clubs, especially at school. Clubs may range from hiking and sports to language study. Going to your Korean friends' English study group is a great way to meet other Koreans.

COMMON INTERESTS & HOBBIES

공통 관심사,
취미

What are your hobbies?
  ch'wimiga mwŏ-eyo?   취미가 뭐에요?

Do you like ...?	...rŭl/ŭl choahaseyo?	...를/을 좋아하세요?
I like ...	...rŭl/ŭl choahaeyo	...를/을 좋아해요.
I don't like ...	...rŭl/ŭl shirŏhaeyo	...를/을 싫어해요.
art	misul	미술
cooking	yori hanŭn-gŏt	요리하는 것
dancing	ch'um ch'unŭn-gŏt	춤추는 것
films	yŏnghwa	영화
gardening	chŏng-wonil	정원일
hiking	tŭngsan	등산
music	ŭmak	음악
photography	sajin	사진
playing sport	undong hanŭn-gŏt	운동하는 것
reading	toksŏ	독서
shopping	shop'ing	쇼핑
talking	iyagi hanŭn-gŏt	이야기하는 것
the theatre	yŏn-gŭk	연극
travelling	yŏhaeng	여행
watching TV	t'ellebijŏn ponŭn-gŏt	텔레비전 보는 것
writing	kŭl ssŭgi	글쓰기

INTERESTS & ACTIVITIES

TYPES OF SPORT   스포츠 종류

Korea is a place where both indigenous and Western sports enjoy immense popularity. Koreans have embraced 'Western' sports such as soccer, skiing, swimming, basketball, baseball and golf. Accordingly, when it comes to sports vocabulary, Korea tends to 'hangulise' English terms: a strike is a **sŭtŭraikŭ** (스트라이크), and a goal is a **gol** (골).

What sport do you play?
musŭn undong haseyo?   무슨 운동 하세요?

I play/practise/do …	**chŏnŭn …rŭl/ŭl haeyo**	저는 …를/을 해요.
aerobics	**eŏrobik**	에어로빅
archery	**yanggung**	양궁
athletics	**yuksang**	육상
baseball	**yagu**	야구
basketball	**nonggu**	농구
cycling	**ssaik'ŭl**	사이클
football (soccer)	**ch'ukku**	축구
(ice) hockey	**(aisŭ) hak'i**	(아이)스하키
karate	**karade**	가라데
kendo (Japanese fencing)	**kŏmdo**	검도
kung fu	**k'unghu**	쿵후
martial arts	**musul**	무술
meditation	**myŏngsang**	명상
skiing	**sŭk'i**	스키
swimming	**suyŏng**	수영
taebo	**t'aebo**	태보
taekwondo	**t'aekwŏndo**	태권도
Tai Chi	**t'aegŭkkwŏn**	태극권
tennis	**t'enisŭ**	테니스
volleyball	**paegu**	배구
yoga	**yoga**	요가

TALKING ABOUT SPORT

운동에 대해
이야기하기

Do you like sport?
undong choahaseyo?
운동 좋아하세요?

I like watching it.
ponŭn-gŏsŭn choahaeyo
보는 것은 좋아해요.

What sports do you follow?
ŏttŏn undong-e kwanshimi issŭseyo?
어떤 운동에 관심이 있으세요?

I follow ...
...e kwanshimi issŏyo
...에 관심이 있어요.

What's your favourite team?
ŏnŭ t'imŭl cheil choahaseyo?
어느 팀을 제일 좋아하세요?

Who's your favourite ...?	**cheil choahanŭn ...ga/i nugueyo?**	제일 좋아하는 ...가/이 누구예요?
player	**sŏnsu**	선수
sportsperson	**undong sŏnsu**	운동선수

INTERESTS & ACTIVITIES

T'AEKWŎNDO

Together with **ssirŭm** (씨름), a traditional form of wrestling, **t'aekwŏndo** (태권도) is one of the two representative sports of Korea. Taekwondo is a version of unarmed combat designed for the purpose of self-defense that has been taught for hundreds of years in Korean military academies.

Nowadays it's studied by men and women all over the world for exercise, mental well-being, and personal safety, and it has become an Olympic sport. It makes scientific use of the body to promote mental and physical conditioning, and like other martial arts, it's a discipline that promotes character as much as physical capabilities.

GOING TO THE MATCH   경기에 가기

Korea's national and municipal stadiums are generally easily accessed by public transport, especially the subway system. Some sporting events also take place on college campuses.

Koreans go to matches to have fun, and they get caught up in the chants and songs as much as the game itself. Even when two teams are long-time rivals, there's hardly ever any violence.

Would you like to go to a match?
  kyŏnggi borŏ kalkkayo?   경기 보러 갈까요?
Where's it being held?
  ŏdisŏ hanŭndeyo?   어디서 하는데요?
How much are the tickets?
  p'yoga ŏlma-eyo?   표가 얼마에요?
What time does it start?
  ŏnje shijak haeyo?   언제 시작해요?
Who's playing?
  nuga kyŏnggi haeyo?   누가 경기해요?
Who do you think will win?
  nuga igilgŏt kat'ayo?   누가 이길 것 같아요?
Who are you supporting?
  nugu p'yŏniseyo?   누구 편이세요?
I'm supporting …
  chŏn … p'yŏnieyo   전 … 편이에요.
Who's winning?
  nuga igigo issŏyo?   누가 이기고 있어요?
What's the score?
  chŏmsuga ŏttŏk'e dwaeyo?   점수가 어떻게 돼요?
How much time is left?
  shigani ŏlmana namassŏyo?   시간이 얼마나 남았어요?

referee	shimp'an	심판
seat	chwasŏk/chari	좌석/자리
ticket	p'yo/t'ik'et	표/티켓
ticket office	maep'yoso	매표소

THEY MAY SAY ...

chŏ sŏnsu shillyŏgi choayo
  He's/She's good.

chŏ sŏnsu shillyŏgi pyŏlloneyo
  He's/She's no good.

taedan-han ... (i)neyo!	What a ...!
gol	goal
hit´u	hit
p´aesŭ	pass
shut	shot

chŏngmal chal hanŭndeyo!
  What a great performance!

chŏngmal koéngjanghan kyŏnggi yŏssŏyo!
  That was a really good game!

nŏmu chiru haeyo!
  What a boring game!

SOCCER   축구

The 2002 Korea-Japan World Cup has spurred a tremendous
amount of interest in soccer. Korea has long had one of the best
national teams in Asia, and matches against other countries –
particularly against rival Japan – are major television events.

Do you follow soccer?
  ch´ukkue kwanshim issŭseyo?   축구에 관심있으세요?
Who's at the top of the league?
  ŏnŭ t´imi sŏngjŏgi   어느 팀이 성적이
  cheil choayo?   제일 좋아요?
Who plays for (the Tigers)?
  (t´aigŏjŭ)e ŏttŏn   (타이거즈)에 어떤
  sŏnsuga issŏyo?   선수가 있어요?
My favourite player is ...
  chŏnŭn ... sŏnsurŭl   저는 ... 선수를
  cheil choahaeyo   제일 좋아해요.

He played brilliantly in the
match against (Japan).

(ilbon) daehang kyŏnggiesŏ   (일본) 대항 경기에서
chŏngmal chal haessŏyo   정말 잘 했어요

coach	k'ŏch'i	코치
corner	k'ŏnŏ	코너
cup	k'ŏp	컵
fan(s)	p'aen(dŭl)	팬(들)
free kick	p'ŭri k'ik	프리 킥
foul	p'aul	파울
goal	gol/gorin	골/골인
goalkeeper	golk'ipŏ	골키퍼
kick off	k'igopŭ	킥오프
league	rigŭ;	리그;
	kyŏnggi-yŏnmaeng	경기연맹
manager	maenijŏ	매니저
offside	opŭsaidŭ	오프사이드
penalty	pŏlchŏm/p'enŏlt'i	벌점/페널티
player	sŏnsu	선수
to score	chŏmsu naeyo	점수내요
to shoot	gorŭl ch'ayo	골을 차요

SPLISH SPLASH

Bathing in Korea borders on being a social ritual.
Most neighbourhoods have several public baths called
mogyokt'ang (목욕탕). Some include on-site barber
shops, and ritzier ones pamper you with food and mas-
sages. A standard neighbourhood **mogyokt'ang** will
have a 'women's side', **yŏt'ang** (여탕) and a 'man's
side', **namt'ang** (남탕). Inside you'll find a large room
with showers, a sauna, an **onsu** (온수), 'hot pool', and
a **naengsu** (냉수), 'cold pool'.

KEEPING FIT 운동하며 건강유지하기

Korea's post-war re-building and rapid urbanisation didn't leave much room for tennis courts, fields and parks. Recent efforts have been made to rectify that problem, however. Parks along major rivers are popular places for jogging, in-line skating or cycling. Municipal swimming pools are usually crowded, but private swimming pools are enjoyable.

Where's the best place to
jog/run around here?
  ijubyŏnesŏ choging hagie 이 주변에서 조깅하기에가
  ŏdiga cheil choayo? 어디 제일 좋아요?

Where's the nearest ...?	**cheil kakka-un ...ga/i ŏdieyo?**	제일 가까운 ...가/이 어디에요?
gym (gymnasium)	**ch'eyukkwan**	체육관
gym (health club)	**helsŭjang**	헬스장
ice rink	**aisŭ ringkŭ; sŭkeit'ŭjang**	아이스 링크; 스케이트장
swimming pool	**suyŏngjang**	수영장
tennis court	**t'enisŭjang**	테니스장

What's the charge per ...?	**...e ŏlma-eyo?**	···에 얼마에요?
day	**haru**	하루
game	**han-geim**	한 게임
hour	**han-shigan**	한 시간

Can I hire (a) ...?	**... pillilsu issŏyo?**	... 빌릴 수 있어요?
bicycle	**chajŏn-gŏ**	자전거
racquet	**rak'et**	라켓
shoes	**shinbal**	신발

INTERESTS & ACTIVITIES

TENNIS & TABLE TENNIS   테니스/탁구

Although standard tennis courts are hard to come by, table tennis facilities can be found quite easily.

Do you like (tennis; table tennis)?
(t'enisŭ/t'akku) choahaseyo?   (테니스/탁구) 좋아하세요?
Would you like to play tennis?
t'enisŭ ch'ishillaeyo?   테니스 치실래요?
Is there a tennis court near here?
ijubyŏne t'enisŭjang issŏyo?   이 주변에 테니스장 있어요?
How much is it to hire a court?
k'otŭ pillinŭnde ŏlma-eyo?   코트 빌리는데 얼마에요?
Is there racquet and ball hire?
rak'eshirang kong pillyŏjwŏyo?   라켓이랑 공 빌려줘요?

tennis court	t'enisŭ kyŏnggijang	테니스 경기장
ace	eisŭ	에이스
fault	p'oltŭ; sŏbŭ shilp'ae	폴트; 서브 실패
line	rain	라인
match	maech'i	매치
match-point	maech'i p'ointŭ; kyŏlsŭng-e ilchŏm	매치 포인트; 결승의 1점
net	netŭ	네트
pingpong ball	t'akkugong	탁구공
point	p'ointŭ	포인트
racquet	rak'et	라켓
set	setŭ	세트
table tennis	t'akku	탁구
table tennis table	t'akkudae	탁구 탁구대

SKIING   스키

Korea's cold winters and mountainous terrain have made it a haven for skiers from all over East Asia, with many ski resorts located just a few hours' drive from Seoul and other major cities.

What are the skiing conditions like at ... ?
...esŏ sŭk'i t'agiga ŏttaeyo?   ...에서 스키타기가 어때요?

Is it possible to go cross-country
skiing at ...?

| **...eso k'ŭrosŭ k'ŏnt'ŭri** | ...에서 크로스 컨트리 |
| **sŭk'i t'alsu issŏyo?** | 스키 탈 수 있어요? |

cross-country	**k'ŭrosŭ k'ŏnt'ŭri**	크로스 컨트리
downhill	**hwalgang**	활강
instructor	**kangsa**	강사
safety binding	**(seip'ŭt'i) bainding**	(세이프티) 바인딩
skis	**sŭk'i**	스키
ski-boots	**puch'ŭ**	부츠
ski-lift	**rip'ŭt'ŭ**	리프트
ski slope	**sŭllop'ŭ**	슬로프
ski-suit	**sŭk'ibok**	스키복
stock	**p'ol/sŭt'ok**	폴/스톡
sunblock	**sŏn k'ŭrim**	선크림

GOLF
골프

Golf reached the status of national obsession in the 1990s. The
1997 economic downturn and the public's impression of golf
courses as venues for shady business deals, however, took some
of the gloss of its popularity. Multi-level driving ranges where you
can knock around a bucket of balls are a popular alternative.

bunker	**pŏngk'ŏ**	벙커
driving range	**kolp'ŭ yŏnsup-jang**	골프 연습장
flagstick	**hol gittae; p'in**	홀 깃대; 핀
follow-through	**p'ollo ssŭru**	폴로 스루
golf course	**kolp'ŭ k'osŭ**	골프 코스
golfball	**kolp'ŭgong**	골프공
hole	**hol**	홀
iron	**aiŏn k'ŭllŏp; aiŏn**	아이언 클럽; 아이언
miniature golf	**mini golp'ŭ**	미니 골프
teeing ground	**t'i gŭraundŭ**	티 그라운드
wood	**udŭn k'ŭllŏp; udŭ**	우든 클럽; 우드

INTERESTS & ACTIVITIES

GAMES 게임

Western card games such as poker or blackjack are not as popular as home-grown forms of recreational gambling, such as *Go-stop*, a popular card game in Korea, especially among the older generations. Until the recent opening of a rural casino complex in Kangwon-do (Gangwon-do) Province designed to spur the local economy, Korea's lone Western-style casino had been open only to foreign passport holders.

Do you play ...?	... haljul aseyo?	... 할 줄 아세요?
billiards	**tanggu**	당구
cards	**k'adŭnori**	카드놀이
chess	**ch'esŭ**	체스
Chinese chess	**changgi**	장기
computer games	**k'ŏmp'yut'ŏ geim**	컴퓨터 게임
dominoes	**tomino geim**	도미노 게임
draughts	**ch'ek'ŏ**	체커
Go (board game)	**paduk**	바둑
pinball	**p'inbol**	핀볼
pool	**p'okeppol**	포켓볼
roulette	**rullet**	룰렛

ART 미술

Korea has an artistic tradition that goes back thousands of years, as well as a strong interest in modern art.

Seeing Art 미술 감상

When's the gallery open?
**misulgwan mun
ŏnje yŏrŏyo?**
미술관 문
언제 열어요?

What kind of art are you interested in?
**ŏttŏn chongnyue misurŭl
choahaseyo?**
어떤 종류의 미술을
좋아하세요?

I'm interested in …	…rŭl/ŭl choahaeyo	…를/을 좋아해요.
animation	aenimeishŏn	애니메이션
calligraphy	sŏye	서예
cyber art	saibŏ at'ŭ	사이버 아트
design	dijain	디자인
graphic art	kŭraep'ik at'ŭ	그래픽 아트
oriental painting	tong-yanghwa	동양화
painting	hoéhwa	회화
performance art	p'ŏp'omŏnsŭ	퍼포먼스
modern art	hyŏndae misul	현대 미술
sculpture	chogak	조각
traditional art	chŏnt'ong misul	전통 미술

artwork	misul chakp'um	미술작품
exhibition	chŏnshihoé	전시회
exhibition opening	kaejang	개장
painter	hwaga	화가
photographer	sajin chakka	사진작가
sculptor	chogakka	조각가
statue	sang	상

INTERESTS & ACTIVITIES

MUSIC   음악

You can find music to suit all tastes in Korea. Music education is also emphasised, as many Koreans are brought up learning to play an instrument or two.

Do you like …?	… choahaseyo?	… 좋아하세요?
listening to music	ŭmak tŭnnŭn-gŏt	음악 듣는 것
dancing	ch'um ch'unŭn-gŏt	춤추는 것

Do you play an instrument?
akki tarulchul anŭn-gŏt   악기 다룰 줄 아는것
issŭseyo?   있으세요?
Do you sing?
norae purŭseyo?   노래 부르세요?
What music/bands do you like?
ŏttŏn ŭmagŭl/gŭrubŭl   어떤 음악을/그룹을
choahaseyo?   좋아하세요?

INTERESTS & ACTIVITIES

I like (the) ...
      ...rŭl/ŭl choahaeyo   ...를/을 좋아해요.
Where can you hear traditional
music around here?
      ijubyŏne chŏntong ŭmak   이 주변에 전통 음악
      tŭrŭl manhan got issŏyo?   들을 만한 곳 있어요?

band	kŭrup	그룹
bar with music	myujik ba	뮤직 바
concert	k'onsŏt'ŭ	콘서트
concert hall	kong-yŏnjang/	공연장;
	k'ŏnsŏt'ŭhol	콘서트 홀
karaoke bar	karaok'e ba	가라오케 바
musician	ŭmakka	음악가
opera	op'era	오페라
opera house	op'era hausŭ	오페라 하우스
orchestra	ok'esŭt'ŭra	오케스트라
pansori	p'ansori	판소리
(traditional Korean dramatic solo)		
rock group	rokkŭrup	록 그룹
song	norae	노래
show	sho	쇼
singer	kasu	가수

CINEMA & THEATRE   영화와 연극

Hollywood dominates the Korean movie scene, although Korea
produces its share of local blockbusters. Hong Kong movies
involving flying martial artists are also popular. Foreign-language
movies are virtually always in their original language, with subtitles.
Korea has some traditional plays, but many of its offerings are
Korean translations of American or European works.

I feel like going	**...rŭl/ŭl porŏ**	...를/을 보러
to a ...	**kago ship'ŏyo**	가고 싶어요.
ballet	**balle**	발레
comedy	**k'omedi**	코메디
film	**yŏnghwa**	영화
play	**yŏn-gŭk**	연극

What's on at the cinema tonight?
**onŭl bam yŏnghwagwanesŏ
mwŏl sang-yŏng haeyo?**
Are there any tickets for ...?
... p'yo issŏyo?
What language is the movie in?
ŏnŭ nara mallo nawayo?
Does it have English subtitles?
yŏng-ŏ chamang-nawayo?
Have you seen ...?
... poshinjŏk issŏyo?

오늘 밤 영화관에서
뭘 상영해요?

... 표 있어요?

어느 나라 말로 나와요?

영어 자막 나와요?

... 보신 적 있어요?

THE YEAR OF THE WHAT?

Koreans tend to think in terms of the Chinese zodiac. Instead of monthly divisions, the Chinese zodiac is made up of 12 animals, called di (띠) or -tti (띠), each representing one year of a 12-year cycle. Traditionally, five cycles (60 years) represented a full life.

What Chinese zodiac symbol were you born under?
musŭnttiseyo?   무슨 띠세요?

Year of the Cow/Ox   **sotti**   소띠
(1925, 1937, 1949, 1961, 1973, 1985, 1997)
Year of the Tiger   **horang-itti**   호랑이띠
(1926, 1938, 1950, 1962, 1974, 1986, 1998)
Year of the Rabbit   **t'okkitti**   토끼띠
(1927, 1939, 1951, 1963, 1975, 1987, 1999)
Year of the Dragon   **yongtti**   용띠
(1928, 1940, 1952, 1964, 1976, 1988, 2000)
Year of the Snake   **paemtti**   뱀띠
(1929, 1941, 1953, 1965, 1977, 1989, 2001)
Year of the Horse   **maltti**   말띠
(1930, 1942, 1954, 1966, 1978, 1990, 2002)
Year of the Sheep/Goat/Ram **yangtti**   양띠
(1931, 1943, 1955, 1967, 1979, 1991, 2003)
Year of the Monkey   **wonsung-itti**   원숭이띠
(1932, 1944, 1956, 1968, 1980, 1992, 2004)
Year of the Chicken/Rooster   **taktti**   닭띠
(1933, 1945, 1957, 1969, 1981, 1993, 2005)
Year of the Dog   **kaetti**   개띠
(1934, 1946, 1958, 1970, 1982, 1994, 2006)
Year of the Pig/Boar   **twaejitti**   돼지띠
(1935, 1947, 1959, 1971, 1983, 1995, 2007)
Year of the Mouse/Rat   **chwitti**   쥐띠
(1936, 1948, 1960, 1972, 1984, 1996, 2008)

Bear in mind that if you were born before Lunar New Year, your di is the one of the previous year.

STAYING IN TOUCH 연락하고 지내기

Tomorrow is my last day here.
naeiri yŏgisŏ 내일이 여기서
majimang-narineyo 마지막 날이네요.

Let's swap addresses.
chuso kyohwan haeyo 주소 교환해요.

What's your (email) address?
(imeil) chusoga (이메일) 주소가
ŏttŏke dwaeyo? 어떻게 돼요?

Here's my address.
ige che chuso-eyo 이게 제 주소에요.

If you ever visit (Scotland),
you must come and see us.
(sŭkotŭllaendŭ)e oshige (스코틀랜드)에 오시게
doémyŏn gok chŏl ch'ajajuseyo 되면 꼭 절 찾아 주세요.

I plan to come back to Korea
(next year; in two years).
(naenyŏne/inyŏnane) tashi (내년에/2년 안에) 다시
han-guge ol yejŏng-ieyo 한국에 올 예정이에요.

I'll send you copies of the photos.
sajin ponae dŭrilkkeyo 사진 보내 드릴게요.

Don't forget to write.
p'yŏnji gok ssŏjuseyo 편지 꼭 써 주세요.

Keep in touch!
yŏllak hago chinaeyo! 연락하고 지내요!

WRITING LETTERS 편지쓰기

Although email and chatting on the Internet reign supreme in
Korea, everyone likes to receive a hand-written letter, especially
from someone overseas. After you get back home, here are a few
phrases to help you drop a line to the people you met.

Dear ... (pol/inf)
...kke/ege ...께/에게

I'm sorry it's taken me so
long to write.
p'yŏnjiga nŏmu nŭjŏsŏ 편지가 너무 늦어서
choésong haeyo 죄송해요.

INTERESTS & ACTIVITIES

It was great to meet you.
  **mannasŏ chŏngmal
  pan-gawŏssŏyo**
만나서 정말
반가웠어요.

Thank you so much for
your hospitality.
  **hwandae haejushŏsŏ nŏmu
  komawŏssŏyo**
환대해 주셔서 너무
고마웠어요.

I miss you. (sg, pl)
  pogo shimneyo
보고 싶네요.

I had a fantastic time in ...
  **...esŏ chŏngmal choŭn
  shiganŭl kajŏssŏyo**
...에서 정말 좋은
시간을 가졌어요.

My favourite place was ...
  **...i/ga kajang maŭme
  dŭrŏssŏyo**
...이/가 가장 마음에
들었어요.

I hope to visit ... again.
  **ŏnje ...e tashi hanbŏn
  kago shimneyo**
언제 ...에 다시 한번
가고 싶네요.

Say 'hi' to ... and ... for me.
  **...wa/gwa ...hant'e anbu
  chŏn haejuseyo**
...와/과 ...한테 안부
전해 주세요.

I'd love to see you again.
  gok tashi pogo ship'ŏyo
꼭 다시 보고 싶어요.

Write soon.
  tapchang ssŏjuseyo
답장 써 주세요.

With love; Regards,
  ... ollim
... 올림

사회 문제

In 1990, the Cold War ended everywhere but in Korea and the Taiwan Strait. Korea's status as a divided peninsula is something that has dominated the country's political, economic and social issues for the past half century. Recently, relations have thawed to some extent but, still, politics – in particular communism – is a sensitive issue.

The 40-year Japanese occupation of Korea prior to WWII and the fate of the **chŏngshindae** (정신대), literally 'comfort women corps', the hundreds of thousands of women – mostly Korean – who were forced into sexual slavery in frontline brothels during the Pacific War, are also sensitive issues. The same goes for the presence of US military bases.

Environmental and women's issues are generally safe topics in Korea, where both movements have strong followings.

POLITICS   정치

Did you hear about ...?
    ... **iyagi dŭrŭshŏssŏyo?**   ... 이야기 들으셨어요?
What do you think of
(the current government)?
    (hyŏn chŏngbu)e daehae   (현 정부)에 대해
    ŏttŏk'e saenggak haseyo?   어떻게 생각하세요?

democracy	**minjui**	민주의
demonstration	**shiwi**	시위
elections	**sŏn-gŏ**	선거
regional	**chibang-e**	지방의
general/national	**kukka-e**	국가의
legalisation	**pŏmnyulhwa**	법률화
legislation	**pŏmnyul chejŏng**	법률 제정
party politics	**chŏngdang chŏngch'i**	정당 정치
parliament	**ŭihoé**	의회

policy	chŏngch'aek	정책
president	taet'ongnyŏng	대통령
prime minister	susang	수상
trade union	nodongjohap	노동 조합

SOCIAL ISSUES   사회 문제

Is there an (unemployment)
problem here?
    yŏgi (shirŏp) munje issŏyo?   여기 (실업) 문제 있어요?
How is the social welfare
program here?
    yŏgi pokchi jŏngch'aegi   여기 복지 정책이
    ŏttaeyo?   어때요?

abortion	nakt'ae	낙태
animal protection	tongmul poho	동물 보호
citizenship	shimin-gwŏn	시민권
demonstration	demo/shiwi	데모/시위
equality	p'yŏngdŭng	평등
equal opportunity	kihoé p'yŏngdŭng	기회 평등
euthanasia	allaksa	안락사
exploitation	kaebal	개발
human rights	in-gwŏn	인권
inequality	pulp'yŏngdŭng	불평등
racism	injong ch'abyŏl	인종 차별
sexism	sŏng ch'abyŏl	성 차별
sexual harassment	sŏnghirong	성 희롱
social security	sahoé pojang	사회 보장
strike	p'aŏp	파업
tax	segŭm	세금
unemployment	shirŏp	실업
welfare	pokchi	복지

SOCIAL ISSUES

ENVIRONMENT

환경

Does Korea have a
pollution problem?
   han-gugŭn hwan-gyŏng   한국은 환경
   oyŏm munjega issŏyo?   오염 문제가 있어요?
Does Seoul have a
recycling program?
   sŏuresŏnŭn   서울에서는
   chaehwalyong-ŭl haeyo?   재활용을 해요?
Is it safe to drink this water?
   imul mashŏdo dwaeyo?   이 물 마셔도 돼요?
Is this recyclable?
   igŏt chaehwalyong dwaeyo?   이것 재활용 돼요?
Are there any protected ... here?
   poho doénŭn ...i/ga issŏyo?   보호되는 ...이/가 있어요?
Is this a protected area?
   igot chayŏn poho   이곳 자연 보호
   kuyŏgieyo?   구역이에요?

biodegradable	saengbunhaesŏng	생분해성
conservation	pojon	보존
deforestation	samnim pŏlch'ae	삼림 벌채
disposable	ilhoéyong	일회용
ecosystem	saengt'aegye	생태계
endangered species	myŏlchong wigie	멸종 위기의
	tongshingmul	동식물
hydroelectricity	suryŏkchŏn-gi	수력전기
irrigation	kwan-gae	관개
nuclear energy	haegenŏji	핵 에너지
nuclear testing	haek shilhŏm	핵 실험
ozone layer	ojonch'ŭng	오존층
pesticides	salch'ungje	살충제
pollution	oyŏm	오염
recycling	chaehwaryong	재활용
toxic waste	yudoksŏng	유독성
	p'yegimul	폐기물
water supply	kŭpsu/sangsudo	급수/상수도

SOCIAL ISSUES

DRUGS   마약

Relative to Western countries, Korea is fairly drug-free, with the exception of caffeine, nicotine and alcohol. Use of **hiroppong** (히로뽕), a form of methamphetamine, is a small but persistent problem, and inhalant use appears to be rising. The vast majority of Koreans have never taken illegal drugs.

It's inadvisable for foreign visitors to consume or carry any kind of illegal substance within Korea, including marijuana. The legal consequences for even one joint can be extreme. That's not to say, however, that an open discussion of drug use in another country is inappropriate, as many South Koreans might be curious about such a lifestyle.

Do you want a cigarette?
  tambae p'iushillaeyo?   담배 피우실래요?
I'm trying to quit.
  gŭnŭryŏgo   끊으려고
  noryŏkchung-ieyo   노력중이에요.
I don't take drugs.
  chŏn mayak anhamnida   전 마약 안 합니다.
I smoke marijuana occasionally.
  chŏn taemach'orŭl   전 대마초를
  kakkŭmshik p'iwŏyo   가끔씩 피워요.

acid	hwan-gakche	환각제
cocaine	k'ok'ain	코카인
drug addiction	mayak chungdok	마약 중독
drug dealer	mayangmilmaeja	마약 밀매자
heroin	heroin	헤로인
overdose	kwada t'uyŏ;	과다 투여;
	kwada pogyong	과다 복용

쇼핑하기   **SHOPPING**

Korea once billed itself as a 'shopper's paradise', and although it's not as dirt cheap as it was in the past, there are still lots of bargains to be had.

Korea's big cities have one or more traditional markets, which sell just about anything you could imagine, and then some – from glasses to live sea urchins.

Shops selling specific items are often clustered into certain areas of the city. Seoul, for example, has a street famous for its Oriental medicine (Chongno, 종로), another street famous for its traditional antiques (Insa-dong, 인사동), a couple of electronics areas (Yongsan, 깜박이) and several furniture districts.

Stationery stores double as gift shops, with an emphasis on the cute.

LOOKING FOR ...   ... 찾기

Where can I buy ...?
ŏdisŏ ...rŭl/ŭl
salsu issŭlkkayo?

어디서 ...를/을
살 수 있을까요?

Where's the	cheil kakkaun	제일 가까운
nearest ...?	...ga/i ŏdi issŏyo?	...가/이 어디 있어요?
antique shop	koldongp'um kage	골동품 가게
bank	ŭnhaeng	은행
barber shop	ibalso	이발소
bookshop	sŏjŏm	서점
camera shop	k'amera kage	카메라 가게
chemist	yakkuk	약국
clothing store	okkage	옷가게
convenience store	p'yŏnijŏm	편의점
craft shop	kong-yep'um kage	공예품 가게
department store	paek'wajŏm	백화점
hairdressing salon	miyongshil	미용실
laundry	set'akso	세탁소
market	shijang	시장

newspaper	shinmun	신문
magazine stand	kap'andae	가판
optician	an-gyŏngjŏm	안경점
Oriental medicine shop	hanyakpang	한약방
pharmacy	yakkuk	약국
music shop	ŭmban kage	음반 가게
shoe shop	shinbal kage	신발 가게
souvenir shop	kinyŏmp'um kage	기념품 가게
stationery store	munbanggu/ mun-kujŏm	문방구/ 문구점
supermarket	shup'ŏ maket	슈퍼마켓
travel agency	yŏhaengsa	여행사

MAKING A PURCHASE   구매하기

Koreans don't mind if you just browse, but be advised that if you're the first customer of the morning in a small shop, they'll press you to buy something, as superstition dictates you'll set the pace for the rest of the day.

I'm just looking.
    kŭnyang kugyŏng hanŭn-gŏeyo   그냥 구경하는 거에요.
Excuse me.
    yŏgiyo   여기요.
How much is this?
    igŏ ŏlma-eyo?   이거 얼마에요?
Can you write down the price?
    kagyŏgŭl chŏgŏjushillaeyo?   가격을 적어 주실래요?
I'd like to buy ...
    ... issŏyo?   ... 있어요?
Do you have any others?
    tarŭn-gŏn ŏpsŏyo?   다른 건 없어요?
Can I look at it?
    poyŏjushillaeyo?   보여 주실래요?

I don't like it.
pyŏllo mame andŭneyo　　별로 맘에 안 드네요.

Do you accept credit cards?
k'ŭredit'ŭ k'adŭro dwaeyo?　　크레디트 카드로 돼요?

Do you accept dollars/yen?
dallŏ/en padayo?　　달러/엔 받아요?

Could I have a receipt please?
yŏngsujŭng chushigessŏyo?　　영수증 주시겠어요?

Does it have a guarantee?
pojŭngsŏ innŭn-gŏn-gayo?　　보증서 있는 건가요?

I'd like to get a refund
for this, please.
**igŏt hwanbul padŭryŏgo
hanŭndeyo**　　이것 환불 받으려고
하는데요.

BARGAINING　　흥정하기

Bargaining is still done in small shops and with open-air vendors, but it's gradually falling out of favour. If something has a price tag on it, the price should be considered non-negotiable.

The price is too high.
nŏmu pissayo　　너무 비싸요.

Can you lower the price?
chom gakka juseyo?　　좀 깎아 주세요?

Do you have something cheaper?
tŏssan-gŏtto issŏyo?　　더 싼 것도 있어요?

I'll give you ...
... dŭrilkkeyo　　... 드릴게요.

No more than ...
... isang-ŭn andwaeyo　　... 이상은 안 돼요.

SOUVENIRS   기념품

Korean souvenirs typically tend to be mass-produced wood and
stone reproductions of traditional figures, such as Cheju-do
(Jeju-do) Island's stone 'grandfathers' called **harubang** (하루방).
Antique markets such as Insa-dong offer a wide variety of
tradional items.

baskets	**paguni**	바구니
brassware	**nossoé jepum;**	놋쇠 제품;
	yugi	유기
Buddha statues	**pulsang**	불상
calligraphy	**sŏye chakp´um**	서예작품
ceramic ware; china	**tojagi**	도자기
folding fan	**puch´ae**	부채
folding screens	**pyŏngp´ung**	병풍
furniture	**kagu**	가구
ginseng tea	**insamch´a**	인삼차
ginseng wine	**insamju**	인삼주
hanbok	**hanbok**	한복
(traditional clothing)		
handicraft	**sugong yep´um**	수공예품
hanji handicrafts	**hanji kong-yep´um**	한지공예품
(of traditional paper)		
harubang	**harubang**	하루방
(grandfather		
stone carvings)		
incense	**hyang**	향
jade	**ok**	옥
keychains	**yŏlsoégori**	열쇠고리
lacquerware products	**najŏn ch´ilgi**	나전칠기
traditional	**chasup´um**	자수품
embroidery		
traditional masks	**t´al**	탈
woodcarved figure	**mokkong yep´um**	목공예품

CLOTHING   의류

City markets have a variety of clothing at affordable prices,
unless they are name-brand. Larger size clothing, from shoes to
bras to pants, is sometimes difficult to come by.

boots	**puchŭ**	부츠
business suit	**yangbok**	양복
clothing	**ot**	옷
coat	**k'ŏt'ŭ**	코트
dress	**tŭresŭ**	드레스
gloves	**changgap**	장갑
hat	**moja**	모자
jacket	**chaek'it**	깜박이
jeans	**chŏngbaji**	청바지
jumper (sweater)	**sŭwet'ŏ**	스웨터
miniskirt	**minisŭk'ŏt'ŭ**	미니스커트
pants	**paji**	바지
raincoat	**ubi**	우비
shirt	**shŏch'ŭ**	셔츠
shoes	**shinbal**	신발
ski clothes	**sŭk'ibok**	스키복
skirt	**ch'ima**	치마
socks	**yangmal**	양말
stockings	**sŭt'ak'ing**	스타킹
sweater (jumper)	**sŭwet'ŏ**	스웨터
swimsuit	**suyŏngbok**	수영복
T-shirt	**t'ishŏch'ŭ**	티셔츠
underwear	**sogot**	속옷

Can I try it on?
  ibŏbwado dwaeyo?   입어봐도 돼요?
My size is ...
  che saijŭnŭn ...(i)eyo   제 사이즈는 ...(이)에요.
It doesn't fit.
  anmajayo   안 맞아요.

It's too ...	nŏmu ...	너무 ...
big	k'ŏyo	커요
long	kirŏyo	길어요
loose	hŏllŏng haeyo	헐렁해요
short	tchalbayo	짧아요
small	chagayo	작아요
tight	gwak kkyŏyo	꽉 껴요

MATERIALS　재료

brass	nossoé	놋쇠
ceramic	tojagi	도자기
cotton	myŏn	면
handmade	sujep'um	수제품
glass	yuri	유리
gold	kŭm	금
leather	kajuk	가죽
lycra	raikŭra	라이크라
metal	kŭmsok	금속
plastic	p'ŭllasŭt'ik	플라스틱
silk	pidan/kyŏn	비단/견
silver	ŭn	은
stainless steel	sŭt'einirisŭ	스테인리스
synthetic	hapsŏng sŏmyn	합성 섬유
wood	namu	나무
wool	mojingmul/mo	모직물/모

COLOURS　색깔

dark	ŏdu-un	어두운
light	palgŭn	밝은
black	kŏmŭn	검은
blue	p'aran	파란
brown	kalsaege	갈색의
green	ch'oroksaege	초록색의
grey	hoésaege	회색의
orange	chuhwangsaege	주황색의

pink	punhongsaege	분홍색의
purple	porasaege	보라색의
red	balgan	빨간
white	hin	흰
yellow	noran	노란

TOILETRIES
화장품과 세면용품

aftershave	aep'ŭt'ŏsheibŭ	애프터쉐이브
bath/shower gel	padi shawŏ	바디 샤워
comb	pit	빗
conditioner	rinsŭ	린스
condoms	k'ondom	콘돔
dental floss	ch'ishil	치실
deodorant	tiodorant'ŭ/	디오도란트/
	ch'ech'wijegŏje	체취제거제
hairbrush	pŭrŏshi	브러쉬
mirror	kŏul	거울
moisturiser	moisŭch'ŏraijŏ	모이스춰라이저
moisturising lotion	roshŏn	로션
mosquito coil	mogihyang	모기향
pregnancy test kit	imshin jindanyak set'ŭ	임신 진단약 세트
razor	myŏndogi	면도기
razor blades	myŏndok'al	면도칼
sanitary napkins/ pads	saengnidae	생리대
shampoo	shamp'u	샴푸
shaving cream	myŏndo k'ŭrim	면도 크림
soap	pinu	비누
sunblock	sŏn k'ŭrim	선크림
tampons	t'amp'on	탐폰
tissues	t'ishyu	티슈
toilet paper	turumari hyuji	두루마리 휴지
toothbrush	ch'isol	치솔
toothpaste	ch'iyak	치약
tweezers	tchokchipke	쪽집게

SHOPPING

FOR THE BABY   아기 용품

baby powder	**peibi p'audŏ**	베이비 파우더
bib	**t'ŏkpaji**	턱받이
disposable nappies	**ilhoéyong kijŏgwi**	일회용 기저귀
dummy/pacifier	**komu jŏkkokchi**	고무 젖꼭지
feeding bottle	**uyubyŏng**	우유병
nappies	**kijŏgwi**	기저귀
powdered formula	**yuayong yudongshik**	유아용 유동식
powdered milk	**punyu**	분유
tinned baby food	**agiyong**	아기용
	pyŏng-ŭmshik	병음식

STATIONERY & PUBLICATIONS   문구와 서적

Most Korean bookstores are lacking in English-language materials, but every city usually has a very large bookstore that will have a separate section dedicated to just foreign books, including books for English teaching.

Do you sell (a/an) ...?	... **issŏyo?**	... 있어요?
magazines	**chapchi**	잡지
newspapers	**shinmun**	신문
postcards	**yŏpsŏ**	엽서
dictionary	**sajŏn**	사전
envelope	**pongt'u**	봉투
... map	... **chido**	... 지도
city	**toshi**	도시
regional	**chiyŏge**	지역의
road	**toro**	도로
newspaper	**yŏngtcha**	영자
in English	**shinmun**	신문
paper	**chong-i**	종이
pen (ballpoint)	**polp'en**	볼펜
stamp	**up'yo**	우표

Is there an English-language
section?
 yŏng-ŏ k'onŏga issŏyo?   영어 코너가 있어요?
Is there an English-language
bookshop nearby?
 kakkaunde yŏng-ŏro doén   가까운 데 영어로 된
 ch'aek p'anŭn sŏjŏm issŏyo?   책 파는 서점있어요?
Do you have any books
in English by ...?
 ...e ch'aek yŏng-ŏro   ...의 책 영어로
 naon-gŏt issŏyo?   나온 것 있어요?

MUSIC   음악
Although small music shops can be found along major streets,
the largest selection is usually found in the mega-bookstores.

I'm looking for a ... CD.
 ... shidi ch'annŭndeyo   ... CD(씨디) 찾는데요.
What singer/group is popular
in Korea?
 han-guge inkki choŭn   한국의 인기 좋은
 kasuga/kŭrubi nugueyo?   가수가/그룹이 누구에요?
Where is the foreign music?
 oégugŭmagŭn ŏdie   외국음악은 어디에
 issŏyo?   있어요?
Can I listen to this CD here?
 ishidi tŭrŏbolsu issŏyo?   이 CD 들어볼 수 있어요?
Is there a blank tape?
 kongt'eip'ŭ issŏyo?   공 테이프 있어요?

PHOTOGRAPHY

사진

How much is it to
process this film?
    **ip´illŭm hyŏnsang hanŭnde
    ŏlma-eyo?**

이 필름 현상 하는데
얼마에요?

When will it be ready?
    ŏnjekkaji dwaeyo?

언제까지 돼요?

I'd like a film for this camera.
    **ik´amera-e p´illŭm
    nŏŭryŏgo hanŭndeyo**

이 카메라에 필름
넣으려고 하는데요.

battery	**baet´ŏri**	배터리
B&W film	**hŭkpaek p´illŭm**	흑백 필름
camera	**k´amera**	카메라
colour film	**k´ollŏ p´illŭm**	컬러 필름
film	**p´illŭm**	필름
flash; flash bulb	**p´ŭllaeshi;**	플래시;
	p´ŭllaeshi chŏn-gu	플래시 전구
lens	**renjŭ**	렌즈
light meter	**nochulgye**	노출계
slides	**sŭllaidŭ**	슬라이드
videotape	**bidio t´eipŭ**	비디오 테이프

NAME GAMES

Translating English names into Korean is sometimes
tricky, as there are fewer double consonants available
in Korean than in English, and no triple consonants.
'Sprite', for example, contains three consonants in a row.
Korean syllables require a vowel in between consonants,
so 'Sprite' becomes – **sŭ-pŭ-ra-i-tŭ** (스프라이트).

    Koreans also typically replace f with **p´** or **hw** – thus
the beverage 'Fanta' is known as **hwanta** (환타).

SMOKING

흡연

Smoking is a common habit, especially among Korean men, but the anti-smoking movement has started to take hold. In some buildings smokers are now banished to designated smoking areas. Large restaurants usually offer a choice of smoking or non-smoking seating.

A packet of ... cigarettes, please.

| **... tambae han-gap chuseyo** | ... 담배 한 갑 주세요. |

Do you have a light?

| **purissŭseyo?** | 불 있으세요? |

Please don't smoke.

choésong hajiman	죄송하지만
an-p'iwŏ jushŏssŭmyŏn	안 피워 주셨으면
hanŭndeyo	하는데요.

Do you mind if I smoke?

| **tambae p'iwŏdo doélkkayo?** | 담배 피워도 될까요? |

I'm trying to give up.

| **gŭnŭryŏgo** | 끊으려고 |
| **noryŏkjung-ieyo** | 노력중이에요. |

cigarettes	**tambae**	담배
Korean cigarettes	**hanguksan tambae**	한국산 담배
foreign cigarettes	**yang tambae**	양 담배
cigars	**siga**	시가
lighter	**rait'ŏ**	라이터
matches	**sŏngnyang**	성냥
pipe	**p'aip'ŭ**	파이프

SMOKE ALARM!

No Smoking	**kŭmyŏn**	금연
Non-Smoking Area	**kŭmyŏn kuyŏk**	금연구역
Smoking Area	**hŭbyŏn kuyŏk**	흡연구역

SIZES & COMPARISONS   크기와 비교

a little bit	**chogŭm**	조금
also	**dohan**	또한
little (amount)	**chogŭm**	조금
many	**mani**	많이
more	**tŏ**	더
too much/many	**nŏmu mani**	너무 많이

The following adjectives are in 'modifying' form, which means
they'll have to be followed by a noun:

big	**k'ŭn**	큰
enough	**ch'ungbunhan**	충분한
heavy	**mugŏun**	무거운
light	**kabyŏun**	가벼운
small	**chagŭn**	작은

음식 **FOOD**

THROUGH THE DAY 하루 동안의 음식

Finding establishments that serve breakfast is somewhat difficult, as even Western fast-food chains forego the morning fare they offer in other countries.

For lunch, most Koreans eat out at one of the ubiquitous small eateries that specialise in one type of food or another. Korean meals are light on meat and heavy on vegetables, with lots of **panch'an** (반찬), or side dishes, offered with the main meal. Virtually every Korean meal comes with **kimch'i** (김치), plus rice or noodles.

For dinner, if they can't make it home, Koreans will eat at one of these places again, although Western chains are also becoming popular. Korea's version of Chinese food and Japanese sushi and noodles are also popular.

Fast-food is mostly considered a snack, and many Koreans will supplement fast-food fare with some rice and **kimch'i** when they get home.

breakfast	**ach'im**	아침
lunch	**chŏmshim**	점심
dinner	**chŏnyŏk**	저녁

CHOPSTICKS DOWN!

Avoid leaving your chopsticks and spoons sticking up in your rice bowl. This is done only in food 'presented' to one's deceased ancestors at ceremonies honouring them. Thus, such placement of eating utensils is associated with death, making it a definite no-no. When you're not using them, place your chopsticks horizontally over your bowl or on a napkin.

FOOD

BREAKFAST   아침

Breakfast traditionally consists of a simple selection of light soup, rice and **kimch'i** (김치), Korea's spicy national dish of pickled vegetables. Cold breakfast cereals are becoming popular, however, as part of a 'Western' breakfast that also consists of milk, juice and toast.

cereal	**siriŏl**	시리얼
coffee	**k'ŏp'i**	커피
creamer (for coffee)	**p'ŭrim/k'ŭrim**	프림/크림
eggs	**kyeran**	계란
juice	**jusŭ**	주스
milk	**uyu**	우유
rice	**pap**	밥
scrambled eggs	**pokkŭn dalgyal**	볶은 달걀
seaweed soup	**miyŏkkuk**	미역국
side dishes	**panch'an**	반찬
tea	**ch'a**	차
black tea (lit: red tea)	**hongch'a**	홍차
ginseng tea	**insamch'a**	인삼차
green tea	**nokch'a**	녹차

KIMCH'I

This spicy national dish is well-known throughout the world, but many people don't realise that there are hundreds of varieties besides the usual pickled cabbage fuelled with ground red pepper. You can also find **kimch'i** made from cucumbers, radishes and just about any other vegetable imaginable. For the less adventurous, there are also non-spicy types.

Traditionally, **kimch'i**-making was a way to preserve vegetables to ensure proper nutrition during harsh winters, but it's now eaten year-round to add zest to any meal. Many Koreans – and foreigners living in Korea – find themselves addicted to the stuff!

SNACKS   간식/군것질

In large cities, you'll find outdoor stands selling cheap, freshly made snacks. Many pavement stands offer light meals as well, with enclosed seating (heated in winter) to stay out of the elements – a great place to run to when you're caught in the rain.

FOOD

hottŏk   호떡
brown-sugar-filled pancake

pung-ŏppang   붕어빵
fish-shaped cake with sweet red bean filling

kyeranppang   계란빵
small cake with egg inside

t'wigim   튀김
tempura (deep-fried vegetables, seafood, etc)

dŏkpokki   떡볶이
rice cakes cooked in red pepper paste

sundae   순대
Korean-style stuffed sausage

떡볶이!

FOOD

VEGETARIAN & SPECIAL MEALS

채식주의와 특별음식

Despite its Buddhist influence, Korea is not an easy place for vegetarians or vegans. While it's easy to find food that doesn't contain beef, pork, poultry, eggs or even dairy products, it's harder to track down meals with absolutely no seafood. The concept of 'kosher' is not familiar.

I'm vegetarian.
chŏn ch'aeshikchu-ŭija-eyo
전 채식주의자에요.

I don't eat meat.
chŏn kogirŭl anmŏgŏyo
전 고기를 안 먹어요.

I don't eat chicken, fish or ham.
chŏn takkogi, saengsŏn,
haemŭl anmŏgŏyo
전 닭고기, 생선,
햄을 안 먹어요.

I can't eat dairy products.
chŏn yujep'umŭl
anmŏgŏyo
전 유제품을
안 먹어요.

Do you have any vegetarian dishes?
kogi andŭrŏgan ŭmshik
issŏyo?
고기 안 들어간 음식
있어요?

Does this dish have meat?
i ŭmshige kogiga
dŭrŏgayo?
이 음식에 고기가
들어가요?

Can I get this without meat?
kogi baego haejushilsu
issŏyo?
고기 빼고 해 주실 수
있어요?

Does it contain eggs?
kyerani dŭrŏgayo?
계란이 들어가요?

I'm allergic to (peanuts).
chŏn (dangk'ong)e
allerŭgiga issŏyo
전 (땅콩)에
알레르기가 있어요.

Is there a kosher restaurant here?
chuwie yut'aeinshik
shiktang issŏyo?
주위에 유태인식
식당 있어요?

Is this organic?
igŏt yugi nongbŏbŭro
chaebae doéŏssŏyo?
이것 유기농법으로
재배 되었어요?

EATING OUT

외식하기

Eating out in Korea can be done on any budget. Small family-run restaurants offer full meals, including side dishes, called **panch'an** (반찬), for just a few dollars. Fast-food restaurants are also affordable. Formal dining in foreign restaurant chains has become very popular, with many such establishments offering 'set menus'.

Foreign chains usually offer English-language menus and at least one server will speak English. Korean chains often have menus with photographs, or freakishly realistic models of the food they serve, located in the window.

FOOD

DINING DECORUM

Korean restaurants often have seats available on the floor or at a table. The floor seating will be on a slightly elevated section of the restaurant, and you must take your shoes off to go in there.

Lower-priced restaurants are often light on service, especially when it gets busy. Customers often pour their own water and get out their own cutlery. If you end up in the seat closest to the container with the spoons and the chopsticks, you should make sure to hand a set to every person at your table.

When passing food or drinks around the table, offer food with both hands for politeness. This is especially true when pouring someone alcohol.

When drinking, make sure to fill up the glasses of the people next to you – with two hands, of course – when they get empty.

A table for (five), please.
  (tasŏnmyŏng) chari juseyo   (다섯 명) 자리 주세요.
Could you recommend something?
  mwŏ ch'uch'ŏn haejushillaeyo?   뭐 추천해 주실래요?
We'd like non-smoking/
smoking, please.
  kŭmyŏnsŏgŭro/hŭbyŏnsŏgŭro   금연석으로/흡연석으로
  juseyo   주세요.

FOOD

May we see the menu?
  menyu chom
  katta jushillaeyo?

메뉴 좀
갖다 주실래요?

I'll have what they're having.
  chŏbundŭrirang kat'ŭn
  menyuro juseyo

저분들이랑 같은
메뉴로 주세요.

What's in this dish?
  i ŭmshige mwŏga
  dŭrŏssŏyo?

이 음식에 뭐가
들었어요?

Is this dish spicy?
  i ŭmshing maewŏyo?

이 음식 매워요?

Can you make it less spicy?
  tŏl maepke haejushilsu
  issŏyo?

덜 맵게 해 주실 수
있어요?

I'd like some more of this side dish.
  ibanch'an chom tŏ jushilsu
  issŏyo?

이 반찬 좀 더 주실 수
있어요?

Do you have an English menu?
  yŏng-ŏro doén menyu
  issŏyo?

영어로 된 메뉴
있어요?

No ice in my drink, please.
  ŏrŭm ŏpshi juseyo

얼음 없이 주세요.

DUTCH TREAT

When going out for a meal or drinks, traditionally,
the older or higher-placed friend or colleague would
typically pay, although the others would go through
the motions of 'fighting' for the chance to pay the
tab. Generally, the person planning to pay would also
choose the restaurant.

Nowadays, 'going Dutch' has become the norm
among the younger generation, although a small
group of friends that meets regularly may take turns
paying for meals.

Please bring	... chom	... 좀
a/an/some ...	katta jushillaeyo?	갖다 주실래요?
ashtray	chaettŏri	재떨이
bill	kyesansŏ	계산서
chopsticks	chŏkkarak	젓가락
cup	k'ŏp	컵
fork	p'ok'ŭ	포크
glass of water	mul	물
(with/	(ŏrŭm opshi;	(얼음 없이;
without ice)	ŏrŭm nŏ-ŏsŏ)	얼음 넣어서)
knife	naip'ŭ	나이프
plate	chŏpshi	접시
spoon	sukkarak	숟가락
toothpicks	issushigae	이쑤시개

fresh	shinsŏnhan	신선한
salty	tchan	짠
spicy	mae-un	매운
stale/spoiled	shingshinghaji mot'an	성성하지 못한
sweet	tan	단

FOOD

DID YOU KNOW ...

Food is ordered in servings, especially with dishes consisting mostly of meat.

serving for one
irinbun 일인분
servings for two
i-inbun 이인분
servings for three
saminbun 삼인분
servings for four
sa-inbun 사인분
servings for five
o-inbun 오인분

FOOD

TYPICAL KOREAN DISHES   대표적인 음식들

Korean food is heavy on rice and vegetables and light on meat.
A lot of foods are very spicy, but plenty of them are mild as well.
If you're open-minded, you'll find plenty of Korean cuisine you
can't do without.

Meat Dishes   고기류

kalbi   갈비
  pork or beef ribs; the classic 'Korean barbecue'. It's prepared in
  front of you and comes with rice and vegetables. It's often eaten
  by wrapping rice and a piece of rib meat in lettuce.

kalbitchim   갈비찜
  steamed ribs; a little on the expensive side, but tasty

pulgogi   불고기
  marinated barbecued beef; cooked on a burner in front of
  you. A favourite food when people go out to drink.

samgyŏpsal   삼겹살
  fried pork slices; thinly cut and fried in front of you, it comes
  with rice and vegetables. A good meal when drinking *soju*, but
  not for fighting heart disease.

sanjŏk   산적
  Korean-style shish kebab; marinated meat on a skewer

sogalbi   소갈비
  beef ribs (see **kalbi**)

twaeji-galbi   돼지갈비
  pork ribs (see **kalbi**)

Soups & Stews   국과찌개

k'ongnamulguk   콩나물국
  bean sprout soup; a very light soup with yellow Korean bean
  sprouts

kalbit'ang   갈비탕
  beef rib soup (see **kalbi**)

kimch'i tchigae   김치찌개
  kimch'i stew; Korea's version of bachelor food, this easy-to-
  make dish is basically a mixture of **kimch'i** and whatever else
  you have lying around

mae-unt'ang   매운탕
  spicy fish soup; its name literally means 'spicy soup'

FOOD

manduguk 만두국
stuffed dumpling soup (see **mandu** in Light Meals, page 166)

miyŏkkuk 미역국
seaweed soup; a favourite morning starter in many Korean homes. You also eat this on your birthday.

samgyet'ang 삼계탕
boiled chicken stuffed with ginseng; Koreans eat this as a way to boost energy. It often comes with a shot of ginseng wine on the side.

sŏllŏngt'ang 설렁탕
beef and noodles in hot beef-bone broth; a favourite lunch that's filling but not heavy

sundubu 순두부
spicy tofu stew; brought to your table still boiling in the pot it was cooked in, it contains a hearty mix of soft tofu, egg, and small shellfish, with a side dish of rice

t'angsuyuk 탕수육
sweet and sour pork; if you've never heard of this, we can't help you

toénjang tchigae 된장찌개
miso stew; **toénjang** (된장) is similar to Japan's *miso* sauce, except a little more pungent. This stew is a meal in itself, containing large amounts of tofu, vegetables, some meat, and tiny shellfish.

Noodles 면류
chapch'ae 잡채
Chinese noodles with slices of vegetables; you'll be hungry later

k'alguksu 칼국수
thick noodles in anchovy broth; a nice, warm meal on a cold day

makkuksu 막국수
vegetable noodles; a wholesome mixture of vegetables, light noodles and meat, in chicken broth

naengmyŏn 냉면
spicy cold noodles in broth; a favourite noodle dish during the hot summer months, it includes a slice of meat, a boiled egg, strips of pear, radish and red pepper paste or **kyŏja** (겨자), a type of mustard. It's also called **mul naengmyŏn** (물냉면), literally 'water cold noodles'.

FOOD

pibim naengmyŏn   비빔냉면
   cold vegetable and noodle mix; a hearty meal similar to
   pibimbap (비빔밥) (see Light Meals below), but with noodles
   instead of rice

ramyŏn   라면
   quick noodles; comes in a variety of flavours, but the Korean
   version is usually spicy

tchajangmyŏn   짜장면
   noodles in dark sauce; originally from China, this is a popular
   take-away food

tchamppong   짬뽕
   seafood noodle soup of Chinese origin, with everything thrown in

Light Meals   가벼운 식사

kimbap   김밥
   rice rolled in seaweed; can be stuffed with carrots, spinach,
   radishes, beef, crab, etc

kunmandu   군만두
   fried stuffed dumplings

mandu   만두
   stuffed dumplings; could be described as Korean-style *dim
   sum*. It can be fried, steamed, thrown into soup, etc. It's stuffed
   with mixtures of meat and tofu, or even **kimch'i**.

modŭmhoé   모듬회
   a plate containing all kinds of raw fish, **hoé** (회)

nakchibokkŭm   낙지 볶음
   stir-fried baby octopus; it sounds cruel, but it's tasty

pibimbap   비빔밥
   rice and vegetable mix; a favourite meal for people who
   want something quick and healthy. It contains rice and copi
   ous amounts of vegetables. It's seasoned with a heavy dose of
   red pepper paste.

pindaettŏk   빈대떡
   sometimes called 'Korean pizza' and sometimes 'Korean
   pancake', it's neither. This dish consists of vegetables and meat
   or seafood thrown into a batter and fried up. It's a good dish
   for when you're out drinking.

pokkŭmbap   볶음밥
 fried rice; by itself it usually contains an egg and small amounts
 of vegetable, but it can also come with beef, pork, chicken
 or shrimp.

saengsŏnhoé   생선회
 sliced raw fish; very similar to the variety found in Japan. It's
 generally safe when eaten at larger restaurants.

saengsŏnjŏn   생선전
 lightly seasoned fried fish that has been dipped in batter

saengsŏnkui   생선구이
 broiled and salted fish

sae-u t'wigim   새우튀김

prawn tempura; prawn pieces dipped in batter and then deepfried.
Often sold by street vendors or in Japanese restaurants.

tchinmandu   찐만두
 steamed stuffed dumplings

wangmandu   왕만두
 literally 'king dumplings', very large steamed stuffed dumplings

yakkimandu   야끼 만두
 Chinese-style fried dumplings

Rice & Side Dishes   밥과 반찬

ch'onggak kimch'i   총각김치
 pickled radish **kimch'i**

gaktugi   깍두기
 cubed radish **kimch'i**

hobakchŏn   호박전
 fried squash slices

kim   김
 thin strips of dried seaweed; a great source of nutrients. It's
 used to wrap things (especially rice) and to add flavour to stews
 and soups.

myŏlch'i bokkŭm   멸치볶음
 anchovy side dish

oisobagi   오이소박이
 stuffed cucumber **kimch'i**

FOOD

FOOD

paech´ukimch´i   배추김치
cabbage **kimch´i**; the spicy classic version of Korea's national
dish of pickled vegetables

paekkimch´i   백김치
white cabbage **kimch´i**; less spicy than 'regular' **kimch´i**, with
a sour taste

paekpan   백반
cooked rice; completely unavoidable

shigŭmch´i namul   시금치 나물
whole spinach; cut into pieces and seasoned with soy sauce,
sesame oil and a touch of sugar

tubujorim   두부조림
steamed fried tofu in soy sauce

After Dinner   후식

dŏk   떡
rice cakes; these come in a variety of textures depending on
the type of rice flour. They often contain sweet bean paste, **p´at**
(팥), or a sugary mixture.

shik´ye   식혜
rice punch; this sweet mixture contains grains of rice that have
been soaking in the punch

sujŏnggwa   수정과
persimmon punch; a light beverage made from one of Korea's
favourite fruits

For some typical Korean dishes eaten on specific holidays or
during festivals, see Time, Dates & Festivals, page 227.

HERE'S THE TIP – NO TIP!

Regardless of how good the service was, tipping is generally not
done in Korea. You may express your thanks for good service by
mentioning a kind word or dropping a note to the manager.

That was delicious!
  chŏngmal mashissŏssŏyo!   정말 맛있었어요!
Our compliments to the chef.
  taedanhan yori somshieyo   대단한 요리 솜씨에요.

Although they don't expect it, taxi drivers appreciate a passenger
offering to let them keep the change.

FOOD

SELF-CATERING   스스로 요리하기

Korean food is not easy to make on your own, but if you really want to give it a go, the ingredients can be found in virtually any food store.

In the Delicatessen   식품점에서

Department stores and deluxe hotels usually carry items you would find in a Western deli, although the less common items are significantly more expensive.

How much is (a kilogram of cheese)?
(ch'ijŭ ilkillo)e   (치즈 1킬로)에
ŏlma-eyo?   얼마에요?
Do you have anything cheaper?
tŏssan-gŏt issŏyo?   더 싼 것 있어요?
What's the local speciality?
chibang t'ŭksanp'umi   지방 특산품이
mwŏga issŏyo?   뭐가 있어요?
Give me (one kilogram; 500 grams) please.
(ilk'illo; obaek kŭraem)   (1킬로; 500그램)
juseyo   주세요.
Can I taste it?
mappolsu issŏyo?   맛 볼 수 있어요?

TASTY WALLPAPER

Step into a typical Korean restaurant or cafe and you'll notice the lack of menus. Most restaurants offer a small selection of specialty items, and often a group of people orders the same thing, so typically one table gets one menu. Some places forego menus altogether, instead prominently displaying menu items on the wall.

FOOD

Making Your Own Meals 직접 요리하기

Where can I find the ...?

	... ŏdisŏ kuhalsu issŏyo?	... 어디서 구할 수 있어요?

I'd like some ...	... saryŏgo hanŭndeyo	... 사려고 하는데요.
bread	bang	빵
butter	bŏt'ŏ	버터
cereal	siriŏl	시리얼
cheese	ch'ijŭ	치즈
chocolate	ch'ok'ollit	초콜릿
eggs	kyeran	계란
flour	milkkaru	밀가루
fruit	kwail	과일
ham	haem	햄
honey	gul	꿀
... juice	... jusŭ	... 주스
apple	sagwa	사과
grape	p'odo	포도
orange	orenji	오렌지
margarine	magarin	마가린
marmalade	mamŏlleidŭ	마멀레이드
milk	uyu	우유
olive oil	ollibŭ oil	올리브 오일
pepper (black)	huch'u	후추
red pepper paste	koch'ujang	고추장
red pepper (ground)	koch'ukkaru	고춧가루
salt	sogŭm	소금
soy sauce	kanjang	간장
sugar	sŏlt'ang	설탕
tea bags (black)	hongch'a t'ibaek	홍차 티백
tea bags (green)	nokch'a t'ibaek	녹차 티백
vegetables	yach'ae	야채
yogurt	yogurŭtŭ/yogŏtŭ	요구르트/요거트

AT THE MARKET   시장에서

Korea's selection of meats is fairly basic, and they tend to be expensive. If you want to find more exotic meats such as salami, fancy luncheon meats or turkey, you may have to go to a hotel deli. Fruit and vegetables are easy to come by.

FOOD

Meat & Poultry   고기

beef	soégogi	쇠고기
chicken	takkogi	닭고기
mutton	yanggogi	양고기
ham	haem	햄
meatballs	mit´ŭbol	미트볼
pork	twaejigogi	돼지고기
ribs (beef)	sogalbi	소갈비
ribs (pork)	twaejigalbi	돼지갈비
sausage	soshiji	소시지
spam	sŭp´aem	스팸
steak	sŭt´eik´ŭ	스테이크
turkey	ch´ilmyŏnjogogi	칠면조고기

Seafood   해물

anchovies	myŏlch´i	멸치
clams	taehapchogae	대합조개
cod	taegu	대구
lobster	padakkajae	바다가재
mussels	honghap	홍합
octopus	munŏ	문어
oysters	kul	굴
pufferfish/blowfish	pogŏ	복어
shark	sang-ŏ	상어
shrimp/prawn	sae-u	새우
squid/cuttlefish	ojing-ŏ	오징어
tuna	ch´amch´i	참치

FOOD

Vegetables
야채

beans (green)	gakchik'ong	깍지콩
bean sprouts	k'ongnamul	콩나물
cabbage	yangbaechu	양배추
carrot	tanggŭn	당근
cauliflower	got yangbaechu	꽃양배추
celery	saellŏri	샐러리
chilli (red) pepper	koch'u	고추
cucumber	oi	오이
eggplant	kaji	가지
garlic	manŭl	마늘
lettuce	(yang) sangch'i	(양) 상치
mushrooms	pŏsŏt	버섯
onion	yangp'a	양파
peas	wanduk'ong	완두콩
potato	kamja	감자
pumpkin	hobak	호박
spinach	shigŭmch'i	시금치
spring onion	p'a	파
squash	aehobak	애호박
sweet potato	koguma	고구마
tomato	t'omat'o	토마토
vegetables	yach'ae	야채
zucchini (courgette)	aehobak	애호박

Pulses
콩

broad beans	chamdu	잠두
cereal	kongmul shikp'um	곡물식품
chickpeas	pyŏng-arik'ong	병아리콩
kidney beans	kangnangk'ong	강낭콩
lentils	renjŭk'ong	렌즈콩
rice (uncooked)	ssal	쌀

Fruit & Nuts

과일과 견과류

almonds	amondŭ	아몬드
apple	sagwa	사과
apricot	salgu	살구
avocado	abok'ado	아보카도
banana	panana	바나나
Chinese quince	mokwa	모과
coconut	k'ok'onŏt	코코넛
fig	muhwagwa	무화과
grape (red)	p'odo	포도
grape (white)	ch'ŏngp'odo	청포도
kiwifruit	k'iwi	키위
Korean honeydew melon	ch'amoé	참외
lemon	remon	레몬
mango	manggo	망고
orange	orenji	오렌지
peach	poksung-a	복숭아
pear	pae	배
persimmon	kam	감
pineapple	p'ainaepŭl	파인애플
plum	chadu	자두
raisin	kŏnp'odo	건포도
raspberry	raejŭberi/santtalgi	래즈베리/산딸기
roasted ...	pokkŭn ...	볶은 ...
hazelnut	haejŭllŏt	해즐넛
peanut	dangk'ong	땅콩
gingko nut	ŭnhaeng	은행
pistachio	p'isŭt'ach'io	피스타치오
strawberry	dalgi	딸기
tangerine; mandarin	kyul	귤
tomato	t'omat'o	토마토
watermelon	subak	수박

FOOD

FOOD

Spices & Condiments 양념과 조미료

black pepper	huchu'kkaru	후춧가루
garlic	manŭl	마늘
ginger	saenggang	생강
ketchup	k'ech'ŏp	케첩
mayonnaise	mayonejŭ	마요네즈
miso paste	toénjang	된장
mustard	kyŏja	겨자
pepper	huch'u	후추
red chillies	koch'u	고추
red pepper (ground)	koch'ukkaru	고춧가루
red pepper paste	koch'ujang	고추장
salsa	salsa	살사
salt	sogŭm	소금
soy sauce	kanjang	간장
tabasco sauce	t'abasŭk'o sosŭ	타바스코 소스

SOMETHING SMELLS GOOD

Perhaps Korea's most famous culinary quirk is the consumption of 'man's best friend'. But walking down the street or into some seafood restaurants may reveal some other foods you may find peculiar.

pŏndegi 번데기
silkworm larvae; street vendors near schools still keep a pot of this boiling, because kids love the stuff

sachŏlt'ang/poshint'ang 사철탕/보신탕
Korea's notorious dog soup; this food 'tradition' stems from a belief that dog flesh is extremely healthy for people, providing them with stamina – especially in the bedroom

sannakchi 산낙지
live baby octopus cut up into small bits; the poor creature squirms around on your plate and between your chopsticks. The suction cups still work, and if you're not careful, the octopus's revenge could be cutting off your windpipe – people actually have choked, especially while drunk.

DRINKS
Nonalcoholic

coffee	k'ŏp'i	커피
decaffeinated coffee	muk'ap'ein k'ŏp'i	무카페인 커피
cola	k'olla	콜라
juice	jusŭ	주스
tea	ch'a	차
with/without milk	uyu nŏ-ŏsŏ/baego	우유 넣어서/빼고
with/without sugar	sŏlt'ang nŏ-ŏsŏ/baego	설탕 넣어서/빼고
(cup of) ...	... (hanjan)	... (한 잔)
black tea	hongch'a	홍차
citron tea	yujach'a	유자차
date tea	taech'uch'a	대추차
ginger tea	saenggangch'a	생강차
green tea	nokch'a	녹차
lemonade	remoneidŭ	레모네이드
mineral spring water	saengsu	생수
persimmon punch	sujŏnggwa	수정과
rice punch	shik'ye	식혜
water	mul	물
boiled water	gŭrin mul	끓인 물

Alcoholic

beer	maekchu	맥주
brandy	bŭraendi	브랜디
champagne	shamp'ein	샴페인
clear rice wine	tongdongju	동동주
cocktail	k'akt'eil	칵테일
green plum wine	maeshilchu	매실주
rum	rŏm	럼
soju	soju	소주
(clear, fermented sweet potatoes)		
unstrained rice wine	makkŏlli	막걸리
whisky	wisŭk'i	위스키
a glass of wine	wain hanjan	와인 한 잔
a shot of whisky	wisŭk'i hanjan	위스키 한 잔

FOOD

Beer is typically ordered by the bottle or by mugs or pitchers. But rather than referring to the number of pints, litres, or quarts, beer is ordered by 'cc' (millilitre, literally cubic centimetre). A half-litre mug is **obaek-shishi** (오백씨씨/500cc), '500ml'.

Please give me	**maekchu ... juseyo**	맥주 ... 주세요.
... of beer.		
a litre (1000ml)	**ch'ŏnshishi**	1000cc (천씨씨)
half a litre (500ml)	**obaekshishi**	500cc (오백씨씨)
one bottle	**hanbyŏng**	한 병
two bottles	**tubyŏng**	두 병
a pitcher of beer	**maekchu p'ich'ŏ**	맥주 피처
	han-gae	한 개
draught beer	**saengmaekchu**	생맥주

IN THE BAR   술집에서

Drinking is a group activity, a chance to let loose with friends or colleagues. You should always look to make sure your friend's glass isn't empty, and when you fill it, you should use both hands for politeness. Many bars still require a table of patrons to order **anju** (안주), side dishes of snacks, French fries, fruit, etc, as a kind of cover charge.

Excuse me! (to attract waiter's
attention)
    yŏgiyo!   여기요!
I'll buy you a drink.
    chega salkkeyo   제가 살게요.
What would you like to drink?
    mwŏ mashigo ship'ŭseyo?   뭐 마시고 싶으세요?
What would you like to eat?
(referring to **anju**)
    anju mwŏ dŭshillaeyo?   안주 뭐 드실래요?
What kind of **anju** (side dishes)
do they have?
    anju mwŏga innŭndeyo?   안주 뭐가 있는데요?

I'll have ...

    chŏn ...(ŭ)ro halkkeyo   전 ... (으)로 할게요.

No ice please.

    ŏrŭm nŏch'i maseyo   얼음 넣지 마세요.

It's my round.

    ibŏnenŭn che ch'arye-eyo   이번에는 제 차례에요.

One Too Many?   술 마시기

Korea has its share of binge drinkers, so getting your group to stop drinking can be difficult. A person who bows out early is often considered a wet blanket, but if you have a good excuse you may be in luck.

Thanks, but I don't feel like it.

    komapjiman onŭrŭn   고맙지만 오늘은

    pyŏllo naek'ijiga anneyo   별로 내키지가 않네요.

I don't drink alcohol.

    chŏn surŭl anmashŏyo   전 술을 안 마셔요.

I don't usually drink much.

    pot'ong chŏn surŭl   보통 전 술을

    mani anmashŏyo   많이 안 마셔요.

This is hitting the spot.

    chŏngmal dagindeyo   정말 딱인데요.

I'm tired. I'd better get home.

    chibe kayagessŏyo.   집에 가야겠어요.

    nŏmu p'igon haeyo   너무 피곤해요.

DID YOU KNOW ...   Spill a little food in a restaurant and you might ask for a **naepk'in** (냅킨), 'napkin'. But in a Korean restaurant, you may be handed a role of **hyuji** (휴지), 'toilet paper'.

FOOD

Where's the toilet?
hwajangshiri ŏdijo?

여기 식사가 나오나요?

Is food served here?
yŏgi shiksaga naonayo?

여기 식사가 나오나요?

I'm feeling drunk.
chŏ ch'wihan-gŏt kat'ayo

저 취한 것 같아요.

You're too drunk to drive.
unjŏn hagienŭn nŏmu
ch'wihaessŏyo

운전하기에는 너무
취했어요.

I feel ill.
momi anjoayo

몸이 안 좋아요.

I think I'm going to throw up.
t'ohalgŏt kat'ayo

토할 것 같아요.

전원에서   **IN THE COUNTRY**

CAMPING   캠프/야영

Camping is possible in Korea – however, tensions along the DMZ (De-Militarised Zone) mean restrictions on where you can camp. You should only stay in designated areas, and pay attention to local regulations regarding cooking. Flash flooding in the parks' canyons during the summer rainy season is also a danger.

Is there a camp site nearby?
kŭnchŏ-e k'aemp'ŭ/yayŏng halsu innŭn-got issŏyo?
근처에 캠프/야영
할 수 있는 곳 있어요?

Do you have any sites available?
k'aemp'ŭ/yayŏng hal jari issŏyo?
캠프/야영 할
자리 있어요?

Where can we get permits for camping?
k'aemp'ŭ/yayŏng haryŏmyŏn ŏdisŏ hŏrakpadaya dwaeyo?
캠프/야영 하려면
어디서 허락받아야 돼요?

Where can I hire a tent?
t'ent'ŭ ŏdisŏ pillyŏyo?
텐트 어디서 빌려요?

Are there shower facilities?
shawŏ halsu innŭn-got issŏyo?
샤워할 수 있는 곳
있어요?

Can we camp here?
yŏgisŏ k'aempŭ/yayŏng halsu issŏyo?
여기서 캠프/야영
할 수 있어요?

Does this temple offer sleeping accommodation?
ijŏresŏ sukpak halsu issŏyo?
이 절에서 숙박할 수
있어요?

How much is it per ...?	... ŏlma-eyo?	... 얼마에요?
person	irindang	일인당
tent	t'ent'ŭdang	텐트당
vehicle	hanch'adang	한차당

IN THE COUNTRY

backpack	**paenang**	배낭
batteries	**baet′ŏri**	배터리
gas cyclinder (for burner stove)	**put′an-gasŭ**	부탄가스
camping	**k′aemp′ŭ/yayŏng**	캠프/야영
camp site	**k′aemp′ŭjang/ yayŏngjang**	캠프장/ 야영장
portable burner stove	**pŏnŏ**	버너
rope	**rop′ŭ**	로프
tent	**t′ent′ŭ**	텐트
torch (flashlight)	**sonjŏndŭng**	손전등

HIKING   등산

Hiking is a national pastime in Korea and often a family activity, which means that mountain regions can become very crowded during holiday periods. All of Korea's nearly two dozen national parks, as well as the many provincial parks, are accessible year-round and include hiking trails varying from easy to challenging. Many mountains provide excellent opportunities for rock climbing.

Getting Information   정보 구하기

Most national and provincial parks offer detailed maps of the local area. Trails are also well marked in English and Korean, and often include giant 'you-are-here' maps.

Where can I see a map with
hiking trails of the region?
   tŭngsanno jido polsu
   innŭn-got issŏyo?   등산로 지도 볼 수
                                            있는 곳 있어요?
Where's the nearest village/temple?
   kajang kakkaun maŭri/
   chŏri ŏdi issŏyo?   가장 가까운 마을이/
                                            절이 어디있어요?
Is it safe to climb this mountain?
   isan ollagagi anjŏn haeyo?   이 산 올라가기 안전해요?
Is it possible to rock climb here?
   yŏgisŏ anbyŏk tŭngban halsu
   issŏyo?   여기서 암벽등반 할수
                                            있어요?

Do we need a guide?
    kaidŭga p'iryohaeyo?

가이드가 필요해요?

Are there guided treks?
    **daragalsu innŭn
    girina issŏyo?**

따라갈 수 있는
길이 나 있어요?

How long is the trail?
    **tŭngsannoga ŏlmana
    kirŏyo?**

등산로가 얼마나
길어요?

Is the track marked?
    **kiri arabogi shipke
    p'yoshi doéŏ issŏyo?**

길이 알아보기 쉽게
표시되어 있어요?

Which is the shortest route?
    **kajang tchalbŭn kiri
    ŏttŏn-gŏ-eyo?**

가장 짧은 길이
어떤 거에요?

Is the path open?
    igil kaebang doéŏ issŏyo?

이 길 개방되어 있어요?

On the Path

산길에서

Where have you come from?
    ŏdisŏ oshŏssŏyo?

어디서 오셨어요?

How long did it take you?
    **yŏgikkaji onŭnde
    ŏlmana kŏllishŏssŏyo?**

여기까지 오는데
얼마나 걸리셨어요?

Does this path go to ...?
    **igiri ...e kanŭn
    girieyo?**

이 길이 ...에 가는
길이에요?

I'm lost.
    kirŭl irŏssŏyo

길을 잃었어요.

Where can we spend the night?
    pame ŏdisŏ chayo?

밤에 어디서 자요?

Is the water OK to drink?
    imul mashŏdo dwaeyo?

이 물 마셔도 돼요?

altitude	kodo	고도
backpack	paenang	배낭
binoculars	ssang-an-gyŏng/	쌍안경/
	mang-wŏn-gyŏng	망원경
candles	ch'o	초
to climb	ollayo	올라요
compass	nach'imban	나침반
first-aid kit	kugŭp sangja	구급 상자
gloves	changgap	장갑
guide	kaidŭ	가이드
guided trek	daragalsu	따라갈 수
	innŭn-gil	있는 길
hiking	tŭngsan	등산
hiking boots	tŭngsanhwa	등산화
lookout	chŏnmangdae	전망대
map	chido	지도
matches	sŏngnyang	성냥
mountain climbing	tŭngsan	등산
provisions	shingnyang	식량
rock climbing	ambyŏk tŭngban	암벽 등반
rope	rop'ŭ	로프
signpost	p'yonmal	푯말
water bottle	mult'ong	물통

AT THE BEACH   해변에서

The peninsula's beaches throng with holidaymakers during July and August. Water activities such as windsurfing, water skiing, boogie-boarding and scuba diving have developed a following.

Can we swim here?
   yŏgisŏ suyŏng haedo dwaeyo?   여기서 수영해도 돼요?
Is it safe to swim here?
   yŏgi suyŏng hagi   여기 수영하기
   anjŏn haeyo?   안전해요?
What time is high/low tide?
   milmuri/ssŏlmuri   밀물이/썰물이
   ŏnje-eyo?   언제예요?

Are there good diving sites here?
   yŏgi daibing halmanhan-got
   ŏpsŏyo?

여기 다이빙 할 만한 곳
없어요?

Can we get diving lessons here?
   yŏgisŏ daibing pae-ulsu
   issŏyo?

여기서 다이빙 배울 수
있어요?

We'd like to hire diving equipment.
   daibing changbi pilliryŏgo
   hanŭndeyo

다이빙 장비 빌리려고
하는데요.

coast	hae-an	해안
coral	sanho	산호
fishing	nakshi	낚시
lagoon	sŏkho	석호
ocean	haeyang	해양
reef	amch'o	암초
rock	pawi	바위
sand	morae	모래
scuba diving	sŭkubŏ daibing	스쿠버 다이빙
sea	pada	바다
snorkelling	sŭnok'ŭlling	스노클링
sunblock	sŏnk'ŭrim	선크림
sunglasses	sŏngŭllasŭ	선글라스
surfing	sŏp'ing	서핑
surfboard	sŏp'ingbodŭ	서핑보드
swimming	suyŏng	수영
towel	sugŏn/t'awŏl	수건/타월
waterskiing	susangsŭk'i	수상스키
waves	p'ado	파도
windsurfing	windŭsŏp'ing	윈드서핑

SIGNS

낚시금지	NO FISHING
수영금지	NO SWIMMING

Aquatic Creatures   수생 동물

blowfish	pogŏ	복어
crab	ke	게
dolphin	tolgorae	돌고래
eel	paemjang-ŏ	뱀장어
fish (pl)	mulgogi	물고기
lobster	padakkajae/rapsŭt'ŏ	바다가재/랍스터
ray	kaori	가오리
seagull	kalmaegi	갈매기
seal	mulgae	물개
sea urchin	sŏngge	성게
shark	sang-ŏ	상어
shellfish	chogae	조개
squid/cuttlefish	ojing-ŏ	오징어
starfish	pulgasari	불가사리
turtle	kŏbugi	거북이
whale	korae	고래

WEATHER   날씨

In general, Korea has a humid continental climate that brings hot, muggy summers and cold, dry winters. The coastal cities farthest south are relatively mild all year. Korea's island province of Cheju-do is semi-tropical.

In springtime the country explodes into the colours of azaleas, forsythia and cherry blossoms. North and South Korea are two of the 10 most heavily forested countries in the world, and in summer deep-green foliage is everywhere. Autumn brings out the golden colours of the gingko trees and the red hues of the Asian maples. In winter, snow cover brings an eerie calm to everything.

Korea has a rainy season from late June to early August. In winter, occasional blizzards can bring big cities to a standstill.

What's the weather like?
  nalshiga ŏttaeyo?   날씨가 어때요?

Today it's ...	ŏnŭl ...	오늘 ...
cloudy	kurŭmi manayo	구름이 많아요
cold	ch'uwŏyo	추워요
hot	tŏwŏyo	더워요
muggy	mudŏwŏyo	무더워요
warm	dattŭt'aeyo	따뜻해요
windy	parami mani purŏyo	바람이 많이 불어요

It's raining heavily.	piga mani oneyo	비가 많이 오네요.
It's raining lightly.	piga chogŭm wayo	비가 조금 와요.
It's dry.	kŏnjo haeyo	건조해요.

ice	ŏrŭm	얼음
monsoon	changma	장마
snowstorm	nunbora	눈보라
snow	nun	눈
storm	p'okp'ung	폭풍
sun	hae	해
typhoon	t'aep'ung	태풍

GEOGRAPHICAL TERMS   지리 용어

beach	haesu yokchang; haebyŏn	해수욕장; 해변
bridge	tari	다리
cave	tonggul	동굴
cliff	chŏlbyŏk	절벽
earthquake	chijin	지진
farm	nongjang	농장
footpath	podo	보도
forest	sup	숲
harbour	hanggu	항구
hill	ŏndŏk	언덕
hot spring	onch'ŏn	온천
island	sŏm	섬
lake	hosu	호수
mountain	san	산
mountain path	san-gil/tŭngsanno	산길/등산로
peak	pong-uri	봉우리
peninsula	pando	반도
river	kang	강
riverside	kangbyŏn	강변

sea	pada	바다
valley	kyegok	계곡
waterfall	p'okp'o	폭포
East Sea (Sea of Japan)	tonghae	동해
Yellow Sea	hwanghae/sŏhae	황해/서해
East China Sea	namhae	남해

FAUNA   동물

What animal is this?
  ige musŭn tongmurieyo?   이게 무슨 동물이에요?

Domestic Creatures   가축동물

buffalo	pŏp'allo/tŭlso	버팔로/들소
calf	song-aji	송아지
cat	koyang-i	고양이
chicken	tak	닭
cow	chŏtso	젖소
dog	kae	개
donkey	tangnagwi	당나귀
duck	ori	오리
goat	yŏmso	염소
hen	amt'ak	암탉
horse	mal	말
ox	hwangso	황소
pig	twaeji	돼지
rooster	sut'ak	수탉
sheep	yang	양

DID YOU KNOW ... In Korea, a pig appearing in a dream, called twaejikkum (돼지꿈), literally 'pig dream', is a sign of good luck to come. If you tell a Seoulite about a porcine presence appearing to you the previous night, he or she may advise you to go out and buy a lottery ticket.

Wildlife   야생동물

ant	kaemi	개미
bee	pŏl	벌
bird	sae	새
butterfly	nabi	나비
cockroach	pak'wibŏlle	바퀴벌레
crocodile	agŏ	악어
dragonfly	chamjari	잠자리
fish	mulgogi	물고기
fly	p'ari	파리
frog	kaeguri	개구리
leech	kŏmŏri	거머리
lion	saja	사자
monkey	wŏnsung-i	원숭이
mosquito	mogi	모기
mouse/rat	chwi	쥐
snail	talp'aeng-i	달팽이
snake	paem	뱀
spider	kŏmi	거미
squirrel	taramjwi	다람쥐
tiger	horang-i	호랑이

IN THE COUNTRY

FLORA & AGRICULTURE   식물과 농업

Much of Korea is covered by farmland, especially rice fields.
Corn and tobacco are also major crops.

What (tree/plant/flower) is that?
   chŏge musŭn (namu/   저게 무슨 (나무/
   shingmuri/gochi)eyo?   식물이/꽃이)에요?
What's it used for?
   kŭgŏl ŏdie ssŏyo?   그걸 어디에 써요?
Can you eat that fruit?
   chŏ kwail mŏgŭlsu issŏyo?   저 과일 먹을 수 있어요?

acacia	ak'ashia namu	아카시아 나무
apple tree	sagwa namu	사과나무
oak	dŏkkallamu	떡갈나무
palm tree	chongnyŏ namu	종려나무
date	taech'uyaja	대추야자

IN THE COUNTRY

gingko	ŭnhaeng namu	은행나무
magnolia	mongnyŏn namu	목련나무
maple	tanp'ung namu	단풍나무
persimmon tree	kamnamu	감나무
pine	sonamu	소나무
bush	kwanmok	관목

Herbs, Flowers & Crops   풀, 꽃, 곡식들

agriculture	nong-ŏp/nongsa	농업/농사
azalea	chindallae	진달래
(Chinese) cabbage	paech'u	배추
cherry blossom	pŏkkot	벚꽃
corn	oksusu	옥수수
crops	kokshik	곡식
flower	got	꽃
forsythia	kaenari	개나리
greenhouse	onshil	온실
grapevine	p'odo namu	포도나무
harvest	ch'usu	추수
irrigation	kwan-gae	관개
jasmine	chaesŭmin namu	재스민 나무
leaf	ipsagwi/ip	잎사귀/잎
orchard	kwasuwŏn	과수원
planting/sowing	shimkki/shippurigi	심기/씨 뿌리기
rice field/paddy	non	논
sunflower	haebaragi	해바라기
rose	changmi	장미
baby's breath	an-gaekkot	안개꽃
thyme	paengnihyang namu	백리향 나무
tobacco	tambae	담배
tree	namu	나무
vineyard	p'odowŏn	포도원
wheat	mil	밀

South Korea has a modern health network that also includes
traditional forms of treatment such as acupuncture.

Many of Korea's major hospitals have 'international clinics'
geared towards patients who don't speak Korean. Almost every
neighbourhood has a small local hospital, and ŭiwon (의원), private specialisation clinics, are found almost everywhere. Doctors
usually have studied with English-language textbooks, so although
they may not be able to carry on a conversation with you, they can
write out 'appendicitis' or 'contusion of patella' for you.

AT THE DOCTOR   병원에서

I'm sick.
   momi anjoayo   몸이 안 좋아요.
My friend is sick.
   che ch'in-guga ap'ayo   제 친구가 아파요.
It hurts here.
   yŏgiga apayo   여기가 아파요.
I need a doctor who speaks English.
   yŏng-ŏ hanŭn ŭisaga   영어하는 의사가
   p'iryo haeyo   필요해요.

Where's the nearest ...?	**kajang kakkaun**	가장 가까운
	...ga/i ŏdi issŏyo?	...가/이 어디있어요?
chemist/ pharmacist	**yakkuk**	약국
dentist	**ch'ikkwa**	치과
doctor	**ŭisa**	의사
hospital	**pyŏng-won**	병원

This is my usual medicine.
**ige chega p'yŏngso-e
pogyŏng hanŭn yagieyo**

이게 제가 평소에
복용하는 약이에요.

I don't want a blood transfusion.
**chŏn suhyŏrŭn wŏnhaji
annŭndeyo**

전 수혈은 원하지
않는데요.

Can I have a receipt for my insurance?
**pohŏm yŏngsujŭng chom
jushilsu issŏyo?**

보험 영주증 좀
주실 수 있어요?

THE DOCTOR MAY ASK ...

ŏdiga apŭseyo?
어디가 아프세요?
  Where does it hurt?

saengnijung ishin-gayo?
생리중이신가요?
  Are you menstruating?

yŏri issŭseyo?
열이 있으세요?
  Do you have a temperature?

**ŏlmana orae irŏn
jŭngsang-i issŏssŏyo?**
얼마나 오래 이런
증상이 있었어요?
  How long have you
  been like this?

**chŏnedo irŏnjŏgi
issŭseyo?**
전에도 이런 적이
있으세요?
  Have you had this before?

yak pogyongjung iseyo?
약 복용중이세요?
  Are you on medication?

tambae p'iuseyo?
담배 피우세요?
  Do you smoke?

sul dŭshimnikka?
술 드십니까?
  Do you drink?

mayak hashimnikka?
마약 하십니까?
  Do you take drugs?

allerŭgi issŭseyo?
알레르기 있으세요?
  Are you allergic to anything?

**imshinjung ishin-gayo?;
ŏlmana dwaessŏyo?**
임신중이신가요?;
얼마나 됐어요?
  Are you pregnant?

AILMENTS 병

I'm ill.
   chŏn ap'ayo 전 아파요.

I've been vomiting.
   kyesok t'orŭl haessŏyo 계속 토를 했어요.

I feel nauseous.
   mesŭkkŏryŏyo 메슥거려요.

I can't sleep.
   chamŭl mot chagessŏyo 잠을 못 자겠어요.

Explaining symptoms in Korean is a little more grammatically complex than in English. Some ailments you 'have' while others 'occur'. The symptom itself comes first, followed by the verb (which is often in the past tense). When describing symptoms below, take note of the verb that follows.

I feel ...	chŏn ...	전 ...
dizzy	ŏjirŏwŏyo	어지러워요
shivery	ch'uwŏsŏ bŏlbŏl dŏllyŏyo	추워서 벌벌 떨려요
weak	himi hanado ŏpsŏyo	힘이 하나도 없어요

I have (a/an) ...	chŏn ...	전 ...
allergy	allerŭgiga issŏyo	알레르기가 있어요
anaemia	pinhyŏri issŏyo	빈혈이 있어요
bronchitis	kigwanjiyŏmi issŏyo	기관지염이 있어요
burn	hwasang-ŭl ibŏssŏyo	화상을 입었어요
cancer	ami issŏyo	암이 있어요
chicken pox	sudue kŏllyŏssŏyo	수두에 걸렸어요
cold	kamgie kŏllyŏssŏyo	감기에 걸렸어요
constipation	pyŏnbiga issŏyo	변비가 있어요

HEALTH

cough	kich'imŭl haeyo	기침을 해요
diarrhoea	sŏlsarŭl haeyo	설사를 해요
fever	yŏri nayo	열이 나요
food poisoning	shikchungdoge kŏllyŏssŏyo	식중독에 걸렸어요
gastroenteritis	wijang-yŏmi issŏyo	위장염이 있어요
glandular fever	sŏnyŏri issŏyo	선열이 있어요
hayfever	kŏnch'oyŏri issŏyo	건초열이 있어요
headache	tut'ong-i issŏyo	두통이 있어요
heart condition	shimjang-e munjega issŏyo	심장에 문제가 있어요
hepatitis	kanyŏmi issŏyo	간염이 있어요
indigestion	sohwaga chal andwaeyo	소화가 잘 안 돼요
inflammation	yŏmjŭng-i issŏyo	염증이 있어요
influenza	tokkam'e kŏllyŏssŏyo	독감에 걸렸어요
lump	hogi nassŏyo	혹이 났어요
migraine	p'yŏn dutong-i issŏyo	편두통이 있어요
pain	t'ongjŭng-i issŏyo	통증이 있어요
parasite	kisaengch'ung-i issŏyo	기생충이 있어요
rash	palchini issŏyo	발진이 있어요
sexually transmitted disease	sŏngbyŏng-e kŏllyŏssŏyo	성병에 걸렸어요
sore throat	mogi ap'ayo	목이 아파요
sprain (ankle)	(palmogŭl) biŏssŏyo	(발목을) 삐었어요
stomachache	pokt'ong-i issŏyo	복통이 있어요
sunburn	haeppich'e t'assŏyo	햇빛에 탔어요
sunstroke	ilsabyŏng-i nassŏyo	일사병이 났어요
thrush	aguch'ang-e kŏllyŏssŏyo	아구창에 걸렸어요
toothache	ch'it'ong-i issŏyo	치통이 있어요
travel sickness	mŏlmiga nayo	멀미가 나요
urinary infection	yoro kamyŏme kŏllyŏssŏyo	요로 감염에 걸렸어요

WOMEN'S HEALTH　　　여성의 건강

For most gynaecological care, a large hospital is preferable to a
local obstetrics/gynaecology clinic. The latter tend to specialise in pre-
natal care and childbirth, rather than other gynaecological issues.

Could I see a female doctor?
**yŏja ŭisarŭl ch'ajassŭmyŏn
hanŭndeyo?**
여자 의사를 찾았으면
하는데요?

I'm pregnant.
chŏn imshin haessŏyo.
전 임신했어요.

I think I'm pregnant.
imshin han-gŏt kat'ayo.
임신한 것 같아요.

I'm on the Pill.
p'i-imyagŭl mŏgŏyo
피임약을 먹어요.

I haven't had my period
for ... weeks.
... ju dong-an saengniga ŏpsŏyo.
... 주 동안 생리가 없어요.

I'd like to get the morning-after pill.
minibora juseyo.
미니보라 주세요.

I'd like to use contraception.
p'i-imŭl hago ship'ŏyo.
피임을 하고 싶어요.

I'd like to have a pregnancy test.
**imshin haennŭnji arabogo
ship'ŭndeyo**
임신했는지 알아보고
싶은데요.

abortion	nakt'ae	낙태
cystitis	panggwang-yŏm	방광염
diaphragm	p'esŏri	페서리
IUD	chagungnae p'i-imgigu	자궁내피임기구
mammogram	yubang eksŭsŏn sajin	유방 엑스선 사진
menstruation	saengni/wŏlgyŏng	생리/월경
miscarriage	yusan	유산
pap smear	p'aep t'esŭt'ŭ	팹테스트
period pain	saengnit'ong	생리통
the Pill	kyŏnggu p'i-imyak	경구 피임약
premenstrual	saengnijŏn	생리전
tension (PMS)	chŭnghugun	증후군
ultrasound	ch'oŭmpa	초음파

SPECIAL HEALTH NEEDS

특별한 건강 관리

I'm ...	chŏnŭn ... ga/i issŏyo	저는 ... 가/이 있어요.
diabetic	tangnyobyŏng	당뇨병
asthmatic	ch'ŏnshik	천식
anaemic	pinhyŏl	빈혈

I'm allergic to ...	chŏn ...e allerŭgiga issŏyo	전 ...에 알레르기가 있어요.
antibiotics	hangsaengje	항생제
aspirin	asŭp'irin	아스피린
bees	pŏl	벌
codeine	k'odein	코데인
dairy products	yujep'um	유제품
penicillin	p'enishillin	페니실린
pollen	gokkaru	꽃가루

I have a skin allergy.
chŏn p'ibu allerŭgiga issŏyo

전 피부 알레르기가 있어요.

I have high/low blood pressure.
chŏn kohyŏrabieyo/ chŏhyŏrabieyo

전 고혈압이에요/ 저혈압이에요.

I have a weak heart.
chŏn shimjang-i yak'aeyo

전 심장이 약해요.

I've had my vaccinations.
chŏn yebang jusa majannŭndeyo

전 예방주사 맞았는데요.

I'm on medication for ...
chŏn ... yagŭl mŏngnŭn jung-ieyo

전 ... 약을 먹는 중이에요.

I'm on a special diet.
chŏn kyujŏngshigŭl mŏkko issŏyo

전 규정식을 먹고 있어요.

I need a new pair of glasses.
an-gyŏng-i p'iryo haeyo

안경이 필요해요.

I've been bitten.
mullyŏssŏyo

물렸어요.

addiction	chungdok	중독
blood test	hyŏraek kŏmsa	혈액 검사
contraceptive	p'i-imyak	피임약
inhaler (for asthma)	chŏnshik hwanjayong	천식환자용
	hŭbipki	흡입기
injection	chusa	주사
injury	pusang	부상
pacemaker	p'eisŭmeik'ŏ	페이스메이커
vitamins	pitamin	비타민
wound	sangch'ŏ	상처

ALTERNATIVE TREATMENTS   대체의술

Having employed its use for thousands of years, Koreans have no qualms about going to practitioners of Oriental medicine when Western medicine doesn't seem to be doing the trick. Often Oriental medicines can be found in pharmacies, side-by-side with Western medications.

acupuncture	ch'im	침
aromatherapy	aroma t'erap'i;	아로마테라피;
	hyanggi yoppŏp	향기요법
chiropractor	ch'ŏkch'u chiapsa	척추 지압사
doctor of Oriental medicine	hanisa	한의사
homeopathy	dongjong yoppŏp	동종요법
massage	anma/masaji	안마/마사지
meditation	myŏngsang	명상
moxibustion	dŭm	뜸
naturopath	chayŏn yoppŏpka	자연 요법가
Oriental medical clinic	haniwŏn	한의원
Oriental medicine	hanyak	한약
reflexology	pansahak	반사학
yoga	yoga	요가

HEALTH

PARTS OF THE BODY　　　　　　신체부위

My ... hurts.	
...ga/i ap'ayo	...가/이 아파요.
I have a pain in my ...	
...e t'ongjŭng-i issŏyo	...에 통증이 있어요.
I can't move my ...	
...rŭl/ŭl umjigilsuga ŏpsŏyo	...를/을 움직일 수가 없어요.

ankle	palmok	발목
appendix	maengjang	맹장
arm	p'al	팔
back	hŏri	허리
bladder	panggwang	방광
blood	hyŏraek	혈액
bone	byŏ	뼈
chest	kasŭm	가슴
ears	kwi	귀
eye	nun	눈
finger	sonkkarak	손가락
foot	pal	발
hand	son	손
head	mŏri	머리
heart	shimjang	심장
jaw	t'ŏk	턱
kidney	shinjang	신장
knee	murŭp	무릎
leg	tari	다리
liver	kan	간
lungs	p'ye	폐
mouth	ip	입
muscle	kŭnyuk	근육
nose	k'o	코
ribs	kalbippyŏ	갈비뼈
shoulders	ŏkkae	어깨
skin	p'ibu	피부
spine	ch'ŏkch'u	척추
stomach	wi	위
teeth	i	이
throat	mok	목
vein	chŏngmaek	정맥

AT THE CHEMIST 약국에서

As in most Western countries, a prescription must be obtained for most medicines.

I need something for ...
... yagi p'iryo handeyo ... 약이 필요한데요.
Do I need a prescription for ...?
... yak saryŏmyŏn ŭisa ... 약 사려면 의사
ch'ŏbangjŏni issŏya dwaeyo? 처방전이 있어야 돼요?
How many times a day?
harue myŏppŏn ijo? 하루에 몇 번이죠?
Will it make me drowsy?
iyak mŏgŭmyŏn 이 약 먹으면
chollin-gayo? 졸린가요?

antibiotics	**hangsaengje**	항생제
antiseptic	**sodong-yak**	소독약
aspirin	**asŭpirin**	아스피린
bandage	**pungdae**	붕대
Band-Aids	**panch'anggo**	반창고
condoms	**k'ondom**	콘돔
contraceptives	**p'i-imyak**	피임약
cotton balls	**som**	솜
cough medicine	**kich'imyak**	기침약
gauze	**kŏjŭ**	거즈
laxatives	**chisaje**	지사제
painkillers	**chintongje**	진통제
sleeping pills	**sumyŏnje**	수면제

See the Shopping chapter page 151 for general toiletries.

AT THE DENTIST

치과에서

I have a toothache.
iga apayo;
ch'itong-i issŏyo

이가 아파요;
치통이 있어요.

I've lost a filling.
pong-i bajŏssŏyo;
daeun goshi dŏrŏjŏssŏyo

봉이 빠졌어요;
때운 곳이 떨어졌어요.

I've broken my tooth.
iga purŏjŏssŏyo

이가 부러졌어요.

My gums hurt.
inmomi ap'ayo

잇몸이 아파요.

I don't want it extracted.
bopji anassŭmyŏn
hanŭndeyo

뽑지 않았으면
하는데요.

Please give me an anaesthetic.
mach'wi haejuseyo

마취 해 주세요.

Ouch! That hurts.   **a! ap'ayo.**   아! 아파요.

SPECIFIC NEEDS

DISABLED TRAVELLERS 장애인 여행자

Korea as a whole is not an easy place for the disabled to get around, especially for those in wheelchairs, but things are improving rapidly. Newly built facilities, including the more recently built subway lines, offer wheelchair ramps and lift access exclusively for the physically disabled.

I'm disabled.
chŏn chang-aein indeyo 전 장애인인데요.

I need assistance.
toumi p'iryo haeyo 도움이 필요해요.

What services do you have
for disabled people?
chang-aeinŭl wihan 장애인을 위한
sŏbisŭ issŏyo? 서비스 있어요?

Is there wheelchair access?
hwilch'e-ŏ ch'uripkuga 휠체어 출입구가
issŏyo? 있어요?

I'm hard of hearing.
chŏn kwiga chal andŭllyŏyo 전 귀가 잘 안 들려요.

I have a hearing aid.
chŏn pochŏnggirŭl 전 보청기를
sayong haeyo 사용해요.

Speak more loudly, please.
chom tŏ kŭge 좀 더 크게
mal haejushillaeyo? 말해 주실래요?

Are guide dogs permitted?
maeng-in annaegyŏn 맹인 안내견
ch'urip kanŭng haeyo? 출입 가능해요?

Braille library	chŏmja tosŏgwan	점자도서관
disabled person	chang-ae in	장애인
guide dog	maeng-in annae gyŏn	맹인 안내견
sign language	suhwa	수화
wheelchair	hwil ch'e-ŏ	휠체어

GAY TRAVELLERS   동성애자 여행자

When it comes to attitudes towards homosexuality, Korea practically invented 'don't ask, don't tell'. Although most Koreans know that homosexuality exists in their country, they simply don't want to know about it. Especially for men, it generally doesn't matter what you do as long as you're discreet about it and you fulfil all your family obligations (such as getting married and giving your parents grandchildren).

For travellers, this means that Korea's gay scene is hard to find on your own. It's probably best to search the Internet for the location of gay and lesbian bars or clubs in the city where you're staying, and then go to that area and ask about the bar or club by name. For more information on gay and lesbian venues and organisations in Korea, see the various resources listed in the Korea and Seoul guides.

Where is (Club Nouveau)?
   (k'ŭllop nubo)ga/i   (클럽 누보)가/이
   ŏdi issŏyo?   어디있어요?
Are homosexuals likely to be harassed here?
   tongsŏngaejarŭl anjoŭn   동성애자를 안 좋은
   shigagŭro ponayo?   시각으로 보나요?

SPECIFIC NEEDS

TRAVELLING WITH THE FAMILY

가족과
여행하기

Travelling within Korea is a mixed bag for people with children. On the one hand, Korea's large population of families with children has led to an explosion in the number of family-oriented restaurants and recreational facilities. On the other hand, Western-style daycare facilities are virtually unknown, and even babysitters are hard to come by.

Are there facilities for babies?
agirŭl wihan shisŏri issŏyo?
아기를 위한 시설이 있어요?

Do you have a child-minding service?
agi pwajunŭn sŏbisŭ issŏyo?
아기 봐주는 서비스 있어요?

Where can I find a/an (English-speaking) babysitter?
(yŏng-ŏ hanŭn) agi pwajunŭnbun ŏdisŏ ch'ajŭlsu issŏyo?
(영어하는) 아기 봐주는 분 어디서 찾을 수 있어요?

Can you put an (extra) bed in the room?
pang-e ch'imdae (hana tŏ) nŏ-ŏjushilsu issŏyo?
방에 침대 (하나 더) 넣어 주실 수 있어요?

Can you put an (extra) cot/crib in the room?
pang-e agich'imdae (hana tŏ) nŏ-ŏjushilsu issŏyo?
방에 아기침대 (하나 더) 넣어 주실 수 있어요?

I need a car with a child seat.
agi chwasŏgi innŭn ch'aga issŭmyŏn hanŭndeyo
아기 좌석이 있는 차가 있으면 하는데요.

Is it suitable for children to do it?
agidŭri hagie chŏkchŏl haeyo?
아기들이 하기에 적절해요?

Is there a family discount?
kajok harin issŏyo?
가족 할인 있어요?

Are children allowed to go in?
ŏrini ipchang halsu issŏyo?
어린이 입장 할 수 있어요?

SPECIFIC NEEDS

Do you have a children's menu?
ŏrini menyu issŏyo?
어린이 메뉴있어요?

Are there any activities for children?
aidŭri chŭlgilsu innŭn hwaldong issŭlkkayo?
아이들이 즐길 수 있는 활동있을까요?

Is there a playground nearby?
chuwie norit'ŏ issŏyo?
주위에 놀이터있어요?

ON BUSINESS
비지니스

We are here for a ...	**chŏhinŭn ...e ch'amga harŏ wassŏyo**	저희는 ...에 참가하러 왔어요.
conference	**k'ŏnp'ŏrŏnsŭ/hoé-ŭi**	컨퍼런스/회의
meeting	**hoé-i**	회의
trade fair	**muyŏk pangnamhoé**	무역 박람회

I have an appointment with ...
...wa/gwa yaksogi innŭndeyo
...와/과 약속이 있는데요.

Here's my business card.
che myŏngham imnida
제 명함입니다.

I need an interpreter.
t'ongyŏksaga p'iryo handeyo
통역사가 필요한데요.

I'd like to use a computer.
k'ŏmp'yutŏrŭl ssŭgo ship'ŭndeyo
컴퓨터를 쓰고 싶은데요.

THANK YOU

In Korean, there are two common ways to say 'thank you': **komapsŭmnida** (고맙습니다) and **kamsa hamnida** (감사합니다). They're only different in their origin, the first one being 'pure' Korean, the second one 'Sino-Korean'.

Where can I plug in my laptop?
    **che not'ŭbugŭl yŏn-gyŏlhalsu
    innŭn goshi issŏyo?**
I'd like to send (a fax; an email).
    **(p'aeksŭrŭl/imeirŭl)
    ponaego ship'sŭmnida**

제 노트북을 연결할 수
있는 곳이 있어요?

(팩스를/이메일을)
보내고 싶습니다.

client	**kogaek**	고객
email	**imeil**	이메일
exhibition	**pangnamhoé**	박람회
manager	**maenijŏ/kyŏng-yŏngja**	매니저/경영자
mobile phone	**hyudaep'on/haendŭp'on**	휴대폰/핸드폰

TRACING ROOTS & HISTORY

뿌리찾기와
역사

Millions of ethnic Koreans live outside Korea, and many of them choose to come to Korea to visit relatives and see where their parents grew up. A large number of ethnic Koreans living overseas are adoptees, and many of them also come to trace their roots, if possible.

The 50th anniversary of the Korean War has led to renewed interest among veterans in visiting Korea.

(I think) my ancestors came
from this area.
    **(che saenggagenŭn) chŏhi
    chosang-i ijiyŏge
    issŏttŏn-gŏt kat'ayo**
I'm looking for my relatives.
    **che ch'inch'ŏgŭl
    ch'akko issŏyo**
I have/had a relative who
lives around here.
    **chŏn ijubyŏne
    sanŭn ch'inch'ŏgi
    issŏyo/issŏssŏyo**

(제 생각에는) 저희
조상이 이 지역에
있었던 것 같아요.

제 친척을
찾고 있어요.

전 이 주변에
사는 친척이
있어요/있었어요.

SPECIFIC NEEDS

Is there anyone here by
the name of ...?

    yŏgi ...ranŭn/iranŭn
    bun kyeseyo

여기 ...라는/이라는
분 계세요?

I'd like to go to the cemetery/
burial ground.

    myojie kago ship'ŏyo

묘지에 가고 싶어요.

I'm looking for my birth parents.

    saengbumorŭl ch'akko issŏyo

생부모를 찾고 있어요.

(I) was adopted from this agency.

    (chŏn) i ibyangdanch'erŭl
    t'onghaesŏ ibyang dwaessŏyo

(전) 이 입양단체를
통해서 입양 됐어요.

My Korean name is ...

    che han-gugirŭmŭn
    ...(i)eyo

제 한국이름은
...(이)에요.

My (father) fought/died (here)
in the Korean War.

    che (abŏjikkesŏnŭn)
    han-gukchŏnttae (yŏgisŏ)
    (ssaushŏssŏyo;
    chŏnsa hashŏssŏyo)

제 (아버지께서는)
한국전때 (여기서)
(싸우셨어요;
전사하셨어요).

My (grandmother) served
as a nurse (in Pusan) in the
Korean War.

    chŏhi (halmŏnikkesŏnŭn)
    han-gukchŏnttae (pusanesŏ)
    kanho irŭl hashŏssŏyo

저희 (할머니께서는)
한국전 때 (부산에서)
간호일을 하셨어요.

(My father) fought (here) in the
(Australian) armed forces.

    (chŏhi abŏjikkesŏnŭn)
    (hoju) mujangbudaero
    (yŏgisŏ) ssaushŏssŏyo

(저희 아버지께서는)
(호주) 무장부대로
(여기서) 싸우셨어요.

RELIGION

종교

South Korea is a country of great religious diversity and a high degree of religious tolerance. Most Koreans are Buddhist, Protestant or Catholic, though many practise no religion at all. The country's Buddhist temples are treasure troves of cultural value, and its early Christian cathedrals and churches are of historical importance. Seoul has a large mosque and an Eastern Orthodox church, but their members are mostly from the foreign community.

속리산

SPECIFIC NEEDS

What's your religion?
chonggyoga mwŏ-eyo?   종교가 뭐에요?

I'm (a/an) ...	**chŏn ... shinja-eyo**	전 … 신자에요.
Anglican	**yŏngguk sŏnggonghoé**	영국 성공회
Baptist	**ch´imnyegyo**	침례교
Buddhist	**pulgyo**	불교
Catholic	**ch´ŏnjugyo**	천주교
Christian	**kidokkyo**	기독교
Episcopalian	**kamdokkyo**	감독교
Hindu	**hindugyo**	힌두교
Jewish	**yut´aegyo**	유태교
Lutheran	**rut´ŏgyo**	루터교
Methodist	**kamnigyo**	감리교
Mormon	**morŭmon-gyo**	모르몬교
Muslim	**isŭllamgyo**	이슬람교
Presbyterian	**changnogyo**	장로교
Protestant	**kaeshin-gyo**	개신교
Unification Church member	**t´ong-ilgyo**	통일교
Zen Buddhist	**sŏnbulgyo**	선불교
Won Buddhist	**wonbulgyo**	원불교

I don't have any religion.
chŏn chonggyoga ŏpsŏyo   전 종교가 없어요.
I'm (Catholic), but not practising.
chŏn (ch´ŏnjugyo) indeyo,   전 (천주교)인데요,
kyŏhoénŭn chal annagayo   교회는 잘 안 나가요.
I'm an atheist.
chŏn mushinnonja-eyo   전 무신론자에요.
I'm agnostic.
chŏn pulgajironja-eyo   전 불가지론자에요.
Can I attend this service/mass?
chŏdo yebae-e/misa-e   저도 예배에/미사에
kado dwaeyo?   가도 돼요?

Can I pray here?
> **yŏgisŏ kido haedo dwaeyo?** 여기서 기도해도 돼요?

Where can I pray/worship?
> **ŏdisŏ kidohal/yebaehal** 어디서 기도할/예배할
> **su issŏyo?** 수 있어요?

Where can I make confession
(in English)?
> **ŏdisŏ (yŏng-ŏro)** 어디서 (영어로)
> **kohaesŏngsa polsu** 고해성사 볼 수
> **issŏyo?** 있어요?

Can I receive communion here?
> **yŏgisŏ yŏngsŏngch'e** 여기서 영성체
> **halsu innayo?** 할 수 있나요?

baptism/christening	seryeshik	세례식
church	kyohoé	교회
communion	yŏngsŏngch'e	영성체
confession	kohae-sŏngsa	고해성사
funeral	changnyeshik	장례식
God	hananim	하나님
god	shin	신
hermitage	amja	암자
minister (Protestant)	moksa	목사
monk (Buddhist)	sŭnim/sŭngnyŏ	스님/승려
monk (Catholic)	susa	수사
nun (Buddhist)	yŏsŭng	여승
nun (Catholic)	sunyŏ	수녀
prayer	kido	기도
priest (Catholic)	shinbu	신부
relic	sŏnggol	성골
sabbath	anshigil	안식일
saint	sŏng-in	성인
shaman	mudang	무당
shamanic exorcism	kut	굿
shamanism	musokshinang	무속신앙
shrine	sadang	사당
temple	chŏl	절

SPECIFIC NEEDS

CRYSTAL BALL GAZING

Although it's now done primarily for amusement, fortune-telling was at one time a big deal in Korea.

Fortune-tellers frequently set themselves up like street vendors in places where couples tend to congregate. For a proper reading, you need to know your **di** (띠), the animal symbol of the Chinese zodiac under which you were born and the hour of your birth (see page 138).

to get a reading for the ...	... pwayo	... 봐요
lines of the palm	sonkkŭm	손금
interpretation of a couple's compatibility	kunghap	궁합
personality interpretation through facial features	kwansang	관상
interpretation of one's fortune through 'four pillars' said to influence one's fate (the year, month, date and hour of one's birth)	saju	사주
connection between two people destined to meet	inyŏn	인연

수와 양

Two types of numbering systems are employed in Korea: the
first consists of pure Korean words for numbers, and the second
is made up of Sino-Korean numbers of Chinese origin, but
whose pronunciation has been 'Koreanised'.

CARDINAL NUMBERS
기수
Pure Korean Numbers
한글 숫자

Pure Korean numbers are used for expressing the hour when
telling time, for counting objects and for expressing your age.
They can only be written in Hangul or as digits, but not in
Chinese characters.

1	hana	하나	6	yŏsŏt	여섯
2	tul	둘	7	ilgop	일곱
3	set	셋	8	yŏdŏl	여덟
4	net	넷	9	ahop	아홉
5	tasŏt	다섯	10	yŏl	열

Numbers from 11 to 19 are made by combining **yŏl** (열) for ten
and the single digit numbers. Keep in mind that the pronunciation of some consonants may change when combining these
words (see Pronunciation, pages 20–24).

11	yŏlhana	열하나	16	yŏlyŏsŏt	열여섯
12	yŏldul	열둘	17	yŏrilgop	열일곱
13	yŏlset	열셋	18	yŏryŏdŏl	열여덟
14	yŏllet	열넷	19	yŏrahop	열아홉
15	yŏldasŏt	열다섯			

Numbers from 21 to 99 are made by combining the multiples of ten and a single digit number:

20	sŭmul	스물		40	mahŭn	마흔
21	sŭmulhana	스물하나		50	shwin	쉰
22	sŭmuldul	스물둘		60	yesun	예순
30	sŏrŭn	서른		70	irŭn	일흔
31	sŏrŭnhana	서른하나		80	yŏdŭn	여든
32	sŏrŭndul	서른둘		90	ahŭn	아흔

From 100 onwards, Sino-Korean numbers take over.

Sino-Korean Numbers

중국어에 기원을 둔 한글 숫자

Sino-Korean numbers are used to express minutes when telling the time, as well as dates and months of the year. They're also used to express amounts of money or floors of a building, and to represent numbers larger than 100. They may be written in Hangul, in digits or in Chinese characters. It's unlikely, however, that foreign visitors will need to know any Chinese characters beyond the first ten numbers, as – eg, in restaurants – the numbers beyond ten are almost never used.

Numeral	Pronunciation	Hangul	Chinese character
1	il	일	一
2	i	이	二
3	sam	삼	三
4	sa	사	四
5	o	오	五
6	yuk	육	六
7	ch'il	칠	七
8	p'al	팔	八
9	ku	구	九
10	ship	십	十
0	yŏng/kong	영/공	
the 9th floor	ku-ch'ŭng	구층	
$10	shiptallŏ	십달러	

Numbers from 11 to 19 are made by combining **ship** (십), 'ten', and the single digit numbers. Keep in mind that the pronunciation of the **p** changes to **b** when followed by a vowel (see Pronunciation, page 21).

11	shibil	십일
12	shibi	십이
13	shipsam	십삼
14	shipsa	십사
15	shibo	십오
16	shimnyuk	십육
17	shipch'il	십칠
18	shipp'al	십팔
19	shipku	십구

Multiples of ten are created by putting **ship** (십), 'ten' after the single digit numbers. Numbers from 21 to 99 are made by combining the multiples of ten (listed below) and the single digit numbers:

20	iship	이십
21	ishibil	이십일
22	ishibi	이십이
30	samship	삼십
31	samshibil	삼십일
32	samshibi	삼십이
40	saship	사십
50	oship	오십
60	yukship	육십
70	ch'ilship	칠십
80	p'alship	팔십
90	kuship	구십
100	paek	백

Multiples of 100 are created by putting **paek/baek** (백), '100', after the single digit numbers. More complex numbers are made by adding smaller numbers after them:

200	**ibaek**	이백
300	**sambaek**	삼백
400	**sabaek**	사백
250	**ibaegoship**	이백오십
257	**ibaegoshipch'il**	이백오십칠
999	**kubaek kushipku**	구백구십구
1000	**ch'ŏn**	천
10,000	**man**	만

COUNTING MARKERS 단위를 나타내는 명사

When describing how many of a certain item, you not only use the pure Korean number, but you add a specific marker used to count that item, to the number. For example, flat pieces of paper are counted using the counting marker **-jang** (-장):

- one piece of paper, etc
  hanjang 한 장
- two pieces of paper, etc
  tujang 두 장
- three pieces of paper, etc
  sejang 세 장

The number and the counting marker come after the noun being counted (noun + number + counting marker):

Two tickets, please.
    p'yo tujang juseyo 표 두 장 주세요.

Note that the pure Korean words for one to four (see page 209), are shortened when they're followed by another word:

one	**han-**	한–
two	**tu-**	두–
three	**se-**	세–
four	**ne-**	네–

COMMON COUNTING MARKERS

Examples of counting markers:

for most inanimate objects	-gae/kae	개
one (object)	han-gae	한 개
two (objects)	tugae	두 개
for people (very pol)	-bun	분
one (person)	hanbun	한 분
two (people)	tubun	두 분
for people (pol, inf)	-myŏng	명
one (person)	hanmyŏng	한 명
two (people)	tumyŏng	두 명

Examples of counting markers with nouns:

for animals	-mari	마리
two dogs	kae tumari	개 두 마리
for flat pieces of paper	-jang	장
two tickets	p'yo tujang	표 두 장
for cups or glasses	-jan	잔
two glasses of beer	maekchu tujan	맥주 두 잔
for books or notebooks	-gwŏn	권
two notebooks	kongchaek tugwŏn	공책 두 권
for bottles	-byŏng	병
two bottles of cola	k'olla tubyŏng	콜라 두 병
for cars	-dae	대
two minivans	ponggoch'a tugae	봉고차 두 대

When in doubt, it's acceptable for a non-native Korean speaker to simply use the counting marker for inanimate objects, **-kae/gae** (개), except when counting people.

ORDINAL NUMBERS   서수

Just as with cardinal numbers (see page 209), there are two systems in use for indicating rank.

Pure Korean Numbers   한글 숫자

The pure Korean method is to add -**pŏntchae/bŏntchae** (번째), to pure Korean numbers. Note, however, that '1st' is an exception:

1st	**chŏppŏntchae**	첫번째
	(not **han-bŏntchae**)	
2nd	**tubŏntchae**	두번째
3rd	**sebŏntchae**	세번째
4th	**nebŏntchae**	네번째
5th	**tasŏppŏntchae**	다섯번째

Sino-Korean   중국어에 기원을
Numbers   둔 한글 숫자

The Sino-Korean method is to precede a Sino-Korean number with the prefix **che-** (제):

1st	**cheil**	제일
2nd	**chei**	제이
3rd	**chesam**	제삼
4th	**chesa**	제사
5th	**cheo**	제오

FRACTIONS 분수

For fractions, you use Sino-Korean characters, but they're in reverse order from those in English. Three-fourths would be **sabune sam** (사분의 삼), meaning 'four-divide-e three'.

1/4	sabune il	사분의 일
1/3	sambune il	삼분의 일
3/4	sabune sam	사분의 삼

Note that there are two ways of expressing 'half':

a half	ibune il; ban	이분의 일; 반

When counting objects, 'half' comes after the counting marker:

two-and-a-half (objects)	tugae ban	두 개 반 (lit: two-**gae**-half)

USEFUL AMOUNTS
양의 표현하는 유용한 표현들

How much?	ŏlmank'ŭmi nayo?	얼만큼이나요?
How many?	myŏkkae nayo?	몇 개나요?

(just) a little	chogŭm	조금
double	tubae	두 배
enough ...	ch'ungbunhan ...	충분한 ...
a few	myŏkkae	몇개
less ...	tŏl ...	덜 ...
many; much; a lot	mani	많이
more ...	tŏ ...	더 ...
once	hanbŏn	한 번
some	yakkan	약간
ten times as much	yŏlbae mank'ŭm	열 배 만큼
too many	nŏmu manŭn	너무 많은
too much	nŏmu mani	너무 많이
triple	sebae	세 배
twice	tubŏn	두 번

WEIGHTS & MEASURES

a bottle of ...	...hanbyŏng	...한 병
a jar	hanbyŏng	한 병
a kilogram	ilk´illo	일킬로
half a kilogram of ...	... obaekkŭraem	... 오백그램
100 grams	paekkŭraem	백그램
a *kun*	han kŭn	한 근 (斤)
a litre	illitŏ	일리터
half a litre (500cc)	obaekshishi	오백씨씨
a packet	han mukkŭm;	한 묶음;
	handabal	한 다발
a pair	hanssang	한 쌍
a tin/can	hank´aen	한 캔
(5000 *won*) worth of ...	och´ŏnwŏn ŏch´i	5000원어치

A **kŭn** (근/斤) is a traditional measure for food, equal to 600g. When shopping in the market, particularly at the butcher's shop, this term is still quite common.

TIME, DATES & FESTIVALS

The Western (Gregorian) calendar, **yangnyŏk** (양력) is the standard used, but traditional holidays such as ch'usŏk (추석), Buddha's Birthday, and of course Lunar New Year, are all calculated according to the lunar calendar, **ŭmnyŏk** (음력). Korean calendars often have lunar dates printed in small numbers at the bottom of each day. Like the Gregorian calendar, the lunar calendar has 12 months. The lunar year starts in late January or in early February. Most Koreans know their birth date according to both calendars.

TELLING THE TIME   시간 말하기

To tell the time in Korean you'll need to use both the pure Korean and the Sino-Korean numbering systems (see Numbers & Amounts, page 209).

The hour is expressed with pure Korean numbers, followed by **-shi** (시), 'hour', and the minutes are expressed with Sino-Korean numbers, followed by **-pun/bun** (분), 'minutes'. The suffix **-ban** (-반), 'half', is used to indicate half past the hour. So **seshi** (세시 or 3시) is 'three o'clock' and **seshiban** (세시 반 or 3시 반) is 'half past three'.

It's ...

three o'clock	**seshiyo**	세시요
3:10	**seshi shippuniyo**	세시 십분이요
9:40	**ahopshi sashippuniyo**	아홉시 사십분이요
half past one	**hanshi samshippuniyo;**	한시 삼십분이요;
	hanshi ban-iyo	한시 반이요
quarter past one	**hanshi shibobuniyo**	한시 십오분이요
half past three	**seshi samshippuniyo;**	세시 삼십분이요;
	seshi baniyo	세시 반이요

(See Numbers & Amounts, page 215, for more information on the use of **ban**.)

TIME, DATES & FESTIVALS

ONE O'CLOCK YO

Remember to keep your speech polite and avoid offence by simply adding **-yo** (요) to your sentences – even when replying with only one word, for example, when telling the time.

What time is it?	**chigŭm myŏshieyo?**	지금 몇 시에요?
It's (one) o'clock.	**(han)shiyo**	(한)시요.
It's (10) o'clock.	**(yŏl)shiyo**	(열)시요.

To describe a time before the hour, as in '20 minutes to four', you add **-jŏn** (-전), 'before', to the number of minutes (in Sino-Korean numbers) before the hour:

It's ...

10 to three	**seshi shippunjŏniyo**	세시 십분 전이요
quarter to one	**hanshi shibobunjŏniyo**	한시 십오분 전이요
20 to one	**yŏldushi ishippunjŏniyo**	열두시 이십분 전이요

DAYS OF THE WEEK   ·요일

Korean and Japanese both use the same Chinese characters to represent the days of the week. Like their English counterparts, the days of the week have a special meaning. Starting with Sunday, they represent the sun, the moon, fire, water, trees, gold and land.

day	**il**	일	日
Sunday	**iryoil**	일요일	日曜日
Monday	**wŏryoil**	월요일	月曜日
Tuesday	**hwayoil**	화요일	火曜日
Wednesday	**suyoil**	수요일	水曜日
Thursday	**mogyoil**	목요일	木曜日
Friday	**kŭmyoil**	금요일	金曜日
Saturday	**t'oyoil**	토요일	土曜日

MONTHS 달

The word for each month is its corresponding Sino-Korean number, followed by **-wŏl** (월 or 月), the Sino-Korean word for 'moon/month'. The only exceptions are that **k** in **yuk** (육), 'six', and **p** in **ship** (십), '10', are dropped.

Lunar calendar dates use the same terminology, so Koreans may differentiate between the two by adding **yangnyŏguro** (양력으로), 'according to the Western calendar' or **ŭmnyŏguro** (음력으로), 'according to the lunar calendar'.

January	**irwŏl**	일월	July	**ch'irwŏl**	칠월
February	**iwŏl**	이월	August	**p'arwŏl**	팔월
March	**samwŏl**	삼월	September	**kuwŏl**	구월
April	**sawŏl**	사월	October	**shiwŏl**	시월
May	**owŏl**	오월	November	**shibirwŏl**	십일월
June	**yuwŏl**	유월	December	**shibiwŏl**	십이월

THE KOREAN CALENDAR 음력

The Korean calendar is divided into four seasons which are calculated according to solstices and equinoxes. Each season starts a few weeks earlier than its Western counterpart. Korean seasons are further subdivided into four phases, corresponding roughly to that season starting, rising, falling and then ending.

Seasons 계절

spring	**pom**	봄
summer	**yŏrŭm**	여름
autumn	**kaŭl**	가을
winter	**kyŏul**	겨울
summer solstice	**haji**	하지
winter solstice	**tongji**	동지
the arrival of spring	**ipch'un**	입춘
the arrival of summer	**ip'a**	입하
the arrival of autumn	**ipch'u**	입추
the arrival of winter	**iptong**	입동
rainy season	**changma**	장마

TIME, DATES & FESTIVALS

Dates
날짜

Dates use Sino-Korean numbers followed by -nyŏn (-년), -wŏl (월), and -il (일) to express the year, month and date, respectively. Dates are expressed from larger to smaller (ie, year, month, date).

What date is it today?
    onŭri myŏchirieyo?   오늘이 며칠이에요?
It's 13 October.
    shiwŏl shipsamiriyo   시월 십삼일이요.
It's 18 September 2003.
    ichŏnsamnyŏn,   이천삼년
    kuwŏl shipp'aririyo   구월 십팔일이요.
I was born in 1972.
    chŏnŭn   저는
    ch'on-gubaek ch'ilshibinyŏne   천구백칠십이년에
    t'ae-ŏnassŏyo   태어났어요.

COUNTING DAYS

Korean uses both a Sino-Korean and a pure Korean system of counting days. The first one is easy: you just combine Sino-Korean numbers with the Sino-Korean word for day, **il** (일).

one day	**iril**	일일
two days	**i-il**	이일
three days	**samil**	삼일
four days	**sail**	사일
five days	**oil**	오일
six days	**yugil**	육일

Pure Korean, however, has a special word for one day, two days, three days, etc. Chances are, though, that you won't encounter anything beyond three days.

one day	**haru**	하루
two days	**it'ŭl**	이틀
three days	**sahŭl**	사흘

TIME, DATES & FESTIVALS

Present 현재

now	chigǔm	지금
today	onǔl	오늘
this day	tang-il	당일
(used when buying tickets, for example)		
this week	ibǒnju	이번 주
this month	ibǒndal	이번 달
this year	ibǒnnyǒndo/	이번 년도;
	ibǒnhae	이번 해

Past 과거

yesterday	ǒje	어제
day before yesterday	kǔjǒkke	그저께
last week	chinanju	지난주
last month	chinandal/	지난달;
	chǒbǒndal	저번 달
last year	chinanhae/	지난해/
	changnyǒn	작년
a while ago	chogǔmjǒne	조금 전에

Future 미래

tomorrow	naeil	내일
day after tomorrow	more	모레
next week	taǔmju	다음 주
next month	taǔmdal	다음 달
next year	taǔmhae/naenyǒn	다음 해; 내년
later	najung-e/taǔme	나중에/다음에
until (June)	(yuwǒl)kkaji	(유월)까지

During the Day   하루 중에
| It's early. | illŏyo | 일러요. |
| It's late. | nŭjŏssŏyo | 늦었어요. |

afternoon	ohu	오후
day	nat	낮
early morning	saebyŏk	새벽
evening	chŏnyŏk/pam	저녁/밤
lunchtime	chŏmshim shigan	점심시간
midday	chŏng-o/hannat	정오/한낮
midnight	chajŏng	자정
morning	ach'im	아침
night	pam/chŏnyŏk	밤/저녁
noon	chŏng-o	정오
sunrise	haedoji/ilch'ul	해돋이/일출
sunset	ilmol	일몰
wee hours	irŭn saebyŏk	이른 새벽

NATIONAL HOLIDAYS   국경일
The holidays celebrated in Korea are a reflection of both its history and its religious diversity. Korea's Christians and non-Christians alike celebrate Jesus's birthday at Christmas, just as Buddhists and non-Buddhists enjoy the festivities of Buddha's Birthday in April or May. Korea's traditional religious practices are recognised in the celebration of **sŏllal** (설날), Lunar New Year, and **ch'usŏk** (추석), the autumn harvest commemoration, which are usually observed according to the traditional lunar calendar. Patriotic holidays honouring Korea's independence movement and its liberation from Japan are also important.

shinjŏng   신정
New Year's Day (1 January) is a day of making resolutions that you won't keep. Ringing in the new year at midnight is not traditional, but it has become popular lately. The ringing of the old bell at Chonggak Pavilion in downtown Seoul at midnight is Korea's traditional answer to the ball dropping in New York's Times Square. Fireworks follow.

kujŏng/sŏllal   구정/설날

The Lunar New Year is celebrated on the first day of the first lunar month, which falls between late January and early February. Lunar New Year is one of the two most important holidays in Korean culture, during which half of the country ventures to their ancestral hometown to pay respects to deceased forebears with a big feast.

samil-chŏl   삼일절

Independence Day or March 1st Movement Day on 1 March commemorates Korea's heroic struggle for independence against imperial Japanese rule.

shingmogil   식목일

Arbour Day on 5 April originated during Korea's post-war redevelopment, when the government sought to mobilise Koreans to reforest their country, which had been denuded of much of its trees during intense fuel shortages at the end of WWII and during the Korean War.

sŏkkat'anshinil   석가탄신일

Buddha's Birthday on the eighth day of the fourth lunar month (in April or May) is a great time to go and visit a local Buddhist temple, where prayer lanterns with lit candles inside offer hope to the faithful. Larger temples have twilight parades that wind through the neighbourhood.

ŏrininal   어린이날

Children's Day (5 May) is a holiday designed to remind parents that it's important to take time out for their kids. Any place where children would want to go, like amusement parks or zoos, is best avoided on this day.

hyŏnch'ung-il   현충일

The Memorial Day holiday on 6 June is intended to pay respects to the millions of Koreans who died during fighting to preserve Korea, especially during the Korean War and the Japanese occupation of Korea.

chehŏnjŏl   제헌절

The meaning of Constitution Day (17 July) is largely ignored by many citizens, who use it as a chance to head out to the beach or the mountains.

kwangbokchŏl   광복절

Korea's liberation from Japan on 15 August 1945, marked the end of four decades of brutal oppression. Liberation Day (15 August) is a holiday that evokes patriotism among many Koreans.

ch'usŏk   추석

The other of Korea's two most important holidays, **ch'usŏk** (추석), which is celebrated on the 15th day of the eighth lunar month (in September or October) is a day set aside to honour deceased ancestors in a ceremony called a **ch'arye** (차례), and to thank them for a good harvest. Like Lunar New Year, it involves tens of millions of people travelling to their hometowns to tend graves and offer a feast.

kaechŏnjŏl   개천절

Korea marks its legendary foundation in 2333 BC with National Foundation Day (3 October). Korea's mythical first king, Tan-gun, a semi-deity whose mother was a bear, came to earth on this day and founded the Old Choson dynasty.

k'ŭrisŭmasŭ   크리스마스

Christmas (25 December) is celebrated in Korea as a religious observance by Christians, and as a secular day of gift-giving by non-Christians. Beautiful displays of Christmas lights are strung up downtown and near major buildings, and are kept up until after Lunar New Year almost two months later.

FESTIVALS & CELEBRATIONS   축제와 축하

pallent´ain dei; hwaitŭ dei   발렌타인 데이/화이트 데이
As in the West, Valentine's Day (14 February) is celebrated with chocolate, candies and other gifts, but with a twist: women give presents to men on this day. Men, on the other hand, give gifts to the object of their affection one month later on White Day (14 March) celebrated only in Korea and Japan.

taeborŭm   대보름
This holiday marks the 15th day of the first month of the lunar calendar, the first full moon of the year. 'Moon viewing' or **talmaji** (달맞이) is a big activity, as many citizens head up to the hills to see the first full moon of the year.

pŏkkŏt ch´ukche   벚꽃 축제
Numerous cherry blossom festivals are held in April when the blooming **pŏkkŏt** (벚꽃), 'cherry blossoms', start appearing along the peninsula, starting in Cheju-do (Jeju-do) and working up towards Seoul. Many cities have festivals marking this period, with the most famous being at the port city of Chinhae, near Pusan (Busan). In Seoul, Yoido Island's Yunjung-no Avenue is a popular place to witness the splendour of these ephemeral whitish-pink blossoms.

puhwalchŏl   부활절
Korea's large Christian population observes the religious holiday of Easter (March or April) much the same as they do in the West.

mose-e kijŏk   모세의 기적
The unusual event of Moses' Miracle (timing varies) takes place on Chindo Island. Legend has it that a fisherman who was stranded on an offshore island prayed for a way off, and a super-low tide opened up a 2.8km-long land bridge about 40 metres wide between the mainland and the island. Thousands of visitors come to cross the bridge and collect seashells. Festivals include rites such as paying homage to the Dragon King, the god of the underwater world.

TIME, DATES & FESTIVALS

ŏbŏinal　어버이날

Although it's not an official holiday, Parents' Day on 8 May combines Mother's Day and Father's Day. Typically children give their parents a carnation.

sŭsŭng-enal　스승의 날

Demonstrating Korea's traditional respect for teachers, Teachers' Day (15 May) is a day on which students give flowers, ties or candies to their favourite educators. If you're teaching English while in Korea, your students may wish to take you out to dinner on this day.

pongnal　복날

The three **pongnal** days mark the beginning, middle and end of a scorchingly hot one-month period beginning around the 15th day of the seventh month of the lunar calendar.

hangŭllal　한글날

As part of Koreans' intense pride in the Hangul alphabet and their affection for its creator, Great King Sejong, Hangul Day on 9 October was a national holiday until recently. Koreans still commemorate this day by showcasing Korea's extremely high literacy rate and the usefulness of their homegrown alphabet.

birthday cake	**saeng-il k'eik'ŭ**	생일 케이크
to celebrate (an event)	**kinyŏm haeyo**	기념해요
to celebrate (in general)	**ch'uk'a haeyo**	축하해요
candles	**ch'o**	초
champagne	**shamp'ein**	샴페인
church	**kyohoé**	교회
to exchange gifts	**sŏnmurŭl**	선물을
	kyohwan haeyo	교환해요
gift	**sŏnmul**	선물
holiday	**hyuil**	휴일s
incense	**hyang**	향
party	**p'at'i**	파티
rice cake	**dŏk**	떡
seaweed soup	**miyŏkkuk**	미역국

CALENDAR COOKING

In traditional Korea, certain foods were to be eaten on certain days of the lunar calendar, especially on the 15th day of a lunar calendar month, which is always a full moon. A few of these are still observed:

dŏkkuk 떡국
soup containing doughy rice cakes, eaten on **sŏllal** (설날), to ensure you grow a year older

ogokpap 오곡밥
boiled rice mixed with four other grains (literally: five-grain rice), eaten on the night before **taeborŭm** (대보름)

kwibalgisul 귀밝이술
alcoholic drink supposed to improve hearing; should be drunk on **taeborŭm** (대보름)

samgyet´ang 삼계탕
boiled whole chicken stuffed with ginseng, eaten on **pongnal** (복날) in order to stay healthy and survive the hot weather

poshint´ang 보신탕
dog soup; also eaten on **pongnal** (복날) to maintain strenght and stamina during the hot days of late summer

songp´yŏn 송편
a half-moon-shaped rice cake stuffed with red bean paste and sesame seeds; eaten on **ch´usŏk** (추석)

miyŏkkuk 미역국
seaweed soup eaten on your birthday (according to the Western or lunar calendar)

BIRTHDAYS

생일

Koreans have a peculiar way of calculating age. When you're born, you're already one year old, and then you get another year older when New Year's Day rolls around. The result is that your **hangungnai** (한국 나이), 'Korean age', is usually one to two years older than your **man-nai** (만 나이), 'actual age'. Under-age kids sometimes try to take some advantage of this, but eligibility for drinking, obtaining a driving licence etc is determined by your actual age.

When's your birthday?
   saeng-iri ŏnje-eyo?   생일이 언제에요?
My birthday is on (13 October).
   che saeng-irŭn
   (shiwŏl) (shipsam)irieyo   제 생일은
   (10)월 (13)일이에요.
My Korean age is (30) years.
   che han-gungnainŭn
   (sŏrŭn)sarieyo   제 한국 나이는
   (30)살이에요.
My actual age is (28) years.
   che mannainŭn
   (sŭmuryŏdŏl)sarieyo   제 만 나이는
   (28)살이에요.

Congratulations!
   ch'uk'a haeyo!   축하해요!
Happy Birthday!
   saeng-il ch'uk'a haeyo!   생일 축하해요!
Many happy returns!
   nŭl haengbok haseyo!   늘 행복하세요!
Blow out the candles!
   ch'oppurŭl gŭseyo!   촛불을 끄세요!

CHRISTMAS & NEW YEAR   크리스마스와 새해

Christmas traditions of gift-giving are starting to take hold in Korea. However, Koreans don't sit down to a special feast as they do in Western countries.

New Year's Day traditions are observed on both Western and Lunar New Years (see also pages 222-223). Traditionally, young people bow to their elders to show respect, and in return they receive money and accolades. So special is this tradition that there are specific words for the bowing, **sebae** (세배) and the blessing and advice that come in response, **tŏktam** (덕담). Many Korean Christians go to church on New Year's Eve to pray in the new year.

Christmas Day	k'ŭrisŭmasŭ	크리스마스
Christmas Eve	k'ŭrisŭmasŭ ibŭ	크리스마스 이브
New Year's Eve	shibiwŏl samshibiril/ saehaejŏnnal	12월 31일/ 새해 전날
New Year's Day (lunar calendar)	sŏllal/kujŏng	설날/구정
New Year's Day (Western calendar)	shinjŏng	신정

Happy Christmas! **meri k'ŭrisŭmasŭ!**	메리 크리스마스!
Happy New Year! (to someone older) **saehaebong mani padŭseyo!**	새해 복 많이 받으세요.
(to someone of the same age or younger) **saehaebong mani pada!**	새해 복 많이 받아.

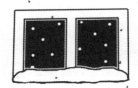
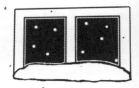

CHRISTENINGS & WEDDINGS   세례와 결혼

Catholics make up about 10% of the South Korean population, but christening is not a major part of Korean culture. In spite of the fact that Catholics and Protestants represent around 40% of the Korean population, church weddings are rare. Koreans tend to get married in wedding halls – gaudy commercial establishments that have all the charm of a chapel in Las Vegas. The couple is often herded in and out very quickly to make room for the next paying couple.

baptism/christening	**seryeshik**	세례식
bride	**shinbu**	신부
christened name	**seryemyŏng**	세례명
(Christian name)		
engagement	**yak'on**	약혼
groom	**shillang**	신랑
honeymoon	**shinhon yŏhaeng**	신혼여행
wedding	**kyŏron**	결혼
wedding anniversary	**kyŏron kinyŏmil**	결혼기념일
wedding cake	**kyŏron k'eik'ŭ;**	결혼 케이크;
	weding k'eik'ŭ	웨딩 케이크
wedding present	**kyŏron sŏnmul**	결혼 선물

TOASTS & CONDOLENCES   축배와 애도의 말

Like everyone else, Koreans like to make toasts when they celebrate over a glass or bottle of alcohol. Long speeches often end with a wish for good health or camaraderie.

Cheers!	**kŏnbae!**	건배!
To ...!	**...rŭl/ŭl wi hayŏ!**	...를/을 위하여!
Good luck!	**haeng-unŭl pirŏyo!**	행운을 빌어요!
Hope it goes well!	**chal doégil pirŏyo!**	잘 되길 빌어요!

Sickness   병

Saying 'bless you' to someone who has sneezed is simply not done in Korea. In fact, Koreans might even laugh at the person who sneezed, if it looks or sounds sufficiently amusing. But if someone is sick, Koreans will show their concern with words and favours, while pleading for you to get better quickly.

Get well soon.
balli naŭshŏya dwaeyo   빨리 나으셔야 돼요.

Death   죽음

Korean wakes are often held in the hospital where a person passes away. As in the West, a kind word at a time of loss is greatly appreciated.

I'm very sorry.
chŏngmal yugam imnida   정말 유감입니다.
My thoughts are with you.
myŏngbogŭl pimnida   명복을 빕니다.

Korea doesn't have any particular dangers such as poisonous snakes or plants. Shark attacks are extremely rare, and beaches are generally safe. Erratic traffic – including deliverymen driving their scooters on the pavements – is probably the biggest hazard you'll encounter. North Korean soldiers occasionally sneak into the south through the rugged mountain regions of northern Kangwon-do (Gangwon-do) and Kyonggi-do (Gyeonggi-do) provinces. The South Korean Government has set up many small military installations in these provinces, especially in areas close to the DMZ, as well as on mountain tops and other strategic locations throughout the country. You should steer clear of these areas and heed any warnings of military personnel.

GENERAL

일반적인 표현

Fire!	puriya!	불이야!
Go away!	chŏri kaseyo!	저리 가세요!
Stop!	kŭman haseyo!	그만하세요!
Thief!	todugiya!	도둑이야!
Watch out!	choshim haeyo!	조심해요!

Help! (in life-threatening situations)
　towa juseyo!　　　　　　　　　　　도와 주세요!

Help! (in other situations)
　chom towa jushillaeyo?　　　　　　좀 도와 주실래요?

It's an emergency.
　aju kŭp'an irieyo　　　　　　　　　아주 급한 일이에요;
　pisang sat'ae-eyo　　　　　　　　　비상 사태에요.

Could you help us please?
　chebal towa jushillaeyo?　　　　　　제발 도와 주실래요?

Could I please use the telephone?
chŏnhwa chom ssŭrkkeyo   전화 좀 쓸게요.

I'm lost.
kirŭl irŏssŏyo   길을 잃었어요.

Where are the toilets?
**hwajangshiri ŏdie   화장실이 어디에
issŏyo?**   있어요?

Is this area off limits?
**yŏgi ch'urip-kŭmji   여기 출입금지
kuyŏgi-eyo?**   구역이에요?

We're sorry, but we didn't know
this area was off limits.
**ch'urip kŭmji   출입금지
kuyŏginji mollassŏyo.   구역인지 몰랐어요.
choésong hamnida**   죄송합니다.

Are North Korean infiltrators
possibly in this area?
**ijiyŏge puk'an kanch'ŏbi   이 지역에 북한 간첩이
issŭlsudo issŏyo?**   있을 수도 있어요?

---

military installation   **minbang-wi hullyŏn**   민방위 훈련

DEALING WITH   경찰과 대화하기
THE POLICE

The Korean Government has been making an effort to improve
English skills among public servants, including the police force.
Nevertheless, most police have only rudimentary English. In a
bind, you could call the taxi interpreting service – the number
can be found in any urban taxi – and get help.

police substation   **p'achulso**   파출소
police box   **pangbŏm-ch'oso**   방범초소

Call the police!
kyŏngch'al pullŏjuseyo!   경찰 불러 주세요!

Where's the police station?
    kyŏngch'alsŏga ŏdi issŏyo?   경찰서가 어디있어요?
We want to report an offence.
    shin-go haryŏgo hanŭndeyo   신고하려고 하는데요.
I've been assaulted.
    p'ok'aeng dang haessŭmnida   폭행당했습니다.
I've been raped.
    kanggan dang haessŭmnida   강간당했습니다.
I've been robbed.
    toduk majassŭmnida   도둑 맞았습니다.
My room has been burgled.
    chebang-e todugi   제 방에 도둑이
    dŭrŏ-on-gŏt katsŭmnida   들어온 것 같습니다.

My ... was/were stolen.	...rŭl/ŭl toduk majassŏyo	...를/을 도둑 맞았어요.
backpack	**paenang**	배낭
bags	**kabang**	가방
camera	**k'amera**	카메라
handbag	**haendŭbaek**	핸드백
money	**ton**	돈
papers/documents	**sŏryu**	서류
travellers cheques	**yŏhaengja sup'yo**	여행자 수표
passport	**yŏkwŏn**	여권
wallet	**chigap**	지갑

My possessions are insured.
    chŏn pohŏme tŭrŏssŏyo   전 보험에 들었어요.

Korean police are generally willing to give extra leeway to foreign residents and visitors, but not if they cop an attitude. Apologising, expressing regret for one's actions, and/or admitting fault is often a quick way to end a sticky situation, because the injured party is often only looking for face-saving satisfaction that he or she was wronged.

EMERGENCIES

I'm sorry; I apologise.
   choésong hamnida;
   sagwa dŭrimnida.

죄송합니다;
사과드립니다.

I didn't realise I was doing
anything illegal.
   chŏn kŭge pulbŏbinji
   mollassŭmnida

전 그게 불법인지
몰랐습니다.

I didn't do it.
   chŏn kŭrŏke
   anhaessŭmnida

전 그렇게
안 했습니다.

We're innocent.
   chŏhinŭn amu
   chalmoshi ŏpsŭmnida

저희는 아무
잘못이 없습니다.

We're foreigners.
   urin oégugin imnida

우린 외국인입니다.

Is there a fine we can pay
to clear this?
   pŏlgŭmŭl naemyŏn
   doémnikka?

벌금을 내면
됩니까?

Is there someone here who
speaks English?
   yŏng-ŏ hashinŭnbun kyeseyo?

영어하시는 분 계세요?

I want to contact my
embassy/consulate.
   che taesagwane/yŏngsagwane
   yŏllak hago shipsŭmnida

제 대사관에/영사관에
연락하고 싶습니다.

Can I call someone?
   chŏnhwa chom ssŏdo
   doégessŭmnikka?

전화 좀 써도
되겠습니까?

Can I have a lawyer who
speaks English?
   yŏng-ŏ hanŭn pyŏnhosa
   kuhalsu issŭmnikka?

영어하는 변호사
구할 수 있습니까?

I understand.
   ihae hamnida

이해합니다.

I don't understand.
    ihaega an-gamnida 이해가 안 갑니다.
What am I accused of?
    chega musŭn iyuro 제가 무슨 이유로
    kobal tanghanŭn gŏmnikka? 고발당하는 겁니까?

THEY MAY SAY ...

tangshin-ŭn/kŭnun/kŭnyŏnŭn 당신은/그는/그녀는
...ro/ŭro ...로/으로
koso-doél-gŏmnida 고소될 겁니다.
    You'll/He'll/She'll be
    charged with ...

panjŏngbu	반정부	anti-government
haeng-wi	행위	activity
p´ok´aeng	폭행	assault
shiwi	시위	demonstrating
ŭmju unjŏn	음주 운전	drink driving
pŏlgŭm minap	벌금 미납	failure to pay fine
mugi sojijoé	무기소지죄	possession of weapon
pulbŏp ch´imip	불법 침입	illegal entry
sarin	살인	murder
pulbŏp ch´eryu	불법 체류	overstaying your visa
chuch´a wiban	주차 위반	parking violation
kukka poanbŏp wiban	국가 보안법 위반	violation of national security
kanggan	강간	rape
chŏltto	절도	theft/shoplifting
kyot´ong wiban	교통 위반	traffic violation
pulbŏmnodong	불법 노동	working without a permit

EMERGENCIES

arrest	ch'epo	체포
consulate	yŏngsagwan	영사관
embassy	taesagwan	대사관
fine (payment)	pŏlgŭm	벌금
guilty	yujoé	유죄
lawyer	pyŏnhosa	변호사
military police	hŏnbyŏng	헌병
not guilty	mujoé	무죄
police officer	kyŏngch'algwan	경찰관
police station	kyŏngch'alsŏ	경찰서
prison	kyodoso	교도소
trial	chaep'an	재판

HEALTH

건강

Call a doctor!
ŭisa pullŏjuseyo!
의사 불러 주세요!

Call an ambulance!
aembyullŏnsŭ pullŏjuseyo!
앰블런스 불러 주세요!

I'm ill.
chŏn ap'ayo.
전 아파요.

My friend is ill.
che ch'in-guga ap'ayo
제 친구가 아파요.

This is a life-threatening situation.
ch'imyŏngjŏgilsudo innŭn sanghwang-ieyo
치명적일 수도 있는 상황이에요.

I have foreign medical insurance.
oéguk ŭiryo bohŏmi innŭndeyo
외국 의료보험이 있는데요.

I have Korean national medical insurance.
han-guk ŭiryo bohŏmi innŭndeyo
한국 의료보험이 있는데요.

EMERGENCIES

ENGLISH – KOREAN DICTIONARY

In this dictionary, the following notation applies in regard to parts of speech:

Nouns are not indicated unless they can be mistaken for adjectives, in which case they're followed by (n). Likewise, adjectives are only followed by (adj) when their use can be mistaken for a noun. Verbs are preceded by 'to'. This serves to distinguish a verb from its noun counterpart, eg, 'to answer' versus 'answer'. The verbs are displayed in their polite form (ending in **-yo**). The verb stem (see Grammar page 38) is in parentheses after the verb in Hangul (Korean) only, not in the transliterations.

- **bullet points**

are used in the dictionary only (in transliteration and Hangul) to separate different alternatives (synonyms) in the foreign language:

baggage claim	**chim channŭn-got •**	짐 찾는 곳 •
	suhamul ch'annŭn-got	수하물 찾는 곳

If it's necessary to clarify the difference between alternatives, this is indicated in parentheses after each.

/ forward slash

indicates when single words on either side of the slash are interchangeable:

Can we camp here?
yŏgisŏ k'aemp'ŭ/yayŏng haedo dwaeyo?
여기서 캠프/야영 해도 돼요?

denotes:

Can we camp here?
yŏgisŏ k'aemp'ŭ haedo dwaeyo?
여기서 캠프 해도 돼요?

or

Can we camp here?
yŏgisŏ yayŏng haedo dwaeyo?
여기서 야영 해도 돼요?

A

to be able	**halsu issŏyo**	할 수 있어요 (할 수 있~)

I can't do it.
chŏn kŭgŏt mot'aeyo
전 그것 못해요.

We can do it.
urin halsu issŏyo
우린 할 수 있어요.

abortion	**nakt'ae**	낙태
above	**wie**	위에
abroad	**oeguge**	외국에
to accept	**padadŭryŏyo**	받아들여요 (받아들이~)
accident	**sago**	사고
accommodation	**sukpak**	숙박

across	majǔnp'yǒne	맞은편에
acupuncture	ch'im	침
adaptor	ǒdaept'ǒ	어댑터
addiction	chungdok	중독
address	chuso	주소
admission (to enter)	ipchangnyo	입장료
to admit	hǒrak haeyo	허락해요 (허락하~)
adopted parent	yangbumo	양부모
adoptee	yangja	양자
adult	sǒng-in	성인
advice	cho-ǒn • ch'unggo	조언 • 충고
aerobics	eǒrobik	에어로빅
aeroplane	pihaenggi	비행기
to be afraid	musǒwǒyo	무서워요
to be afraid of	musǒwǒhaeyo	무서워해요 (무서워하~)
after	twie	뒤에
afternoon	ohu	오후
again	tashi hanbǒn	다시 한번
to be against …	…e pandae haeyo	…에 반대해요
age (inf)	nai	나이
age (pol)	yǒnse	연세
to agree	tong-i haeyo	동의해요 (동의하~)

I don't agree.
chǒn k'ǔrǒke saenggak anhaeyo
전 그렇게 생각 안 해요.

agriculture	nong-ǒp • nongsa	농업 • 농사
ahead	ap'e	앞에
aid (help)	toum	도움
AIDS	eiju	에이즈
air (for car tyre)	e-ǒ	에어
air-conditioned	naengbangjung-in	냉방중인
air mail	hanggong up'yǒn	항공우편
airport	konghang	공항
airport tax	konghangse	공항세
alarm clock	allam shigye	알람시계
all	modu	모두
allergy	allerǔgi	알레르기
to allow	hǒrak haeyo	허락해요 (허락하~)
almost	kǒi	거의
alone	hollo	홀로
already	pǒlssǒ • imi	벌써 • 이미
also	dohan	또한
altitude	kodo	고도
always	ǒnjena	언제나
amateur	amach'uǒ	아마추어
ambassador	taesa	대사
American (person)	migugin • miguksaram	미국인 • 미국사람
among …	… chung-esǒ	… 중에서

amusement park	yuwonji	유원지
anaemia	pinhyŏl	빈혈
ancient	kodae-ŭi	고대의
and	kŭrigo	그리고
angry	hwanan	화난
to be angry	hwanassŏyo	화났어요 (화나~)
animals	tongmul	동물
animation	aenimeishŏn	애니메이션
annual	haemada-e	해마다의
to answer	taedap haeyo	대답해요 (대답하~)
antenna	ant'ena	안테나
antibiotics	hangsaengje	항생제
antiques	koldongp'um	골동품
antiseptic	sodong-yak	소독약
any	ŏnŭ gŏshina	어느 것이나
apartment	apat'ŭ	아파트
appendicitis	maengjang-yŏm	맹장염
appointment	yaksok	약속
archery	yanggung	양궁
architect	kŏnch'ukka	건축가
architecture	kŏnch'uk	건축
to argue	nonjaeng haeyo	논쟁해요 (논쟁하~)
arrest	ch'epo	체포
arrivals	toch'ak	도착
to arrive	toch'ak haeyo	도착해요 (도착하~)
art	misul	미술
art gallery (museum)	misulgwan	미술관
artwork	misul chakp'um	미술작품
to ask (a question)	murŏbwayo	물어봐요 (물어보~)
to ask (for something)	put'ak haeyo	부탁해요 (부탁하~)
aspirin	asŭp'irin	아스피린
assault	p'ok'aeng	폭행
asthma	ch'ŏnshik	천식
athletics	yuksang	육상
atmosphere	taegi	대기
aunt	ajumŏni	아주머니
Australia	hoju	호주
Australian (person)	hojuin • hojusaram	호주인 • 호주사람
automatic teller machine (ATM)	hyŏn-gŭm chigŭpki	현금지급기
autumn	kaŭl	가을
awful	hyŏngp'yŏn ŏmnŭn	형편 없는

B

baby	agi	아기
baby food	yuashik	유아식
baby powder	peibi p'audŏ	베이비 파우더
babysitter	ai tolponŭn saram	아이 돌보는 사람

backpack	paenang	배낭
bad	nappŭn	나쁜
bag	kabang	가방
baggage	chim • suhamul	짐 • 수하물
baggage claim	chim channŭn-got •	짐 찾는 곳 •
	suhamul ch'annŭn-got	수하물 찾는 곳
bakery	bangjip • beik'ŏri	빵집 • 베이커리
balcony	balk'oni	발코니
ball	kong	공
ballet	balle	발레
band (music)	kŭrup	그룹
bandage	pungdae	붕대
Band-Aid(s)	panch'anggo	반창고
bank	ŭnhaeng	은행

Where is the bank?
ŭnhaeng-i ŏdi issŏyo?
은행이 어디있어요?

banknotes	sup'yo	수표
baptism	seryeshik	세례식
bar	sulchip • ba	술집 • 바
bar with music	myujik ba	뮤직 바
barber shop	ibalso	이발소
baseball	yagu	야구
basket	paguni	바구니
basketball	nonggu	농구
bath	mogyok	목욕
bathing suit	suyŏngbok	수영복
bathroom	yokshil	욕실
batteries	baet'ŏri	배터리
to be	(i)eyo	(이)에요 (이~)
beach	haesuyokchang •	해수욕장 •
	haebyŏn	해변
beautiful	arŭmdaun	아름다운
because	waenya hamyŏn	왜냐하면
bed	ch'imdae	침대
bedroom	ch'imsul	침실
beef	soégogi	쇠고기
beer	maekchu	맥주
before	chŏne	전에
beggar	kŏji	거지
to begin	shijak haeyo	시작해요 (시작하~)
behind ...	... dwie	... 뒤에
below ...	... arae	... 아래
beside ...	... yŏp'e	... 옆에
best	ch'oégo-e	최고의
bet	ton-gŏlgi	돈 걸기
to bet	naegihaeyo •	내기해요 (내기하~) •
	ton-gŏrŏyo	돈 걸어요 (돈 걸~)

ENGLISH – KOREAN DICTIONARY

better	tŏ naŭn	더 나은
between	saie	사이에
bib	t'ŏkpaji	턱받이
Bible	sŏnggyŏng	성경
bicycle	chajŏn-gŏ	자전거
bicycle path	chajŏn-gŏ doro	자전거 도로
big	k'ŭn	큰
bill (account)	kyesansŏ	계산서
binoculars	ssang-an-gyŏng	쌍안경
biodegradable	saengbunhaesŏng-e	생분해성의
bird	sae	새
birth certificate	ch'ulsaengjŭngmyŏngsŏ	출생증명서
birthday	saeng-il	생일
birthday cake	saeng-il k'eik'ŭ	생일 케이크
bite (insect, mammal)	mullim	물림
black	kŏmŭn	검은
B&W film	hŭkpaek p'illŭm	흑백 필름
blanket	tamnyo	담요
to bleed	p'iga nayo	피가 나요 (피가 나~)
to bless	ch'ukpok haeyo	축복해요 (축복하~)
blind	nunmŏn • changnime	눈 먼 • 장님의
blister	mulchip	물집
blood	hyŏraek	혈액
blood pressure	hyŏrap	혈압
blood test	hyŏraek kŏmsa	혈액 검사
blood type	hyŏraek hyŏng	혈액형
blue	p'aran	파란
to board (ship, etc)	t'ayo	타요 (타~)
boarding house	hasukchip	하숙집
boarding pass	t'apsŭnggwŏn	탑승권
boat	pae	배
body	mom	몸
boiled water	gŭrin mul	끓인 물

> Bon voyage!
> **chŭlgŏun yŏhaeng dóeseyo!**
> 즐거운 여행 되세요!

bone	pyŏ	뼈
to book	yeyak haeyo	예약해요 (예약하~)
book	ch'aek	책
bookshop	sŏjŏm	서점
boots	puch'ŭ	부츠
border	kukkyŏng	국경
bored	shimshimhan	심심한
boring	chiruhan •	지루한 •
	chaemi ŏmnŭn	재미없는
to borrow	pillyŏyo	빌려요 (빌리~)
both	tulda	둘 다
bottle	pyŏng	병

bottle opener	pyŏngttagae	병따개
at the bottom	padage	바닥에
box	sangja	상자
boxing	kwŏnt'u	권투
boy	namja ai	남자아이
boyfriend	namja ch'in-gu	남자친구
braces	kyojŏnggi •	교정기 •
	ch'iyŏl kyojŏnggi	치열교정기
Braille library	chŏmja tosŏgwan	점자도서관
brakes	bŭreik'ŭ	브레이크
branch	kaji	가지
brave	yonggamhan	용감한
bread	bang	빵
to break	puswŏyo	부숴요 (부수~)
breakfast	ach'im	아침
to breathe	sumshiŏyo	숨쉬어요 (숨쉬~)
bribe	noémul	뇌물
to bribe	noémul jwŏyo	뇌물 줘요 (뇌물 주~)
bride	shinbu	신부
bridge	tari	다리
to bring	kajigowayo	가지고 와요 (가지고 오~)
broken (in pieces)	pusŏjin	부서진
broken (out of order)	kojangnan	고장난
bronchitis	kigwanjiyŏm	기관지염
brother	hyŏngje	형제
brown	kalsaege	갈색의
bruise	mŏng	멍
bucket	yangdong-i	양동이
Buddha statues	pulsang	불상
Buddhist (adj)	pulgyo-e	불교의
Buddhist (n)	pulgyo shinja	불교 신자
bug	pŏlle	벌레
to build	chiŏyo	지어요 (짓~)
building	bilding	빌딩
bunker	pŏngk'ŏ	벙커
bus	bŏsŭ	버스
bus-only lane	bŏsŭ chŏnyongsŏn	버스전용선
bus station	bŏsŭ t'ŏminŏl	버스 터미널
bus stop	bŏsŭ chŏngnyujang	버스 정류장
business	saŏp • bijinisŭ	사업 • 비지니스
businessperson	saŏpka	사업가
busker	kŏri kong-yŏn-ga	거리 공연가
busy (person)	pappŭn	바쁜
busy (phone)	t'onghwajung	통화중
but	hajiman	하지만
butane (for stove)	put'an gasŭ	부탄가스
butter	bŏt'ŏ	버터
to buy	sayo	사요 (사~)

ENGLISH – KOREAN DICTIONARY

I'd like to buy ...
... rŭl/ŭl saryŏgo hanŭndeyo
...를/을 사려고 하는데요.

C

cable TV	k'eibŭl t'ibi	케이블 티비
cafe	k'ŏp'i shop	커피숍
calendar	tallyŏk	달력
camera	k'amera	카메라
camera shop	k'amera kage	카메라 가게
to camp	k'aemp'ŭ haeyo •	캠프해요 (캠프하~) •
	yayŏng haeyo	야영해요 (야영하~)

Can we camp here?
yŏgisŏ k'aemp'ŭ/yayŏng haedo dwaeyo?
여기서 캠프/야영 해도 돼요?

camping	k'aemp'ŭ • yayŏng	캠프 • 야영
camp site	k'aemp'ŭjang •	캠프장 •
	yayŏngjang	야영장
can (cannister)	k'aen	캔
can opener	k'aenttagae	캔 따개
Canada	k'aenada	캐나다
Canadian (n)	k'aenada-in •	캐나다인 •
	k'aenadasaram	캐나다사람
to cancel	ch'wiso haeyo	취소해요 (취소하~)
cancer	am	암
candle	ch'o	초
car	ch'a	차
car registration	chadongch'a	자동차
	dŭngnokchŭng	등록증
card	k'adŭ	카드
card games	k'adŭnori	카드놀이
to care (about)	shin-gyŏng ssŏyo	신경써요 (신경쓰~)
to care (for someone)	akkyŏyo	아껴요 (아끼~)
to carry	nallŏyo	날라요 (나르~)
cartoons	manhwa	만화
cash (money)	hyŏn-gŭm • ton	현금 • 돈
cashier	hoégyewŏn	회계원
cash register	kŭmjŏn dŭngnokki	금전 등록기
cassette	k'aset'ŭ	카세트
castle	sŏng	성
cat	koyang-i	고양이
cathedral	sŏngdang	성당
Catholic (n)	ch'ŏnjugyo shinja	천주교 신자
cave	tonggul	동굴
cell phone	hyudaep'on • haendŭp'on	휴대폰 • 핸드폰
centimetre	sent'imit'ŏ	센티미터
ceramic ware	tojagi	도자기

cereal (breakfast)	siriŏl	시리얼
certificate	chŭngmyŏngsŏ	증명서
chair	ŭija	의자
champagne	shamp'ein	샴페인
championships	sŏnsugwŏndaehoé	선수권대회
chance	kihoé	기회
change (coins)	chandon • kŏsŭrŭm ton	잔돈 • 거스름 돈
to change	pakkwŏyo	바꿔요 (바꾸~)
changing rooms	t'arishil	탈의실
channel	ch'aenŏl	채널
cheap	ssan	싼
to cheat	sogyŏyo	속여요 (속이~)
to check	chŏmgŏm haeyo	점검해요 (점검하~)
check-in (hotel)	ch'ek'ŭ-in	체크 인
check-out (hotel)	ch'ek'ŭ-aut	체크 아웃

Cheers!
kŏnbae!
건배!

cheese	ch'iju	치즈
chef	yorisa	요리사
chemist (pharmacist)	yaksa	약사
chemist (pharmacy)	yakkuk	약국
cheque (money order)	sup'yo	수표
cherry blossom	pŏkkot	벚꽃
cherry blossom festival	pŏkkŏt ch'ukche	벚꽃 축제
chess	ch'esŭ	체스
chicken	tak	닭
chicken meat	takkogi	닭고기
child (children)	ŏrini	어린이
child minding	aidolbogi	아이 돌보기
children	chanyŏ	자녀
child's fare	ŏrinip'yo	어린이표
chiropractor	ch'ŏkch'u chiapsa	척추 지압사
chocolate	ch'ok'ollit	초콜릿
to choose	sŏnt'aek haeyo	선택해요 (선택하~)
christening (baptism)	seryeshik	세례식
Christmas Day	k'ŭrisŭmasŭ	크리스마스
Christmas Eve	k'ŭrisŭmasŭ ibŭ	크리스마스 이브
church	kyohoé	교회
cigarettes	tambae	담배
cigars	siga	시가
cinema	kŭkchang • yŏnghwagwan	극장 • 영화관
circus	sŏk'ŏsŭ	서커스
citizenship	shiminkkwŏn	시민권
city	toshi	도시
city centre (downtown)	shinae	시내
city walls	sŏnggwak	성곽
class (school)	suŏp	수업

class (social)	kyegŭp	계급
class system	kyegŭp chedo	계급제도
clean	gaekkŭt'an	깨끗한
cleaning	ch'ŏngso	청소
client	kogaek	고객
cliff	chŏlbyŏk	절벽
to climb	ollayo •	올라요 (오르~) •
	tŭngsan haeyo	등산해요 (등산하~)
cloakroom	oét'u bogwanso	외투 보관소
clock	shigye	시계
close	kakkaun	가까운
to close	tadayo	닫아요 (닫~)
closed (business)	yŏng-ŏp anhamnida	영업 안 합니다
clothing	ot	옷
clothing store	okkage	옷가게
cloud	kurŭm	구름
cloudy	kurŭmi manŭn	구름이 많은
clutch	k'ŭllŏch'i	클러치
coast	haean	해안
coat	k'ot'ŭ	코트
cockroach	pak'wibŏlle	바퀴벌레
cocktail	k'akt'eil	칵테일
codeine	k'odein	코데인
coffee	k'ŏp'i	커피
coins	tongjŏn	동전
cold (flu)	kamgi	감기

I've caught a cold.
kamgi kŏllyŏssŏyo
감기 걸렸어요.

cold (temperature)	ch'agaun	차가운
cold (weather)	ch'u-un	추운
to be cold	ch'uwŏyo	추워요 (춥~)

It's cold.
ch'uwŏyo
추워요.

cold water	naengsu	냉수
colleague	tongnyo	동료
college	taehak	대학
colour	saekkal	색깔
colour film	k'ŏllŏ p'illŭm	컬러 필름
comb	pit	빗
to come	toch'ak haeyo •	도착해요 (도착하~) •
	wayo	와요 (오~)
comedy	k'omedi	코메디
comfortable	p'yŏnanhan	편안한
comics	manhwa	만화
communion	yŏngsŏngch'e	영성체

communism	kongsanjui	공산주의
communist (n)	kongsanjuija	공산주의자
company	hoésa	회사
compass	nach'imban	나침반
computer	k'ŏmp'yut'ŏ	컴퓨터
computer games	k'ŏmp'yut'ŏ geim	컴퓨터 게임
concert	k'onsŏt'ŭ	콘서트
concert hall	kong-yŏnjang •	공연장 •
	k'ŏnsŏt'ŭhol	콘서트 홀
conditioner	rinsŭ	린스
condoms	k'ondom	콘돔
confession (religious)	kohaesŏngsa	고해성사
to confirm (a booking)	hwagin haeyo	확인해요 (확인하~)

Congratulations!
ch'uk'a haeyo!
축하해요!

conservative (adj)	posudang-e	보수당의
constipation	pyŏnbi	변비
consulate	yŏngsagwan	영사관
contact lenses	k'ont'aekt'ŭ renjŭ	콘택트 렌즈
contact number	yŏllakch'ŏ	연락처
contraceptive	p'i-imyak	피임약
contract	kyeyaksŏ	계약서
convenience store	p'yŏnijŏm	편의점
convent	sudowŏn	수도원
to cook	yori haeyo	요리해요 (요리하~)
cooking	yori	요리
cool (col)	mŏtchin	멋진
corner	mot'ung-i	모퉁이
corrupt	pup'aehan	부패한
cost (n)	kap	값

It costs a lot.
kŭgŏt pissayo.
그것 비싸요.

cough	kich'im	기침
to cough	kich'im haeyo	기침 해요 (기침 하~)
cough medicine	kich'imyak	기침약
to count	seyo	세요 (세~)
country	nara	나라
countryside	shigol	시골
court (legal)	pŏpchŏng	법정
crazy	mich'in	미친
credit card	k'ŭredit'ŭ k'adŭ •	크레디트 카드 •
	shinyong k'adŭ	신용 카드
cross (adj)	shimuruk'an	시무룩한
cross (crucifix)	shipchaga	십자가

crowded	pumbinŭn	붐비는
culture	munhwa	문화
cup	k'ŏp	컵
cupboard	ch'anjang	찬장
customs	segwan	세관
to cut	challayo	잘라요 (자르~)

D

dad (inf)	appa	아빠
daily	maeil	매일
dairy products	yujep'um	유제품
to dance	ch'um ch'wŏyo	춤 춰요 (춤 추~)
dangerous	wihŏmhan	위험한
dark	ŏdu-un	어두운
to date (someone)	...(i)rang deit'ŭ haeyo	···(이)랑 데이트해요 (데이트하~)
date (romantic)	deit'ŭ	데이트
date (time)	naltcha	날짜
date of birth	saengnyŏn wŏril • saeng-il	생년월일 • 생일
daughter	dal	딸
dawn	saebyŏk	새벽
day	haru	하루
day after tomorrow	morae	모레
day before yesterday	kŭjŏkke	그저께
daytime	nat	낮
dead	chugŭn	죽은
deaf	kwigamŏn	귀가 먼
death	chugŭm	죽음
decaffeinated coffee	muk'ap'ein k'ŏp'i	무카페인 커피
to decide	kyŏlchŏng haeyo	결정해요 (결정하~)
deep	kip'ŭn	깊은
deforestation	samnim pŏlch'ae	삼림 벌채
degree (temperature)	do	도
delicatessen	shikp'umjŏm	식품점
delirious	chŏngshini nagan	정신이 나간
democracy	minjujui	민주주의

Democratic People's Republic of Korea
chosŏn inmin konghwaguk
조선인민공화국

demonstration	demo • shiwi	데모 • 시위
dental floss	ch'ishil	치실
dentist	ch'ikwa	치과
to deny	pujŏng haeyo	부정해요 (부정하~)
deodorant	tiodorant'ŭ • ch'ech'wijegŏje	디오도란트 • 체취제거제
to depart (leave)	dŏnayo	떠나요 (떠나~)
department store	paek'wajŏm	백화점

departure	ch'ulbal	출발
deposit	pojŭnggŭm	보증금
desert	samak	사막
destination	mokchŏkchi	목적지
to destroy	p'agoé haeyo	파괴해요 (파괴하~)
detail	chasehan naeyong	자세한 내용
diabetes	tangnyobyŏng	당뇨병
diamonds	daiamondŭ	다이아몬드
diaper (nappy)	kijŏgwi	기저귀
diarrhoea	sŏlsa	설사
diary	ilgi	일기
dictionary	sajŏn	사전
to die	chugŏyo	죽어요 (죽~)
different	tarŭn	다른
difficult	ŏryŏun	어려운
dinner	chŏnyŏk	저녁
direct	chikchŏpchŏgin	직접적인
dirty	tŏrŏun	더러운
disabled person	chang-aein	장애인
discount	harin	할인
to discover	palgyŏn haeyo	발견해요 (발견하~)
discrimination	ch'abyŏl	차별
disease	pyŏng	병
disposable	ilhoéyong	일회용
to dive	daibing haeyo	다이빙해요 (다이빙하~)
diving	daibing	다이빙
divorced	ihonhan	이혼한
dizzy	ŏjirŏun	어지러운
DMZ (De-Militarised Zone)	pimujang jidae	비무장지대
to do	haeyo	해요 (하~)

> I didn't do it.
> **chega anhaessŏyo**
> 제가 안 했어요.

doctor	ŭisa	의사
doctor of Oriental medicine	hanisa	한의사
documentary	tak'yument'ŏri	다큐멘터리
dog	kae	개
doll	inhyŏng	인형
domestic terminal	kungnae ch'ŏngsa	국내 청사
dominoes	tomino geim	도미노 게임
door	mun	문
dormitory	kisuksa	기숙사
double bed	dŏbŭl bedŭ	더블 베드
double room	dŏbŭllum	더블 룸
downhill (skiing)	hwalgang	활강
downtown (city centre)	shinae	시내
drama	dŭrama	드라마

dramatic	kŭkchŏgin	극적인
draught beer	saengmaekchu	생맥주
to dream	gumkkwŏyo	꿈꿔요 (꿈꾸~)
dress	tŭresŭ	드레스
drink	ŭmnyosu	음료수
to drink	mashŏyo	마셔요 (마시~)
to drive	unjŏn haeyo	운전해요 (운전하~)
drivers licence	unjŏn myŏnhŏjŭng	운전면허증
driving range	kolp'ŭ yŏnsŭpchang	골프 연습장
drought	kamum	가뭄
drug (medication)	yak	약
drug addiction	mayak chungdok	마약 중독
drug dealer	mayangmilmaeja	마약 밀매자
drugs	mayak	마약
drum	tŭrŏm • buk	드럼 • 북
to be drunk	sul ch'wi haeyo	술 취해요 (술 취하~)

I'm drunk.
sul ch'wi haessŏyo
술 취했어요.

to dry (clothes)	(osŭl) mallyŏyo	(옷을) 말려요 (말리~)
dry cleaners	set'akso	세탁소
dummy (pacifier)	komu jŏkkokchi	고무 젖꼭지
dumplings	mandu	만두

E

each	kakkage	각각의
early (time)	irŭn	이른
to be early (time)	illŏyo	일러요 (이르~)

It's early.
illŏyo
일러요.

early morning	irŭn ach'im	이른 아침
to earn	pŏrŏyo	벌어요 (벌~)
earrings	kwigori	귀고리
earth (land)	dang	땅
Earth	chigu	지구
earthquake	chijin	지진
east	tongtchok	동쪽
East China Sea	namhae	남해
East Sea (Sea of Japan)	tonghae	동해
Easter	puhwalchŏl	부활절
easy	shiun	쉬운
to eat	mŏgŏyo	먹어요 (먹~)
eating out	oéshik hagi	외식하기
economy	kyŏngje	경제

education	kyoyuk	교육
eggs	kyeran	계란
elderly man	harabŏji (lit: grandpa)	할아버지
elderly woman	halmŏni (lit: grandma)	할머니
elections	sŏn-gŏ	선거
electorate	sŏn-gŏ indan	선거인단
electricity	chŏn-gi	전기
elevator (lift)	ellibeit'ŏ	엘리베이터
embarrassed	ch'angp'ihan	창피한
embarrassment	ch'angp'i • nanch'ŏ	창피 • 난처
embassy	taesagwan	대사관
emergency	ŭnggŭp sanghwang	응급상황
emergency exit	pisanggu	비상구
emotional	kamjŏngjŏgin	감정적인
employee	chigwŏn • p'igoyong-in	직원 • 피고용인
employer	koyongju	고용주
empty	pin	빈
end	kŭt	끝
to end	kŭnnaeyo	끝내요 (끝내~)
endangered species	myŏlchong wigie tongshingmul	멸종 위기의 동식물
engagement	yak'on	약혼
engagement ceremony	yak'onshik	약혼식
engine	enjin	엔진
engineer	enjiniŏ	엔지니어
engineering	konghak	공학
England	yŏngguk	영국
English (language)	yŏng-ŏ	영어
English (person)	yŏnggugin • yŏnguksaram	영국인 • 영국사람
to enjoy (oneself)	chŭlgyŏyo	즐겨요 (즐기~)
enough	ch'ungbunhan	충분한
to enter	tŭrŏgayo	들어가요 (들어가~)
entertaining	chaemi innŭn	재미있는
entrance	ipku	입구
envelope	pongt'u	봉투
environment	hwan-gyŏng	환경
epileptic (adj)	kanjire kŏllin	간질에 걸린
equality	p'yŏngdŭng	평등
equipment	changbi	장비
ethnic Chinese Korean residents	hwagyo	화교
Europe	yurŏp	유럽
European (adj)	yurŏbe	유럽의
European (n)	yurŏbin • yurŏpsaram	유럽인 • 유럽사람
euthanasia	allaksa	안락사
evening	chŏnyŏk • pam	저녁 • 밤
everybody	modu	모두
every day	maeil	매일
example	ye	예

For example, ...
yerŭl dŭlmyŏn ...
예를 들면, ...

excellent	dwiŏnan	뛰어난
exchange rate	hwanyul	환율
to exchange	kyohwan haeyo	교환해요 (교환하~)
to exchange gifts	sŏnmurŭl kyohwan haeyo	선물을 교환해요 (교환하~)

Excuse me. (apologising)
choésong hamnida
죄송합니다.

Excuse me. (attracting attention)
shille hamnida
실례합니다.

exhibition	chŏnshihoé	전시회
exit	ch'ulgu	출구
expensive	pissan	비싼
exploitation	kaebal	개발
express (adj)	kosoge	고속의
express mail	barŭn up'yŏn	빠른 우편

F

factory	kongjang	공장
fall (autumn)	kaŭl	가을
family	kajok	가족
family name	sŏng	성
famous	yumyŏnghan	유명한
fan (hand-held)	puch'ae	부채
fan (machine)	sŏnp'unggi	선풍기
far	mŏn (adj) • mŏlli (adv)	먼 • 멀리
to be far	mŏrŏyo	멀어요 (멀~)
farm	nongjang	농장
farmer	nongbu	농부
fast	barŭn	빠른
fat	dungttunghan	뚱뚱한
father	abŏji	아버지
father-in-law	shiabŏji • chang-inŏrŭn	시아버지 • 장인어른
fault (mistake)	chalmot	잘못
faulty	pullyang-in	불량인
fauna	tongmul	동물
fax	p'aeksŭ	팩스
fear	turyŏum	두려움
feeding bottle	uyubyŏng	우유병
to feel	nŭkkyŏyo	느껴요 (느끼~)
feelings	kamjŏng	감정
fence	tamjang	담장

fencing	p'enshing	펜싱
ferry port	hanggu	항구
festival	ch'ukche	축제
fever	yŏl	열
few	myŏkkae	몇개
fiance(e)	yak'onja (m) •	약혼자 •
	yak'onnyŏ (f)	약혼녀
fiction	sosŏl	소설
field	tŭlp'an	들판
fight	ssaum	싸움
to fight	ssawŏyo	싸워요 (싸우~)
figures (numbers)	sutcha	숫자
Filipino/Filipina	p'illip'in-in •	필리핀인 •
	p'illip'insaram	필리핀사람
to fill	ch'aewŏyo	채워요 (채우~)
film (for camera)	p'illŭm	필름
film (movies)	yŏnghwa	영화
film (negatives)	(negŏt'ibŭ) p'illŭm	(네거티브) 필름
film speed	p'illŭm sŭp'idŭ • kamdo	필름 스피드• 감도
filtered	p'ilt'ŏ innŭn	필터있는
to find	ch'ajayo	찾아요 (찾~)
fine (n)	pŏlgŭm	벌금
finger	son-garak	손가락
fins	oribal	오리발
fire	pul • hwajae	불 • 화재
firewood	changjak	장작
first (adv)	mŏnjŏ	먼저
first (in order)	ch'ŏt	첫
first (pure Korean numeral)	ch'ŏppŏntchae	첫 번째
first (Sino-Korean numeral)	cheil	제일
first-aid kit	kugŭp sangja	구급 상자
first-class metropolitan bus	chwasŏk bŏsŭ	좌석버스
first-class seat	ildŭngsŏk	일등석
fish (alive)	mulgogi	물고기
fish (as food)	saengsŏn	생선
fishing	nakkshi	낚시
fish shop	saengsŏn kage	생선가게
flag (national emblem)	kukki	국기
flash (bulb)	p'ŭllaeshi •	플래시 •
	p'ŭllaeshi chŏn-gu	플래시 전구
flashlight (torch)	sonjŏndŭng	손전등
flat (land, etc)	p'yŏngp'yŏnghan	평평한
flat tyre	p'ŏngk'ŭ	펑크
flea	pyŏruk	벼룩
flight	pihaeng	비행
floor	padak • maru	바닥 • 마루
floor (storey)	ch'ŭng	층
flora	shingmul	식물
flour	milkkaru	밀가루

flower	got	꽃
flower shop	gotchip	꽃집
fly	p'ari	파리
to fly	narayo	날아요 (날~)
folding screens	pyŏngp'ung	병풍
to follow	daragayo	따라가요 (따라가~)
food	ŭmshik	음식
food poisoning	shikchungdok	식중독
foot	pal	발
football (American)	p'uppol	풋볼
football (soccer)	ch'ukku	축구
footpath	podo	보도
foreign	oéguge	외국의
foreigner	oégugin	외국인
forest	sup	숲
forever	yŏng-wŏnhi	영원히
to forget	ijŏbŏryŏyo	잊어버려요 (잊어버리~)

Forget about it; Don't worry.
shin-gyŏng ssŭji maseyo; kŏkchŏng maseyo
신경쓰지 마세요; 걱정 마세요.

I forgot.
ijŏ-bŏryŏssŏyo
잊어버렸어요.

to forgive	yongsŏ haeyo	용서해요 (용서하~)
fork	p'ok'ŭ	포크
fortnight	ijuil	2주일
fortune teller	chŏmjaeng-i	점쟁이
fortune telling	chŏm • unse	점 • 운세
foyer	hyugeshil	휴게실
fraud	sagi	사기
free (not bound)	chayuroun	자유로운
free (of charge)	muryo	무료
free kick	p'ŭrik'ik	프리킥
free parking	muryo chuch'a	무료주차
to freeze	ŏrŏyo	얼어요 (얼~)
fresh	shinsŏnhan	신선한
fried rice	pokkŭmbap	볶음밥
friend	ch'in-gu	친구
fruit	kwail	과일
fuel (all types)	kirŭm	기름
full	kadŭkch'an	가득찬
fun (adj)	chaemi innŭn	재미있는
funeral	changnyeshik	장례식
furnished	kagu wanbidoén	가구 완비된
furniture	kagu	가구
future	mirae	미래

G

game (games)	geim	게임
game (sport)	kyŏnggi	경기
garage	ch'ago	차고
gardening	chŏng-wonil	정원일
gardens	chŏng-wŏn	정원
garlic	manŭl	마늘
gas cyclinder	but'an-gasŭ	부탄가스
gate	mun	문
gay (n)	tongsŏng-aeja	동성애자
gear stick	kiŏ sŭt'ik	기어 스틱
general (usual)	ilbanjŏgin	일반적인

Get lost!
chŏri kaseyo!
저리 가세요!

Get well soon.
balli naŭshŏya dwaeyo
빨리 나으셔야 돼요.

ghosts	yuryŏng	유령
gift	sŏnmul	선물
gig	kong-yŏn	공연
ginger	saenggang	생강
gingko nut	ŭnhaeng	은행
gingko tree	ŭnhaeng namu	은행나무
ginseng tea	insamch'a	인삼차
ginseng wine	insamju	인삼주
girl	yŏja ai	여자아이
girlfriend	yŏja ch'in-gu	여자친구
to give	chwŏyo	줘요 (주~)

Could you give me ...?
... chom jushillaeyo?
... 좀 주실래요?

given name	irŭm	이름
glass	yuri	유리
gloves	changgap	장갑
to go	kayo	가요 (가~)

Let's go.
kapshida
갑시다.

We'd like to go to ...
... e karyŏgo hanŭndeyo
... 에 가려고 하는데요.

| to go out with ... | ...(i)rang sagwiŏyo | ...(이)랑 사귀어요 (사귀~) |

golf course	kolp'ŭ k'osŭ	골프 코스
goal (sports)	gol • gorin	골 • 골인
goalkeeper	golk'ip'ŏ	골키퍼
goat	yŏmso	염소
God	hananim	하나님
god	shin	신
gold	kŭm	금
gold (adj)	kŭme	금의
golf ball	kolp'ŭgong	골프공
good	choŭn	좋은

Good luck!
haeng-unŭl piröyo!
행운을 빌어요!

Goodbye. (pol, when the speaker is leaving)
annyŏnghi kyeseyo
안녕히계세요

Goodbye. (pol, when the speaker is staying)
annyŏnghi kaseyo
안녕히가세요.

to be good	choayo	좋아요 (좋~)
government	chŏngbu	정부
gram	gŭraem	그램
grandchild	sonju	손주
grandfather	harabŏji	할아버지
grandmother	halmŏni	할머니
grape (red)	p'odo	포도
grape (white)	ch'ŏngp'odo	청포도
grass	chandi	잔디
grave	mudŏm	무덤
great	choŭn	좋은

Great!
choŭndeyo!
좋은데요!

green	ch'oroksaege	초록색의
greengrocer	ch'ŏnggwasang	청과상
grey	hoésaege	회색의
groom	shillang	신랑
to guess	ch'uch'ŭk haeyo	추측해요 (추측하~)
guesthouse	minbakchip	민박집
guide (person)	kaidŭ	가이드
guidebook	kaidŭbuk	가이드 북
guide dog	maeng-in annaegyŏn	맹인 안내견
guided trek	daragalsu innŭn-gil	따라갈 수 있는 길
guilty	yujoé	유죄
guitar	git'a	기타

gums (of mouth)	immom	잇몸
gym (gymnasium)	ch'eyukkwan	체육관
gym (health club)	helsŭjang	헬스장
gymnastics	ch'ejo	체조

H

hair	mŏri	머리
hairbrush	bŭrŏshi	브러쉬
haircut (for both sexes)	he-ŏk'ŏt'ŭ	헤어커트
haircut (for men only)	ibal	이발
hairdressing salon	miyongshil	미용실
half	ban	반
ham	haem	햄
hammer	mangch'i	망치
hammock	kŭmul ch'imdae	그물 침대
hand	son	손
handbag	haendŭbaek	핸드백
handball	haendŭbol	핸드볼
handicrafts	sugong yep'um	수공예품
handlebars	haendŭl	핸들
handsome	chal saenggin	잘생긴
happy	haengbokhan	행복한

Happy Birthday!
saeng-il ch'uk'a haeyo!
생일 축하해요!

to be happy	haengbok haeyo	행복해요 (행복하~)
harbour	hanggu	항구
hard (difficult)	ŏryŏun	어려운
hard (not soft)	tandanhan	단단한
harassment	koérop'im • hirong	괴롭힘 • 희롱
harvest	ch'usu	추수
hat	moja	모자
to have	issŏyo	있어요 (있~)

Do you have ...?
... issŭseyo?
... 있으세요?

I have ...
chŏn ... ga/i issŏyo
전 ... 가/이 있어요.

to have fun	chŭlgyŏyo	즐겨요 (즐기~)
he	kŭ	그
head	mŏri	머리
headache	tut'ong	두통
headlight	hedŭrait'ŭ	헤드라이트
health	kŏn-gang	건강

ENGLISH – KOREAN DICTIONARY

to hear	tŭrŏyo	들어요 (들~)
hearing aid	poch'ŏnggi	보청기
heart	shimjang	심장
heat	yŏl	열
heater	hit'ŏ	히터
heavy	mugŏun	무거운
to be heavy	mugŏwŏyo	무거워요 (무겁~)

Hello.
annyŏng haseyo
안녕하세요.

Hello! (answering telephone)
yŏboseyo
여보세요.

| helmet | helmet | 헬멧 |
| to help | towajwŏyo | 도와줘요 (도와주~) |

Help!
towajuseyo!
도와주세요!

herbs	yakch'o	약초
hermitage	amja	암자
heroin	heroin	헤로인
high	nop'ŭn	높은
to hike	tŭngsan haeyo	등산해요 (등산하~)
hiking	tŭngsan	등산
hiking boots	tŭngsanhwa	등산화
hiking routes	tŭngsanno	등산로
hill	ŏndŏk	언덕
Hindu (person)	hindugyo shinja	힌두교 신자
to hire	koyong haeyo	고용해요 (고용하~)
to hitchhike	hich'ihaik'ŭ haeyo	히치하이크해요 (히치하이크~)
HIV positive	eijŭ yangsŏng	에이즈 양성
hobbies	ch'wimi	취미
hockey (field)	hak'i	하키
hockey (ice)	aisŭ hak'i	아이스하키
holiday (vacation)	hyuil	휴일
homeless	nosukcha	노숙자
homosexual (adj)	tongsŏng-ae-e	동성애의
honey	gul	꿀
honeymoon	shinhon yŏhaeng	신혼여행
horoscope	pyŏlchŏm	별점
horrible	gŭmtchikhan	끔찍한
horse	mal	말
horse racing	kyŏngma	경마
horse riding	sŭngma	승마

hospital	pyŏng-won	병원
private hospital	kaein pyŏng-wŏn	개인 병원
hot (to the touch)	dŭgŏun	뜨거운
hot (weather)	tŏun	더운
to be hot (weather)	tŏwŏyo	더워요 (덥~)

It's hot.
tŏwŏyo
더워요.

hotel	hot´el	호텔
hot springs	onch´ŏn	온천
hour	shigan	시간
house	chip	집
housework	chibanil	집안일
how	ŏttŏk´e	어떻게

How do I get to ...?
...e ŏttŏk´e kayo?
...에 어떻게 가요?

How many?
myŏkkae-eyo?
몇 개에요?

How much? (cost)
ŏlma-eyo?
얼마에요?

How much does it cost to go to ...?
...e kanŭnde ŏlmana dŭrŏyo?
...에 가는 데 얼마나 들어요?

hundred (100)	paek	백
hungry	paegop´ŭn	배고픈
husband	namp´yŏn	남편

I

| I | chŏ | 저 |

I'm sorry.
choésong haeyo
죄송해요.

ice	ŏrŭm	얼음
ice rink	aisŭ ringk´ŭ •	아이스 링크 •
	sŭk´eit´ŭjang	스케이트장
ice cream	aisŭk´ŭrim	아이스크림
identification card	shinbujŭng	신분증
if	manyak	만약

| immigration | ipkuk kwalli | 입국 관리 |
| important | chung-yohan | 중요한 |

It's important.
chung-yo haeyo
중요해요.

It's not important.
chung-yo haji anayo
중요하지 않아요.

incense	hyang	향
included	p'ohamdoén	포함된
indicator (car)	gambagi	깜박이
industry	sanŏp	산업
inequality	pulp'yŏngdŭng	불평등
infection	kamyŏm	감염
inflammation	yŏmjŭng	염증
influenza	tokkam	독감
in front of ...	... ap'e	... 앞에
inhaler (for asthma)	chŏnshik hwanjayong	천식환자용
	hŭbipki	흡입기
injection	chusa	주사
injury	pusang	부상
in-line skating	rollŏ bŭlleiding •	롤러 블레이딩 •
	innain sŭk'eit'ing	인라인 스케이팅
inner tube	t'yubŭ	튜브
inside (something)	...ane	...안에
insurance	pohŏm	보험
intense	kanghan	강한
interesting	chaemi innŭn •	재미있는 •
	hŭngmiroun	흥미로운
to be interesting	chaemi issoyo •	재미있어요 (재미있~) •
	hŭngmirowŏyo	흥미로워요 (흥미롭~)

It's interesting.
chaemi issŏyo
재미있어요.

international	kukchejŏgin	국제적인
Internet cafe	p'ishibang • int'ŏnet k'ap'e	PC 방 • 인터넷 카페
interview	int'ŏbyu • myŏnjŏp	인터뷰 • 면접
Ireland	aillaendŭ	아일랜드
Irish (person)	aillaendŭin •	아일랜드인 •
	aillaendŭsaram	아일랜드사람
irrigation	kwan-gae	관개
island	sŏm	섬
itinerary	yŏhaeng sŭk'ejul	여행스케줄

J

jacket	chaek'it	재킷
jail	kyodoso	교도소
Japan	ilbon	일본
Japanese (person)	ilbonin • ilbonsaram	일본인 • 일본사람
jeans	ch'ŏngbaji	청바지
jeep	chip'ŭch'a	지프차
jewellery	changsin-gu	장신구
Jewish (person)	yut'aegyo shinja	유태교 신자
job	chigŏp	직업
job advertisement	kuin kwanggo	구인광고
jogging	choging	조깅
joke	nongdam	농담
to joke	nongdam haeyo	농담해요 (농담하~)
journalist	kija	기자
journey	yŏhaeng	여행
judge	p'ansa	판사
judo	yudo	유도
juice	jusŭ	주스
to jump	dwiŏ ollayo	뛰어 올라요 (뛰어 오르~)
jumper (sweater)	sŭwet'ŏ	스웨터
justice	chŏng-i	정의

K

karaoke	noraebang	노래방
karaoke bar	karaok'e ba	가라오케 바
karate	karade	가라데
kendo (Japanese fencing)	kŏmdo	검도
key	yŏlsoé	열쇠
keyboard	k'ibodŭ	키보드
to kick	ch'ayo	차요 (차~)
to kill	chugyŏyo	죽여요 (죽이~)
kilogram	k'illogŭraem	킬로그램
kilometre	k'illomit'ŏ	킬로미터
kind (adj)	ch'injŏlhan	친절한
kindergarten	yuch'iwŏn	유치원
king	wang	왕
kiss	k'isŭ	키스
to kiss	k'isŭ haeyo	키스해요 (키스하~)
kitchen	chubang	주방
kitten	saekki koyang-i	새끼 고양이
knapsack	paenang	배낭
knife	naip'ŭ	나이프
to know	arayo	알아요 (알~)
(someone or something)		
Korean (language)	han-gugŏ	한국어

How do you say ... in Korean?		
...rŭl/ŭl han-gungmallo mwŏrago haeyo?		
...를/을 한국말로 뭐라고 해요?		

Korean (person)	han-gugin • han-guksaram	한국인 • 한국사람
Korean (adj)	han-guge	한국의

Korean War veterans
han-gukchŏn ch'amjŏn yongsa
한국전 참전 용사

Korean-Japanese relations
hanil kwan-gye
한일 관계

kung fu	k'unghu	쿵후

L

labourer	nodongja	노동자
labour unions	nodong chohap	노동 조합
lace	gŭn	끈
lacquerware products	najŏnch'ilgi	나전칠기
lagoon	sŏk'o	석호
lake	hosu	호수
land	dang	땅
languages	ŏnŏ	언어
large	kŏdaehan	거대한
last	majimak	마지막
last month	chinandal • chŏbŏndal	지난달 • 저번 달
last night	ŏjeppam	어젯 밤
last week	chinanju	지난주
last year	chinanhae • changnyŏn	지난해 • 작년
late	nŭjŭn	늦은
to be late	nŭjŏyo	늦어요 (늦~)
later	najung-e • taŭme	나중에 • 다음에
to laugh	usŏyo	웃어요 (웃~)
laundry	ballae	빨래
law	pŏp	법
law (study)	pŏp'ak	법학
lawyer	pyŏnhosa	변호사
laxatives	chisaje	지사제
lazy	keŭrŭn	게으른
leader	chidoja	지도자
leaf	ipsagwi • ip	잎사귀 • 잎
to learn	paewŏyo	배워요 (배우~)
leather	kajuk	가죽
leathergoods	kajuk chep'um	가죽제품
to leave	dŏnayo	떠나요 (떠나~)
left (not right)	oéntchoge	왼쪽의
legalisation	pŏmnyulhwa	법률화

legislation	pŏmnyul chejŏng	법률 제정
lemon	remon	레몬
lemonade	remoneidŭ	레모네이드
lens	renjŭ	렌즈
lesbian	rejŭbiŏn	레즈비언
less	tŏl	덜
letter	p'yŏnji	편지
liar	kŏjimmalchaeng-i	거짓말쟁이
library	tosŏgwan	도서관
to lie (not tell truth)	kŏjimmal haeyo	거짓말해요 (거짓말하~)
to lie down	nuwŏyo	누워요 (눕~)
life	insaeng	인생
lift (elevator)	ellibeit'ŏ	엘리베이터
light (bright)	palgŭn	밝은
light (electric)	pul	불
light (not heavy)	kabyŏun	가벼운
light bulb	chŏn-gu	전구
lighter	rait'ŏ	라이터
light meter	noch'ulgye	노출계
to like	choahaeyo	좋아해요 (좋아하~)
lips	ipsul	입술
lipstick	ripsŭt'ik	립스틱
to listen	tŭrŏyo	들어요 (듣~)
literature	munhak	문학
litre	lit'ŏ	리터
little (amount)	chogŭm	조금
little (small)	chagŭn	작은
to live	sarayo	살아요 (살~)
local (adj)	chibang-e	지방의
local bus	maŭl bŏsŭ	마을버스
lock	chamulsoé	자물쇠
to lock	chamgwŏyo	잠궈요 (잠그~)
long (adj)	kin	긴
to be long	kirŏyo	길어요 (길~)

> Long live ...!
> manse ...!
> 만세 ...!

long-distance bus	changgŏri bŏsŭ	장거리 버스
to look	pwayo	봐요 (보~)
to look after	tolbwayo	돌봐요 (돌보~)
to look for	ch'ajayo	찾아요 (찾~)
lookout	chŏnmangdae	전망대
to lose	irŏyo	잃어요 (잃~)
loser	p'aebaeja	패배자
loss	sonhae	손해
a lot	mani	많이
loud	soriga k'ŭn	소리가 큰
love (emotion)	sarang	사랑

to love	sarang haeyo	사랑해요 (사랑하~)
lover	aein	애인
low tide	ssŏlmul	썰물
low	najŭn	낮은
loyal	sŏngshilhan	성실한
luck	un • haeng-un	운 • 행운
lucky	uni choŭn	운이 좋은
luggage	chim	짐
luggage lockers	chim pogwanso	짐 보관소
lump	hok	혹
lunch	chŏmshim	점심
lunchtime	chŏmshim shigan	점심시간
luxury	sach'i	사치
lycra	raik'ŭra	라이크라

M

machine	kigye	기계
mad	hwanan	화난
made (of)	...ro/ŭro mandŭrŏjin	...로/으로 만들어진
magazine	chapchi	잡지
mail	p'yŏnji	편지
mailbox	uch'et'ong	우체통
majority	tasu	다수
to make	mandŭrŏyo	만들어요 (만들~)
make-up	hwajang	화장
man	namja	남자
manager	maenijŏ	매니저
many	mani	많이

Many thanks.
chŏngmal komapsŭmnida
정말 고맙습니다.

| map | chido | 지도 |

Can you show me on the map?
chidosang-esŏ ŏdi-inji karŭch'ŏ jushillaeyo?
지도상에서 어디인지 가르쳐 주실래요?

map of neighbourhood	yakto	약도
margarine	magarin	마가린
marijuana	taemach'o	대마초
marital status	kyŏron yumu	결혼유무
market	shijang	시장
marriage	kyŏron	결혼
married	kyŏron han	결혼한
to marry	kyŏron haeyo	결혼해요 (결혼하~)
martial arts	musul	무술
mask	t'al	탈
mass (Catholic)	misa	미사

massage	anma • masaji	안마 • 마사지
mat (sleeping)	yo • tamnyo	요 • 담요
matches	sŏngnyang	성냥
materials	chaeryo	재료
mattress	maet'ŭrisŭ	매트리스
maybe	amado	아마도
meat	kogi	고기
mechanic	kigyegong	기계공
medal	medal	메달
medical insurance	ŭiryobohŏm	의료보험
medicine (pills, etc)	yak	약
medicine (study)	ŭihak	의학
meditation	myŏngsang	명상
to meet	mannayo	만나요 (만나~)
member	membŏ	멤버
menstrual pain	saengnit'ong	생리통
menstruation	saengni • wŏlgyŏng	생리 • 월경
menthol	ment'ol	멘톨
menu	menyu	메뉴
message	meshiji	메시지
metal	kŭmsok	금속
metre	mit'ŏ	미터
midday	chŏng-o • hannat	정오 • 한낮
midnight	chajŏng	자정
migraine	p'yŏn dut'ong	편두통
military police	hŏnbyŏng	헌병
military service	kunbongmu	군복무
milk	uyu	우유
millimetre	millimit'ŏ	밀리미터
million	paengman	백만
mind	maŭm	마음
mineral water	saengsu	생수
mirror	kŏul	거울
miso paste	toénjang	된장
to miss (feel absence)	kŭriwŏhaeyo	그리워해요 (그리워하~)
mistake	shilsu	실수
to mix	sŏkkŏyo	섞어요 (섞~)
mobile phone	hyudaep'on • haendŭp'on	휴대폰 • 핸드폰
modem	modem	모뎀
moisturiser	moisŭch'ŏraijŏ	모이스춰라이저
moisturising lotion	roshŏn	로션
money	ton	돈
money order	up'yŏnhwan	우편환
monk (Buddhist)	sŭnim • sungnyŏ	스님 • 승려
monk (Catholic)	susa	수사
monsoon	changma	장마
month	tal	달
monument	kinyŏmbi	기념비
moon	tal	달

more	tŏ	더
morning	ach'im	아침
mosque	mosŭk'ŭ • isŭllamsawŏn	모스크 • 이슬람사원
mosquito	mogi	모기
mosquito coil	mogihyang	모기향
mosquito net	mogijang	모기장
motel	mot'el • yŏgwan • yŏinsuk	모텔 • 여관 • 여인숙
mother	ŏmŏni	어머니
mother-in-law	shiŏmŏni • changmonim	시어머니 • 장모님
motor	mot'ŏ	모터
motorboat	mot'ŏbot'ŭ	모터보트
motorcycle	ot'obai • mot'ŏsaik'ŭl	오토바이 • 모터사이클
motorway (tollway)	kosoktoro	고속도로
mountain bike	sanak chajŏn-gŏ	산악 자전거
mountain climbing	tŭngsan	등산
mountain path	san-gil • tŭngsanno	산길 • 등산로
mountain range	sanmaek	산맥
mountain(s)	san	산
mouse	chwi	쥐
mouth	ip	입
movie	yŏnghwa	영화
moxibustion	dŭm	뜸
much	mani	많이
mud	chinhŭk	진흙
mum (mom)	ŏmma	엄마
murals	pyŏk'wa	벽화
murder	sarin	살인
muscle	kŭnyuk	근육
museum (art)	misulgwan	미술관
museum	pangmulgwan	박물관

When is the museum closed?
pangmulgwan mun ŏnje tadayo?
박물관 문 언제 닫아요?

music	ŭmak	음악
musician	ŭmakka	음악가
music shop	ŭmban kage	음반가게
Muslim (n)	isŭllamgyo shinja	이슬람교 신자
mute (adj)	muŏne	무언의

N

name	irŭm • sŏngmyŏng	이름 • 성명
nappies (diapers)	kijŏgwi	기저귀
national (adj)	kukka-e	국가의
national championships	kungnae sŏnsugwŏn daehoé	국내 선수권 대회
national holiday	kukkyŏng-il	국경일
national park	kungnip kong-won	국립공원

nationality (citizenship)	kukchŏk	국적
nature	chayŏn	자연
nausea	mesŭkkŏum	메스꺼움
to feel nauseous	mesŭkkŏryŏyo	메슥거려요 (메슥거리~)
near	kakkai	가까이
nearby	kakkaun	가까운
necessary	p'iryohan	필요한
necklace	mokkŏri	목걸이
to need	p'iryo haeyo	필요해요 (필요하~)
needle (sewing)	panŭl	바늘
needle (syringe)	chusabanŭl	주사바늘
net	net'ŭ	네트
never	chŏldaero	절대로
New Year's Day		
(lunar calendar)	sŏllal • kujŏng	설날 • 구정
(Western calendar)	shinjŏng	신정
New Year's Eve	shibiwŏl samshibiril •	12월 31일•
	sŏttal kŭmŭmnal	섣달 그믐날
New Zealand	nyujillaendŭ	뉴질랜드
New Zealander	nyujillaendŭin •	뉴질랜드인 •
	nyujillaendŭsaram	뉴질랜드사람
news	aeroun	새로운
news	nyusŭ	뉴스
newsagency	t'ongshinsa	통신사
newspaper	shinmun	신문
next	taŭm	다음
next month	taŭmdal	다음 달
next week	taŭmju	다음 주
next year	taŭmhae • naenyŏn	다음 해 • 내년
next to ...	... daŭme	... 다음에
nice	choŭn	좋은
night	pam • chŏnyŏk	밤 • 저녁
nightclub	nait'ŭ	나이트

No.
anio
아니오.

No entry!
tŭrŏgaji mashio • ch'urip kŭmji
들어가지 마시오 • 출입 금지

No parking!
chuch'a kŭmji
주차금지

No smoking!
kŭmyŏn
금연

ENGLISH – KOREAN DICTIONARY

no smoking area
kŭmyŏn guyŏk
금연 구역

noise	soŭm	소음
noisy	shikkŭrŏun	시끄러운
nonalcoholic	pialk'o-ol	비알코올
non-direct	chikchŏpchŏgiji anŭn	직접적이지 않은
none	amugŏtto	아무것도
non-recyclable trash	ilban ssŭregi	일반쓰레기
noon	chŏng-o	정오
north	puktchok	북쪽
North Korea	puk'an	북한
(as said in South Korea)		
notebook	kongch'aek	공책
nothing	amugŏtto	아무것도
novels	sosŏl	소설
Novocaine	kukso mach'wije	국소마취제
now	chigŭm	지금
nuclear energy	haegenŏji	핵 에너지
nun (Buddhist)	yŏsŭng	여승
nun (Catholic)	sunyŏ	수녀
nurse	kanhosa	간호사

O

obvious	bŏnhan • tang-yŏnhan	뻔한 • 당연한
ocean	haeyang	해양
offence	wiban	위반
office	samushil	사무실
office worker	hoésa jigwŏn	회사 직원
often	kakkŭm • chaju	가끔 • 자주
oil (for cooking)	kirŭm	기름
oil (for engine)	oil	오일
OK	kwaench'anŭn	괜찮은
old (not new)	oraedoén	오래된
old (not young)	nŭlgŭn	늙은
old city	kodo • oraedoén doshi	고도 • 오래된 도시
Olympic Games	ollimp'ik	올림픽
once, one time	hanbŏn	한 번
one (pure Korean)	hana	하나
one (Sino-Korean)	il	일
one day (pure Korean)	haru	하루
one day (Sino-Korean)	iril	일일
one-way (road)	ilbang t'onghaeng	일방통행
one-way ticket	p'yŏndop'yo	편도표
only	man	만
on strike	paŏpjung-in	파업중인
on time	chŏnggage	정각에
open (for business)	yŏng-ŏpchung	영업중

to open	yŏrŏyo	열어요 (열~)
opening (of an exhibition)	kaejang	개장
opera	op'era	오페라
opera house	op'era hausŭ	오페라 하우스
operation (medical)	susul	수술
operator	kyohwanwŏn	교환원
opinion	ŭigyŏn	의견
opposite (side)	pandaep'yŏne	반대편에
opposition party	yadang	야당
optician	an-gyŏngjŏm • an-gyŏngsa	안경점 • 안경사
or	animyŏn	아니면
oral	kudue	구두의
orange (colour)	chuhwangsaege	주황색의
orange (fruit)	orenji	오렌지
orchard	kwasuwŏn	과수원
orchestra	ok'esŭt'ŭra	오케스트라
order	chumun • myŏngnyŏng	주문 • 명령
to order	chumun haeyo	주문해요 (주문하~)
ordinary	pot'ong-e	보통의
to organise	chŏngni haeyo	정리해요 (정리하~)
orgasm	orŭgajŭm	오르가즘
Oriental medical clinic	haniwŏn	한의원
Oriental medicine	hanyak	한약
original	wŏllae-e • chintcha-e	원래의 • 진짜의
other	tarŭn	다른
outside	pakke	밖에
over ...	... wie	… 위에
overcoat	oét'u	외투
overdose	kwada t'uyŏ •	과다 투여 •
	kwada pogyong	과다 복용
overseas Korean	kyop'o	교포
from China	chaejung kyop'o	재중교포
from Japan	chaeil kyop'o	재일교포
from the US	chaemi kyop'o	재미교포
over there	chŏgi	저기
to owe	pitchŏyo	빚져요 (빚지~)
owner	chuin	주인
oxygen	sanso	산소
ozone layer	ojonch'ŭng	오존층

P

pacemaker	p'eisŭmeik'ŏ	페이스메이커
pacifier (dummy)	komu chŏkkokchi	고무 젖꼭지
package	sop'o	소포
packet (general)	gurŏmi	꾸러미
a packet of cigarettes	tambae han-gap	담배 한 갑
padlock	chamulsoé	자물쇠
page	p'eiji	페이지

English	Romanization	Korean
painful	koéroun • kot'ongsŭrŏun	괴로운 • 고통스러운
painkillers	chint'ongje	진통제
to paint	kŭrim kŭryŏyo	그림 그려요 (그림 그리~)
painter	hwaga	화가
painting (general)	kŭrim kŭrigi	그림 그리기
painting (the art)	hoéhwa	회화
pair (a couple)	hanssang	한 쌍
palace	kung	궁
pan	p'ŭrai p'aen	프라이 팬
pants	paji	바지
paper	chong-i	종이
papers (documents)	sŏryu	서류
pap smear	p'aep t'esŭt'ŭ	팹테스트
parcel	sop'o	소포
parents	pumonim	부모님
park	kong-won	공원
to park	chuch'a haeyo	주차해요(주차하~)
parking (paid)	yuryo chuch'a	유료주차
parking structure	chuch'ajang bilding	주차장 빌딩
parking violation	chuch'a wiban	주차 위반
parliament	ŭihoé	의회
party	p'at'i	파티
party (politics)	chŏngdang	정당
party politics	chŏngdang chŏngch'i	정당 정치
passenger	sŭnggaek	승객
passive	sudongjŏgin	수동적인
passport	yŏkwŏn	여권
passport number	yŏkwŏnbŏnho	여권번호
past	kwagŏ	과거
path	kil	길
patient (adj)	ch'amŭl sŏng innŭn	참을성있는
to pay	ton naeyo	돈 내요 (돈 내~)
payment	chibul	지불
peace	p'yŏnghwa	평화
peak	pong-uri	봉우리
pedestrian (n)	pohaengja	보행자
pedestrian overpass	yukkyo	육교
pedestrian underpass	chihado	지하도
pen (ballpoint)	bolp'en	볼펜
pencil	yŏnp'il	연필
penicillin	p'enishillin	페니실린
peninsula	pando	반도
pensioner	yŏn-gŭm suryŏngja	연금 수령자
people	saramdŭl	사람들
per cent	p'ŏsent'ŭ	퍼센트
performance	kong-yŏn	공연
permanent	yŏnggujŏgin	영구적인
permission	hŏga	허가
person	saram	사람

P

D
I
C
T
I
O
N
A
R
Y

personality	sŏnggyŏk	성격
pesticides	salch'ungje	살충제
petition	t'anwŏn	탄원
petrol	hwibalyu	휘발유
pharmacist	yaksa	약사
pharmacy	yakkuk	약국
Philippines, the	p'illip'in	필리핀
phone book	chŏnhwa bŏnhobu	전화번호부
phone box	chŏnhwa baksŭ	전화박스
phonecard	chŏnhwa k'adŭ	전화카드
photograph	sajin	사진

Can/May I take a photo?
yŏgisŏ sajin tchigŏdo dwaeyo?
여기서 사진찍어도 돼요?

Can/May I take your photo?
(tangshine) sajin chom tchigŏdo doéllkayo?
(당신의) 사진 좀 찍어어 될까요?

photographer	sajin chakka	사진작가
pick(axe)	kokkwaeng-i	곡괭이
pie	p'ai	파이
piece	chogak	조각
pill	allyak	알약
Pill, the	kyŏnggu p'i-imyak	경구 피임약
pillow	pegae	베개
pillowcase	pegaennit	베갯잇
pingpong ball	t'akkugong	탁구공
pink	punhongsaege	분홍색의
pipe	p'aip'ŭ	파이프
pitcher of beer	maekchu p'ich'ŏ	맥주 피처
place	changso	장소
place of birth	ch'ulsaengji	출생지
plain (adj)	p'yŏngbŏmhan •	평범한 •
	kandanhan	간단한
plane	pihaenggi	비행기
planet	haengsŏng	행성
plant	shingmul	식물
to plant	shimŏyo	심어요 (심~)
plastic	p'ŭllasŭt'ik	플라스틱
plate	chŏpshi	접시
plateau	kowŏn	고원
platform	sŭnggangjang •	승강장 •
	p'ŭllaepp'om	플랫폼
play (theatre)	yŏn-gŭk	연극
to play (music)	yŏnju haeyo	연주해요 (연주하~)
to play cards	k'adŭgeim haeyo	카드 게임 해요
		(카드 게임 하~)
plug (bath)	magae	마개

English	Romanization	Korean
plug (electricity)	p'ŭllŏgŭ	플러그
pocket	chumŏni	주머니
poetry	shi	시
point (in a game or test)	chŏmsu	점수
to point	karik'yŏyo	가리켜요 (가리키~)
police officer	kyŏngch'algwan	경찰관
police station	kyŏngch'alsŏ	경찰서
policy	chŏngch'aek	정책
politicians	chŏngch'i-in	정치인
politics	chŏngch'i	정치
pollen	gokkaru	꽃가루
polls	t'up'yo	투표
pollution	oyŏm	오염
pool (game)	p'ok'eppol	포켓볼
pool (swimming)	suyŏngjang	수영장
poor	kananhan	가난한
popular	in-gi choŭn	인기좋은
pork	twaejigogi	돼지고기
port	hanggu	항구
possible	kanŭnghan	가능한
postage stamp	up'yo	우표
postcard	yŏpsŏ	엽서
post code	up'yŏn bŏnho	우편번호
poster	posŭt'ŏ	포스터
post office	uch'eguk	우체국
pottery	tojagi	도자기
poverty	kanan	가난
power	him	힘
prayer	kido	기도
prayer book	kidosŏ	기도서
to prefer	tŏjoahaeyo	더 좋아해요 (더 좋아하~)
pregnancy test kit	imshin jindanyak set'ŭ	임신 진단약 세트
pregnant	imshinhan	임신한
premenstrual tension (PMS)	saengnijŏn chŭnghugun	생리전 증후군
prepaid electronic transit pass	kyot'ong k'adŭ	교통카드
to prepare	chunbi haeyo	준비해요 (준비하~)
present (gift)	sŏnmul	선물
present (time)	hyŏnjae	현재
presentation	palp'yo	발표
presenter (TV, etc)	nyusŭ k'aesŭt'ŏ	뉴스 캐스터
president (of a company)	sajang	사장
president (of a country)	taet'ongnyŏng	대통령
pressure	amnyŏk	압력
pretty	yeppŭn	예쁜
to prevent	magayo •	막아요 (막~) •
	panghae haeyo	방해해요 (방해하~)
price	kagyŏk	가격

pride	chajonshim • kŭngji	자존심 • 긍지
priest (Catholic)	shinbu	신부
prime minister	susang	수상
prison	kyodoso	교도소
prisoner	choésu	죄수
private	satchŏgin	사적인
private hospital	kaein pyŏng-wŏn	개인 병원
privatisation	konggiŏp minyŏnghwa	공기업 민영화
to produce	saengsan haeyo	생산해요 (생산하~)
profession	chigŏp	직업
profit	iyun	이윤
program	p'ŭrogŭraem	프로그램
promise	yaksok	약속
proposal	che-i	제의
to protect	poho haeyo	보고해요 (보호하~)
protected forest	poho samnim	보호삼림
protected species	ch'ŏnyŏn-ginyŏmmul	천연기념물
protest	hang-ŭi	항의
to protest	tanŏn haeyo	단언해요 (단언하~)
Protestant (n)	kaeshin-gyo shinja	개신교 신자
proud	charangsŭrŏwŏ hanŭn •	자랑스러워 하는 •
	chashin innŭn	자신있는
provisions	shingnyang	식량
pub	sulchip • ba	술집 • 바
public telephone	kongjungjŏnhwa	공중전화
public toilet	kongjung hwajangshil	공중화장실
to pull	tanggyŏyo	당겨요 (당기~)
pulses	k'ong	콩
pump	p'ŏmp'ŭ	펌프
puncture	p'ŏngk'u	펑크
to punish	pŏlchwŏyo	벌 줘요 (벌 주~)
puppy	kang-aji	강아지
pure	sunsuhan	순수한
purple	porasaege	보라색의
to push	mirŏyo	밀어요 (밀~)
to put	noayo	놓아요 (놓~)

Q

qualifications	chagyŏk	자격
quality	chil	질
quarantine	kyŏngni	격리
quarrel	malssaum	말싸움
quarter (1/4)	sabune-il	사분의 일
queen	yŏwang	여왕
question	chilmun	질문
to question	chilmun haeyo	질문해요 (질문하~)

ENGLISH – KOREAN DICTIONARY

queue	chul	줄
quick	barŭn	빠른
quiet (adj)	choyonghan	조용한
to quit	kŭman dwŏyo	그만 둬요 (그만 두~)

R

race (breed)	injong	인종
race (sport)	kyŏngju	경주
racism	injong ch'abyŏl	인종 차별
racquet	rak'et	라켓
radiator	rajiet'a • radieit'ŏ	라지에타 • 라디에이터
railroad	ch'ŏldo	철도
railway station	kich'ayŏk	기차역
rain	pi	비
raincoat	ubi	우비
rainy season (monsoon)	changma	장마
rally	chip'oé • demo	집회 • 데모
rape	kanggan	강간
rare	tŭmun • higwihan	드문 • 희귀한
rash (medical)	palchin	발진
rat	chwi	쥐
raw	saeng-e • nalgŏse	생의 • 날것의
raw fish	saengsŏnhoé	생선회
razor	myŏndogi	면도기
to read	ilgŏyo	읽어요 (읽~)
reading books	toksŏ	독서
ready	chunbidoén	준비된
to realise	gaedarayo	깨달아요 (깨닫~)
realism	sashilchui	사실주의
realistic	hyŏnshilchŏgin	현실적인
reason	iyu	이유
receipt	yŏngsujŭng	영수증
to receive	padayo	받아요 (받~)
recent	ch'oégŭne	최근의
recently	yojŭme	요즘에
to recognise	arabwayo	알아봐요 (알아보~)
to recommend	ch'uch'ŏn haeyo	추천해요 (추천하~)
recyclable	chaehwaryong	재활용
red	balgan	빨간
reef	amch'o	암초
referee	shimp'an	심판
reference	ch'amjo	참조
refill	rip'il	리필
refrigerator	naengjanggo	냉장고
refugee	p'inanmin	피난민
refund	hwanbul	환불

to refund	hwanbul haeyo	환불해요 (환불하~)
to refuse	kŏjŏl haeyo	거절해요 (거절하~)
regional	chibang-e	지방의
regionalism	chiyŏkchui	지역주의
registered mail	tŭnggi up'yŏn	등기우편
to regret	huhoé haeyo	후회해요 (후회하~)
regular metropolitan bus	shinae bŏsŭ	시내버스
relationship	kwan-gye	관계
to relax	kinjang p'ŭrŏyo	긴장 풀어요 (긴장 풀~)
religion	chonggyo	종교.
religious	chonggyojŏgin •	종교적인 •
	chonggyŏ-e	종교의
to remember	kiŏk haeyo	기억해요 (기억하~)
remote	mŏn	먼
remote control	rimok'ŏn	리모컨
rent	chipse	집세
to rent	pillyŏyo	빌려요 (빌리~)
to repair	suri haeyo	수리해요 (수리하~)
to repeat	panbok haeyo	반복해요 (반복하~)
republic	konghwaguk	공화국

Republic of Korea
taehan min-guk
대한민국

reservation	yeyak	예약
to reserve	yeyak haeyo	예약해요 (예약하~)
reservoir	chŏsuji	저수지
resignation	shijik	사직
to respect	chon-gyŏng haeyo	존경해요 (존경하~)
rest (relaxation)	hushik	휴식
rest (what's left)	namŏji	나머지
to rest	shiŏyo	쉬어요 (쉬~)
restaurant	shiktang	식당
resume	iryŏksŏ	이력서
retired	t'oéjikhan	퇴직한
to return (something)	tollyŏjwŏyo	돌려줘요 (돌려주~)
return ticket	wangbokp'yo	왕복표
review	pip'yŏng • chaego	비평 • 재고
rice (cooked)	pap	밥
rice (grains)	ssal	쌀
rice paddy	non	논
rice punch	shik'ye	식혜
rich (food)	yŏngyangga innŭn	영양가 있는
rich (wealthy)	puyuhan	부유한
to ride	t'ayo	타요 (타~)
right (correct)	majŭn • orŭn	맞은 • 옳은
right (not left)	orŭntchoge	오른쪽의
to be right	majayo	맞아요 (맞~)

You're right.
kŭrŏnneyo • manneyo
그렇네요/맞네요.

| ring (of phone) | chŏnhwabel | 전화벨 |

I'll give you a ring.
chega chŏnhwa halkkeyo
제가 전화할게요.

ring (on finger)	panji	반지
rip-off	pagaji	바가지
risk	wihŏm	위험
river	kang	강
riverside	kangbyŏn	강변
road (main)	toro	도로
road map	torojido	도로지도
roasted	pokkŭn	볶은
to rob	humch'ŏyo	훔쳐요 (훔치~)
robbery	chŏldo	절도
rock	pawi	바위
rock climbing	ambyŏk tŭngban	암벽 등반
rock group	rokkŭrup	록 그룹
roller blading	rollŏ bülleiding •	롤러 블레이딩 •
	innain sük'eit'ing	인라인 스케이팅
romance	romaensü	로맨스
romantic	romaent'ikhan	로맨틱한
room	pang	방
room number	pangbŏnho	방 번호
rope	rop'ü • chul	로프 • 줄
round (adj)	wŏnhyŏng-e • tunggün	원형의 • 둥근
roundtrip ticket	wangbokp'yo	왕복표
route (trail)	kil • rut'ü	길 • 루트
rubbish	ssŭregi	쓰레기
rug	galgae	깔개
rugby	rŏkpi	럭비
ruins	p'yehŏ • yett'ŏ	폐허 • 옛터
rules	kyuch'ik	규칙
ruling party	yŏdang	여당
to run	dwiŏyo	뛰어요 (뛰~)
Russia	rŏshia	러시아
Russian (person)	rŏshia-in • rŏshiasaram	러시아인 • 러시아사람

S

sad	sŭlp'ŭn	슬픈
to be sad	sŭlp'ŏyo	슬퍼요 (슬프~)
saddle	anjang	안장
safe (adj)	anjŏnhan	안전한
safety binding	bainding •	바인딩 •
	seip'ŭt'i bainding	세이프티 바인딩

saint	sŏng-in	성인
salary	ponggŭp	봉급
on sale	seiljung	세일중
sales department	p'anmaebu	판매부
salt	sogŭm	소금
salty	tchan	짠
sand	morae	모래
sanitary napkins	saengnidae	생리대
satellite dish	wisŏngjŏpshi ant'ena	위성접시 안테나
sauna	sauna	사우나
sausage	soshiji	소시지
to save (rescue)	kuhaeyo	구해요 (구하~)
to say	malhaeyo	말해요 (말하~)

What's he saying?
chŏbuni mwŏrago hashinŭn-gŏ eyo?
저 분이 뭐라고 하시는 거에요?

scarf	sŭk'ap'ŭ	스카프
school	hakkyo	학교
science	kwahak	과학
scientific	kwahakchŏgin	과학적인
scientist	kwahakcha	과학자
sci-fi movies	kongsang kwahak yŏnghwa	공상 과학 영화
scissors	kawi	가위
to score	chŏmsunaeyo	점수내요 (점수내~)
scoreboard	chŏmsup'an	점수판
Scotland	sŭk'ot'ŭllaendŭ	스코틀랜드
Scot(tish person)	sŭk'ot'ŭllaendŭin • sŭk'ot'ŭllaendŭsaram	스코틀랜드인 • 스코틀랜드사람
scrambled eggs	pokkŭndalgyal	볶은 달걀
screen	hwamyŏn	화면
scuba diving	sŭk'ubŏ daibing	스쿠버 다이빙
sculptor	chogakka	조각가
sculpture	chogak	조각
sea	pada	바다
Sea of Japan	tonghae	동해
seafood	haemul	해물
seasick	paemŏlmihanŭn	배멀미하는
seaside	haebyŏn	해변
seasons	kyejŏl	계절
seat	chwasŏk • chari	좌석 • 자리
seatbelt	anjŏn belt'ŭ	안전벨트
seaweed soup	miyŏkkuk	미역국
second (time)	ch'o	초
second-class seat	idŭngsŏk	이등석
secretary	pisŏ	비서
to see	pwayo	봐요 (보~)

I see. (understand)
algessŏyo
알겠어요.

See you later.
taŭme do poélkkeyo (pol) • taŭme do pwayo (inf)
다음에 또 뵐께요 • 다음에 또 봐요.

See you tomorrow.
naeil poéyo • naeil pwayo
내일 뵈요 • 내일 봐요.

self-employed	chayŏng-ŏbul hanŭn	자영업을 하는
selfish	igijŏgin	이기적인
self-service	selp'ŭ sŏbisŭ	셀프 서비스
to sell	p'arayo	팔아요 (팔~)
to send	ponaeyo	보내요 (보내~)
sensible	hyŏnmyŏnghan	현명한
sentence (prison)	sŏn-go	선고
sentence (words)	munjang	문장
to separate	kallanoayo	갈라놓아요 (갈라놓~)
separated	pyŏlgŏjung-in	별거중인
serious	shimgakhan	심각한
service (assistance)	sŏbisŭ	서비스
service (religious)	yebae	예배
set	set'ŭ	세트
several	yŏrŏgae-e	여러 개의
to sew	panŭjil haeyo	바느질해요 (바느질하~)
sex (gender)	sŏngbyŏl	성별
sex (the act of)	seksŭ	섹스
sexism	sŏngch'abyŏl	성 차별
sexual harassment	sŏnghirong	성희롱
sexy	sekshihan	섹시한
shade (shadow)	kŭrimja	그림자
shaman	mudang	무당
shamanism	musokshinang	무속신앙
shamanistic exorcism	kut	굿
shampoo	shamp'u	샴푸
shape	moyang	모양
to share (with)	nanwŏyo	나눠요 (나누~)
to share a room	pang kach'i ssŏyo	방 같이 써요 (방 같이 쓰~)
to shave	myŏndo haeyo	면도해요 (면도하~)
shaving cream	myŏndo k'ŭrim	면도 크림
she	kŭnyŏ	그녀
sheet (bed)	shit'ŭ	시트
sheet (of paper)	chang	장
shell	chogaekkŏpchil	조개껍질
shelves	sŏnban	선반
ship	pae	배

shirt	shŏch'ŭ	셔츠
shoe shop	shinbal kage	신발가게
shoes	shinbal	신발
to shoot	sswayo	쏴요 (쏘~)
shop (place)	kage	가게
shoplifting	kage mulgŏn humch'im	가게 물건 훔침
shopping	shop'ing	쇼핑
to go shopping	shop'ing haeyo	쇼핑해요 (쇼핑하~)
to go window shopping	windo shop'ing haeyo	윈도 쇼핑해요 (윈도 쇼핑하~)
short (height)	(k'iga) chagŭn	(키가) 작은
short (length)	tchalbŭn	짧은
short films	tanp'yŏn yŏnghwa	단편 영화
short stories	tanp'yŏn sosŏl	단편 소설
shortage	pujok	부족
shorts	panbaji	반바지
shoulders	ŏkkae	어깨
to shout	sorijillŏyo	소리질러요 (소리지르~)
show	sho	쇼
to show	poyŏjwŏyo	보여줘요 (보여주~)
shower	shawŏ	샤워
to shower	shawŏ haeyo	샤워해요 (샤워하~)
shower gel	shawŏjel	샤워 젤
shrine	sadang	사당
to shut	tadayo	닫아요 (닫~)
shuttle bus	shŏt'ŭl bŏsŭ	셔틀버스
shy	sujubŭn	수줍은
sick	ap'ŭn	아픈
sickness	pyŏng	병
side	yŏmmyŏn	옆면
side dishes	panch'an	반찬
sightseeing	kwan-gwang	관광
sign	kanp'an	간판
to sign	sŏmyŏng haeyo	서명해요 (서명하~)
sign language	suhwa	수화
signature	sŏmyŏng	서명
signpost	pyommal	푯말
silk	pidan • kyŏn	비단 • 견
silver (n)	ŭn	은
silver (adj)	ŭne	은의
similar	pisŭt'an	비슷한
simple	kandanhan	간단한
sin	choé-ak	죄악
since ...	... butŏ	... 부터
to sing	norae pullŏyo	노래불러요 (노래부르~)
singer	kasu	가수
single (person)	shinggŭl • shinggŭre	싱글 • 싱글의
single (unique)	tan hana-e	단 하나의
single room	shinggŭl rum	싱글 룸

ENGLISH – KOREAN DICTIONARY

sister	chamae	자매
to sit	anjayo	앉아요 (앉~)
size (clothes, shoes)	saijŭ	사이즈
size (of anything)	k'ŭgi	크기
ski clothes	sŭk'ibok	스키복
ski resort	sŭk'i rijot'ŭ	스키 리조트
ski slope	sŭllop'ŭ	슬로프
to ski	sŭk'it'ayo	스키타요 (스키타~)
ski-boots	puch'ŭ	부츠
skiing	sŭk'i	스키
ski-lift	rip'ŭt'ŭ	리프트
skin	p'ibu	피부
skirt	ch'ima	치마
skis	sŭk'i	스키
sky	hanŭl	하늘
to sleep	chayo	자요 (자~)
sleeper car	ch'imdaech'a	침대차
sleeping bag	ch'imnang	침낭
sleeping pills	sumyŏnje	수면제
sleepy	chollin	졸린
to be sleepy	chollyŏyo	졸려요 (졸리~)
slide (film)	sŭllaidŭ	슬라이드
slow	nŭrin	느린
slowly	nŭrige	느리게
small	chagŭn	작은
smell	naemsae	냄새
to smell	naemsae mat'ayo	냄새 맡아요 (냄새 맡~)
to smile	usŏyo	웃어요 (웃~)
to smoke	tambae p'iwŏyo	담배 피워요 (담배 피우~)
smoking area	hŭbyŏn kuyŏk	흡연구역
snake	paem	뱀
snorkelling	sŭnok'ŭlling	스노클링
snow	nun	눈
snowboard	sŭnobodŭ	스노보드
snowstorm	nunbora	눈보라
soap	pinu	비누
soap opera	yŏnsokkŭk • dŭrama	연속극 • 드라마
soccer	ch'ukku	축구
socialist	sahoéjuija	사회주의자
social security	sahoé pojang	사회 보장
social welfare	sahoé pokchi	사회 복지
socks	yangmal	양말
soil	dang	땅
solid	koch'e-e	고체의
some	chogŭme	조금의
somebody (someone)	ŏtton saram	어떤 사람
sometimes	kakkŭm	가끔
son	adŭl	아들
song	norae	노래

soon	kot	곧

Sorry.
choésong hamnida • mian hamnida
죄송합니다 • 미안합니다

sound	sori	소리
south	namtchok	남쪽
South Korea	namhan	남한
souvenir	kinyŏmp'um	기념품
souvenir shop	kinyŏmp'um kage	기념품 가게
soy sauce	kanjang	간장
space	uju	우주
to speak	malhaeyo	말해요 (말하~)
special	t'ŭkpyŏlhan	특별한
specialist	chŏnmun-ga	전문가
speed	sokto	속도
speed limit	chehan sokto	제한 속도
spicy (hot)	maeun	매운
spoiled (food)	shingshing haji mot'an	싱싱하지 못한
sport	sŭp'och'ŭ • undong	스포츠 • 운동
sportsperson	undong sŏnsu	운동선수
spring (season)	pom	봄
square (in town)	kwangjang	광장
stadium	kyŏnggijang	경기장
stage	mudae	무대
stainless steel	sŭt'einrisŭ	스테인리스
stairway	kyedan	계단
stale	shingshing haji mot'an	싱싱하지 못한
stamps	up'yo	우표
standard (usual)	p'yojune	표준의
standing-room ticket	ipsŏk	입석
stars	pyŏl	별
to start	shijak haeyo	시작해요 (시작하~)
station (rail)	yŏk	역
stationery store	munbanggu • mun-gujŏm	문방구 • 문구점
statue	tongsang	동상
to stay (somewhere)	mŏmurŏyo	머물어요 (머물~)
steak	sŭt'eik'ŭ	스테이크
to steal	humch'ŏyo	훔쳐요 (훔치~)
steam	chŭnggi	증기
steamed rice	paekpan	백반
steep	kap'arŭn • kyŏngsaga shimhan	가파른 • 경사가 심한
step	kŏrŭm	걸음
stock (ski poles)	p'ol • sŭt'ok	폴 • 스톡
stockings	sŭt'ak'ing	스타킹
stomach	wi	위
stomachache	pokt'ong	복통
stone	tol	돌

| stop | chungji | 중지 |
| to stop | kŭman haeyo | 그만해요 (그만하~) |

Stop!
kŭman haseyo!
그만하세요!

storm	p'okp'ung	폭풍
storey	ch'ŭng	층
story (tale)	iyagi	이야기
stove	nallo • sŭt'obŭ	난로 • 스토브
straight ahead	dokparo	똑바로

Go straight ahead.
dokparo kaseyo
똑바로 가세요.

strange	isanghan	이상한
stranger	nassŏn saram	낯선 사람
stream	shinae	시내
street	kil	길
strength	him	힘
strike (work stoppage)	p'aŏp	파업
string	gŭn	끈
stroll	sanch'aek	산책
strong	himsen	힘센
stubborn	wan-gohan	완고한
student	haksaeng	학생
student's fare	haksaeng p'yo	학생표
studio	sŭt'yudio	스튜디오
studio apartment	wonrum	원룸
stupid	pabo kat'ŭn	바보같은
subtitles	chamak	자막
suburb	kyo-oé	교외
subway (underground)	chihach'ŏl	지하철
subway entrance	chihach'ŏripku	지하철입구
subway line	chihach'ŏl nosŏn	지하철노선
subway station	chihach'ŏlyŏk	지하철역
success	sŏnggong	성공
to suffer	koérowŏhaeyo	괴로워해요 (괴로워하~)
sugar	sŏlt'ang	설탕
suitcase	yŏhaeng-yong kabang	여행용 가방
summer	yŏrŭm	여름
sun	hae	해
sunblock	sŏn k'ŭrim	선크림
sunburn	haeppich'e t'am	햇빛에 탐
sunglasses	sŏn-gŭllasŭ	선글라스
sunny	haeppit balgŭn	햇빛 밝은
sunrise	haedoji • ilch'ul	해돋이 • 일출

sunset	ilmol	일몰
sunstroke	ilsabyŏng	일사병
supermarket	shup'ŏ mak'et	슈퍼마켓
superstitious	mishinŭl jal minnŭn	미신을 잘 믿는
surface mail	sŏnbak up'yŏn	선박 우편
surfboard	sŏp'ing bodŭ	서핑보드
surfing	sŏp'ing	서핑
surname	sŏng	성
surprise	nollam	놀람
to survive	saengjon haeyo	생존해요 (생존하~)
sweater (jumper)	sŭwet'ŏ	스웨터
sweet (adj)	tan	단
to swim	suyŏng haeyo	수영해요 (수영하~)
swimming	suyŏng	수영
swimming pool	suyŏngjang	수영장
swimsuit	suyŏngbok	수영복
sword	k'al	칼
sympathetic	tongjŏngshim innŭn	동정심 있는
synthetic	hapsŏng-e	합성의
syringe	chusagi	주사기

T

table	t'akcha	탁자
table tennis	t'akku	탁구
taebo	t'aebo	태보
Taekwondo	t'aekwŏndo	태권도
Tai Chi	t'aegŭkkwŏn	태극권
tail	gori	꼬리
Taiwan	taeman	대만
to take (away)	kajŏgayo	가져가요 (가저가~)
to take photographs	sajin tchigŏyo	사진 찍어요 (사진 찍~)
to talk	iyagi haeyo	이야기해요 (이야기하~)
tall	(k'iga) k'ŭn	(키가) 큰
tampons	t'amp'on	탐폰
tandem	i-inyong • saminyong	2인용 • 3인용
	chajŏn-gŏ	자전거
tasty	mashinnŭn	맛있는
tax	segŭm	세금
taxi stand	t'aekshi sŭnggangjang	택시 승강장
tea	ch'a	차
teacher	sŏnsaengnim	선생님
team	t'im	팀
teeth	i	이
telegram	chŏnbo	전보
telephone	chŏnhwa	전화
public telephone	kongjungjŏnhwa	공중전화
to telephone	chŏnhwa haeyo	전화해요 (전화하~)
telephone centre	chŏnhwaguk	전화국

telephone extension	kunae yŏn-gyŏl bŏnho	구내 연결 번호
telescope	mang-won-gyŏng	망원경
television	t'ellebijŏn	텔레비전
television set	t'ellebijŏn set'ŭ	텔레비전 세트
to tell	iyagi haeyo	이야기 해요 (이야기 하~)
temperature (fever)	yŏl	열
temperature (weather)	kion	기온
temple	chŏl	절
tennis	t'enisŭ	테니스
tennis court	t'enisŭ kyŏnggijang	테니스 경기장
tent	t'ent'ŭ	텐트
terminal (domestic)	kungnae ch'ŏngsa	국내 청사
terrible	hyŏngp'yŏn omnŭn	형편없는
test	shihŏm	시험
to thank	kamsa dŭryŏyo	감사드려요 (감사드리~)

Thank you. (pol)
kamsa hamnida • komapsŭmnida
감사합니다. • 고맙습니다.

theatre (cinema)	kŭkchang • yŏnghwagwan	극장 • 영화관
theatre (playhouse)	kŭkchang	극장
theft	chŏldo	절도
they	kŭdŭl	그들
thick	tukkŏun	두꺼운
thief	toduk	도둑
thin	yalbŭn	얇은
to think	saenggak haeyo	생각해요 (생각하~)
thirsty	mongmarŭn	목마른
this (one)	igŏt	이것
this afternoon	onŭrohu	오늘 오후
this day		
(eg, when buying tickets)	tang-il	당일
this month	ibŏndal	이번 달
this morning	onŭrach'im	오늘 아침
this week	ibŏnju	이번 주
this year	ibŏnnyŏndo • ibŏnhae	이번 년도 • 이번 해
thought	saenggak	생각
thousand	ch'ŏn	천
ticket	p'yo • t'ik'et	표 • 티켓

Where can I buy a ticket?
p'yo ŏdisŏ salsu issŏyo?
표 어디서 살 수 있어요?

ticket counter	p'yo p'anŭn-got	표 파는 곳
ticket office	maep'yoso	매표소
ticket vending machine	p'yo chap'an-gi	표 자판기
tide	chosu	조수
time	shigan	시간

What time is it?
chigŭm myŏshieyo?
지금 몇 시에요?

timetable	shiganp'yo	시간표
tin (can)	k'aen	캔
tin opener	k'aenttagae	캔따개
tinned baby food	agiyong pyŏng-ŭmshik	아기용 병음식
tip (gratuity)	t'ip	팁
tired	p'igonhan	피곤한
tissues	t'ishyu	티슈
toast (bread)	t'osŭt'ŭ	토스트
to toast (when drinking)	kŏnbae haeyo	건배해요 (건배하~)

To ...! (as a toast)
...rŭl/ŭl wihayŏ!
...를/을 위하여!

tobacco	tambae	담배
today	onŭl	오늘
together	kach'i	같이
toilet	hwajangshil	화장실
public toilet	kongjung hwajangshil	공중화장실
toilet paper	turumari hyuji	두루마리 휴지
tollbooth	yogŭm naenŭn-got	요금 내는 곳
tomorrow	naeil	내일
tomorrow afternoon	naeirohu	내일 오후
tomorrow evening	naeil bam •	내일 밤 •
	naeil chŏnyŏk	내일 저녁
tomorrow morning	naeirach'im	내일 아침
tonight	onŭl bam	오늘 밤
too (as well)	dohan	또한
too	nŏmu	너무
too many (adj)	nŏmu manŭn	너무 많은
too much/many (adv)	nŏmu mani	너무 많이
tooth (teeth)	i	이
tooth cap (crown)	k'ŭraun	크라운
toothache	ch'it'ong	치통
toothbrush	ch'isol	치솔
toothpaste	ch'iyak	치약
toothpick	issushigae	이쑤시개
torch (flashlight)	sonjŏndŭng	손전등
to touch	kŏndŭryŏyo	건드려요 (건드리~)
tourist	yŏhaenggaek	여행객
tourist information office	kwan-gwang-annaeso	관광안내소
tours	yŏhaeng • t'uŏ	여행 • 투어
towards ...	... tchogŭro	... 쪽으로
towel	sugŏn • t'awŏl	수건 • 타월
tower	t'awŏ • t'ap	타워 • 탑
toxic waste	yudoksŏng p'yegimul	유독성 폐기물

ENGLISH – KOREAN DICTIONARY

trade union	nodongjohap	노동 조합
traditional art	chŏnt'ong misul	전통 미술
traditional Korean soap opera	sagŭk	사극
traditional music performance	kugak kong-yŏn	국악 공연
traditional teahouse	chŏnt'ong ch'atchip	전통 찻집
traffic lights	shinhodŭng	신호등
traffic violation	kyot'ong wiban	교통 위반
trail (route)	kil • rut'ŭ	길 • 루트
train	kich'a	기차
train station	kich'ayŏk	기차역
transfer point	karat'anŭn-got	갈아타는 곳
transit lounge	kyŏng-yu sŭnggaeng-yong taehapshil	경유 승객용 대합실
to translate	pŏnyŏk haeyo	번역해요 (번역하~)
to travel	yŏhaeng haeyo	여행해요 (여행하~)
travel agency	yŏhaengsa	여행사
travel sickness	mŏlmi	멀미
travellers cheque	yŏhaengja sup'yo	여행자 수표
travelling	yŏhaeng	여행
tree	namu	나무
trendy	yuhaeng-ŭl jalttarŭnŭn	유행을 잘 따르는
trial	chaep'an	재판
trip	yŏhaeng	여행
trousers	paji	바지
truck	t'ŭrŏk	트럭
trust	midŭm • shinyong	믿음 • 신용
to trust	midŏyo	믿어요 (믿~)
truth	chinshil	진실
to try (to attempt)	shido haeyo	시도해요 (시도하~)
T-shirt	t'ishŏch'ŭ	티셔츠

Turn left.
oéntchogŭro toseyo
왼쪽으로 도세요.

Turn right.
orŭntchogŭro toseyo
오른쪽으로 도세요.

TV series	t'ibi sirijŭ	티비 시리즈
twice	tubŏn	두 번
twin beds	irinyong ch'imdae	일인용 침대
twins	ssangdung-i	쌍둥이
to type	t'aip'ŭ ch'ŏyo	타이프 쳐요 (타이프 치~)
typhoon	t'aep'ung	태풍
typical	chŏnhyŏngjŏgin	전형적인
tyre pressure	t'aiŏ amnyŏk	타이어 압력
tyres	t'aiŏ	타이어

ultrasound	ch'oŭmp'a	초음파
umbrella	usan	우산
underground (subway)	chihach'ŏl	지하철
underground walkway	chihado	지하도
to understand	ihae haeyo	이해해요 (이해하~)
underwear	sogot	속옷
unemployed	chigŏbi ŏmnŭn	직업이 없는
unemployment	shirŏp	실업
unfurnished	kaguga ŏmnŭn	가구가 없는
universe	uju	우주
university	taehakkyo	대학교
unleaded	muyŏn hwibalyu	무연 휘발유
unmarried	mihone	미혼의
unsafe	anjŏn haji anŭn	안전하지 않은
until …	…kkaji	…까지
unusual	t'ŭgi han	특이한
up	wiro	위로
uphill	orŭmak	오르막
urgent	kŭp'an	급한
USA, the	miguk	미국
US military bases	migunbudae	미군 부대
useful	yuyonghan •	유용한 •
	ssŭlmo innŭn	쓸모있는

V

vacant	pin	빈
vacation (holiday)	hyuga	휴가
vaccination	yebangjusa	예방주사
valley	kyegok	계곡
valuable	kapchin	값진
value (price)	kagyŏk • kap	가격 • 값
van	baen • ponggoch'a	밴 • 봉고차
vegetables	yach'ae	야채
vegetarianism	ch'aeshikchui	채식주의

I'm vegetarian.
chŏn ch'aeshikchuija eyo
전 채식주의자에요.

vegetation	ch'omok	초목
vein	chŏngmaek	정맥
venereal disease	sŏngbyŏng	성병
very	aju	아주
videotape	bidio t'eip'ŭ	비디오 테이프
view	chŏnmang	전망
village	maŭl	마을

vineyard	p'odowŏn	포도원
virus	bairŏsŭ	바이러스
visa	bija	비자
to visit	pangmun haeyo	방문해요 (방문하~)
vitamins	bit'amin	비타민
voice	moksori	목소리
volleyball	paegu	배구
volume	pollyum	볼륨
vote	t'up'yo	투표
to vote	t'up'yo haeyo	투표해요 (투표하~)

W

| to wait | kidaryŏyo | 기다려요 (기다리~) |

Wait!
kidariseyo!
기다리세요!

waiter	weitŏ	웨이터
waiting room	taegishil	대기실
Wales	weilsŭ	웨일스
to walk	kŏrŏyo	걸어요 (걷~)
wall	pyŏk	벽
wallet	chigap	지갑
to want	wŏnhaeyo	원해요 (원하~)
war	chŏnjaeng	전쟁
wardrobe	otchang	옷장
warm	dattŭthan	따뜻한
to warn	kyŏnggo haeyo	경고해요 (경고하~)
to wash (something)	shisŏyo	씻어요 (씻~)
washing machine	set'akki	세탁기
washing powder	punmal seje	분말 세제
watch	sonmok shigye	손목시계
to watch	pwayo	봐요 (보~)
water	mul	물
water bottle	mulbyŏng	물병
waterfall	pokp'o	폭포
water-skiing	susang sŭk'i	수상스키
water-skis	susangsŭk'i	수상스키
water supply	kŭpsu • sangsudo	급수 • 상수도
waves	p'ado	파도
way	kil	길

Please tell me the way to ...
... e kanŭn gil chom allyŏ jushillaeyo?
... 에 가는 길 좀 알려 주실래요?

Which way?
ŏnŭtchogŭro kaya dwaeyo?
어느 쪽으로 가야돼요?

Way Out
naganŭn-got
나가는 곳

we	uri	우리
weak	yak'an	약한
wealthy	puyuhan	부유한
to wear	ibŏyo	입어요 (입~)
weather	nalshi	날씨
wedding	kyŏron	결혼
wedding anniversary	kyŏron kinyŏmil	결혼기념일
wedding cake	kyŏron k'eik'ŭ •	결혼 케이크 •
	weding k'eik'ŭ	웨딩 케이크
wedding hall	yeshikchang	예식장
wedding present	kyŏron sŏnmul	결혼 선물
week	chu	주
weekend	chumal	주말
to weigh	mugega nagayo	무게가 나가요
		(무게가 나가~)
weightlifting	yŏkto	역도
weights	yŏkki	역기
welcome	hwanyŏng	환영
welfare	pokchi	복지
well (adv)	chal	잘
well (adj)	kŏn-ganghan	건강한
Welsh (person)	weilsŭin • weilsŭsaram	웰스인 • 웰스사람
west	sŏtchok	서쪽
wet	chŏjŭn	젖은
wetsuit	chamsubok	잠수복
what	muŏt	무엇

What are you doing?
mwŏ haseyo?
뭐 하세요?

What's the matter?
musŭn iriseyo?
무슨 일이세요?

wheel	pak'wi	바퀴
wheelchair	hwilch'e-ŏ	휠체어
when	ŏnje	언제

When does it leave?
ŏnje ttŏnayo?
언제 떠나요?

where	ŏdi	어디
white	hin	흰
who	nugu	누구

ENGLISH – KOREAN DICTIONARY

Who are they?
chŏbundŭri nuguseyo?
저분들이 누구세요?

Who is it?
nuguseyo?
누구세요?

whole	chŏnbu	전부
why	wae	왜
wide	p'ogi nŏlbŭn	폭이 넓은
wife	anae	아내
to win	igyŏyo	이겨요 (이기~)
wind	param	바람
window	ch'angmun	창문
windscreen	amnyuri	앞유리
windsurfing	windŭsŏp'ing	윈드서핑
windy	parami mani punŭn	바람이 많이 부는
wine	wain	와인
wings	nalgae	날개
winner	usŭngja	우승자
winter	kyŏul	겨울
wire	ch'ŏlsa • waiŏ	철사 • 와이어
wise	hyŏnmyŏnghan	현명한
to wish	himang haeyo	희망해요 (희망하~)
with ...	... wa/gwa hamkke	... 와/과 함께
within ...	... anŭro	... 안으로
within an hour	hanshiganane	한 시간 안에
without	... ŏpshi	... 없이
woman	yŏja	여자
wonderful	hullyunghan	훌륭한
wood	namu	나무
woodcarved figure	mokkong-yep'um	목공예품
wool	mojingmul	모직물
word	tanŏ	단어
work (tasks)	il	일
work (profession)	chigŏp	직업
to work	ilhaeyo	일해요 (일하~)
work permit	ch'wiŏp hŏgajŭng	취업 허가증
workout	undong	운동
workshop	wŏk'ŭshop	워크숍
world	segye	세계
World Cup	wŏldŭ k'ŏp	월드컵
worms	pŏlle	벌레
to be worried	kŏkchŏng dwaeyo	걱정돼요 (걱정되~)
worship	yebae	예배
wound (injury)	sangch'ŏ	상처
to write	ssŏyo	써요 (쓰~)
writer	chakka	작가

| writing | kŭl ssŭgi | 글쓰기 |
| wrong | t'ŭllin • chal mot toén | 틀린 • 잘못된 |

I'm wrong.
chega t'ŭllin-gŏt kanneyo
제가 틀린 것 같네요.

I'm wrong. (my fault)
chega jal mot haessŭmnida
제가 잘못했습니다.

Y

year	hae • nyŏndo	해 • 년도
yellow	noran	노란
yellow dust storm	hwangsa	황사
Yellow Sea	hwanghae • sŏhae	황해 • 서해

Yes.
Ne
네.

yesterday	ŏje	어제
yesterday afternoon	ŏje ohu	어제 오후
yesterday evening	ŏjejŏnyŏk	어제 저녁
yesterday morning	ŏje ach'im	어제 아침
yet	ajik	아직
yoga	yoga	요가
yogurt	yogurŭt'ŭ • yogŏt'ŭ	요구르트 • 요거트
you (inf)	nŏ	너
you (pol)	tangshin	당신
young	chŏlmŭn • ŏrin	젊은 • 어린
young woman	agashi	아가씨
youth (person)	chŏlmŭni	젊은이
youth hostel	yusŭ hosŭt'el	유스 호스텔

Z

zero	yŏng • kong	영 • 공
zodiac (Chinese)	di	띠
zodiac (Western)	shibi kungdo	12궁도
zoo	tongmulwŏn	동물원

INDEX

don't just stand there,
say something!

ee the full range of our language products, go to:

www.lonelyplanet.com

What kind of traveller are you?

A. You're eating chicken for dinner *again* because it's the only word you know.

B. When no one understands what you say, you step closer and shout louder.

C. When the barman doesn't understand your order, you point frantically at the beer.

D. You're surrounded by locals, swapping jokes, email addresses and experiences – other travellers want to borrow your phrasebook.

If you answered A, B, or C, you NEED Lonely Planet's phrasebooks.

- **Talk to everyone everywhere**
  Over 120 languages, more than any other publisher

- **The right words at the right time**
  Quick-reference colour sections, two-way dictionary, easy pronunciation, every possible subject

- **Lonely Planet Fast Talk** – essential language for short trips and weekends away

- **Lonely Planet Phrasebooks** – for every phrase you need in every language you want

'Best for curious and independent travellers' – *Wall Street Journal*

Lonely Planet Offices

Australia
90 Maribyrnong St, Footscray,
Victoria 3011
☎ 03 8379 8000
fax 03 8379 8111
✉ talk2us@lonelyplanet.com.au

USA
150 Linden St, Oakland,
CA 94607
☎ 510 893 8555
fax 510 893 8572
✉ info@lonelyplanet.com

UK
72-82 Rosebery Ave,
London EC1R 4RW
☎ 020 7841 9000
fax 020 7841 9001
✉ go@lonelyplanet.co.uk

www.lonelyplanet.com